Puncher Pie and Cowboy Lies

Steven M. Sederwall

Illustrated by Bob Diven

Puncher Pie and Cowboy Lies

Steven M. Sederwall

Illustrated by Bob Diven

Republic of Texas Press

Library of Congress Cataloging-in-Publication Data

Sederwall, Steven M.
    Puncher pie and cowboy lies / by Steven M. Sederwall.
        p.   cm.
    ISBN 1-55622-683-7 (pbk.)
    1. West (U.S.)—Social life and customs—Fiction. 2. Cowboys—
    West (U.S.)—Fiction.   3. Tall tales—West (U.S.)   I. Title.
    PS3569.E3155P86   1999
    813.54—dc21   99-17306
                                                              CIP

Republic of Texas Press is an imprint of Wordware Publishing, Inc.
No part of this book may be reproduced in any form or by
any means without permission in writing from
Wordware Publishing, Inc.

Printed in the United States of America

ISBN 1-55622-683-7
10 9 8 7 6 5 4 3 2 1
9902

All inquiries for volume purchases of this book should be addressed to
Wordware Publishing, Inc., at 2320 Los Rios Boulevard, Plano, Texas 75074.
Telephone inquiries may be made by calling:

(972) 423-0090

This book is dedicated to the Punchers —
to the ones who have spurred ahead, and to
the ones who still ride among us.

Steve Sederwall

Contents

Foreword

Puncher Pie—baloney wrapped in a light crust of a lie—cowboy style.

My first attempt to write the introduction for this book was, without a doubt, a total and utter failure. After writing a rough draft, I read it to the boys for their input—major mistake. Reading in my best radio voice, the affair proceeded in this manner:

"The men I speak of in this book—Dale Tunnell, Malcolm Burdett, Ken Kleiber, Pete Steele, and Lee Crump—are all real people, western men. Over the years we have forged a firm and lasting bond. I trust if I fell prey to Road Agents, these men would be at my side, men who would take a bullet for a friend." (I know, I know. I was waxing like I thought I was Mark Twain, and for my trouble I received the following punishment.)

"Road Agents!" Lee scoffed.

"Nice touch, wouldn't you say?" I asked proudly

"Have you started drinking?" Lee chuckled. "You're drinking, aren't you . . . ?"

"How many Road Agents?" Ken cut in before Lee could jump into his next smart remark.

"Seven," I laughed, pulling the number straight out of thin air as I went back to my page.

"Seven's a lot," Pete said, rubbing his chin and sporting what I'd describe as a seemingly worried look.

"Do they have sticks?" Dale wanted to know.

"Sticks?" I shot back. "What are you talking about sticks?"

"Yeah, sticks. You know, sticks?"

"No sticks," I declared with authority.

"No sticks," Dale said, nodding his head. "It's good they don't have sticks."

"But seven is still a lot of guys," Ken said again. "Sticks or no sticks, seven is a lot of guys. And Road Agents. I don't know about this Road Agent business."

I grunted and attempted to read the rest of my introduction but was cut off.

"Are they professionals?" Lee wanted to know. "The title Road Agent sounds like some kind of professional outfit. Something you have to take a test for; like they might be guys who know what they're doing."

"I bet you're right. With a title like Road Agents they must pay dues and everything," Dale said. "Any outfit that pays dues I'd bet would have sticks, or some kind of weapons."

"If they're pros," Malcolm said, "then I'm with Ken. That's a lot of guys."

"OK, OK," I said, pulling my hat off and rubbing my head in disbelief. "There are three Road Agents. No sticks, and they're rookie Road Agents, who are behind in their dues, at that. They don't have a clue what they're doing. Now can I read the rest of this?"

"Do they have any other weapons?" Dale wanted to know. "You've only ruled out sticks, but with the title of Road Agents I'm sure this outfit would have some kind of weapons."

"Weapons," I said, dropping my head against my chest.

"Yeah, weapons? I think it's an important question," Dale said. "We would almost have to know if they had weapons. Wouldn't you say, Malcolm?"

"I agree with Dale," Malcolm said. "We would have to have a full account of all weapons to know what we were up against."

"With seven guys, Road Agent type guys, we need this information," Ken chimed in with the group.

"No weapons," I sighed.

"Maybe they've got the weapons hidden," Dale said, nodding his head at the rest of the boys. "Being a professional bunch they would know how to hide weapons and have them out before you knew they had 'em with them. I don't think a Road Agent would be unarmed. If he was unarmed he'd be . . . well, just another traveler on the road and not a Road Agent. I would think you'd call them Travelers or Road Travelers or. . . . "

"It's my story," I snapped, cutting Dale off. "So here's the way it is. There are three rookie Road Agents. No weapons. I know they have no weapons because they are buck naked. That's how I am sure they are unarmed. They're behind on their dues and have had their official Road Agent credentials stripped from them. Now, does everyone feel better about this Road Agent matter?"

"About this 'take a bullet for you,'" Pete said. "We need to talk about that."

"What kind of bullet? We're just low rent cowboys," Lee said. "Not high dollar New York bodyguards."

"Look, I was just trying to show that you guys were real good friends," I said. "And regular guys."

"That's exactly why we need to know if they have weapons," Dale snorted. "We, after all, are just regular guys."

"Never mind," I grunted.

No matter how entertaining their thought process, or lack of it, I assure you they are much more entertaining in the flesh. Yet, I firmly stand on the record that they are real and, most of all, they are my good friends. Now that I think about it, I may be the only fictional character in this book.

I'd like to convey to the reader at the outset that every word in this book, no matter how hard it may be to believe, is nothing but the naked and unblemished truth. However, to assert such a statement would become the most outrageous lie in this book. Keeping this in mind, I would suggest to the reader to take the contents the way they were written. After all, it's just a slice of **Puncher Pie**.

A Full-Time Puncher

Before deciding his blood was too thin for cold country and moving off to New Mexico, Pete Steele spent his life in southern Utah. Pete had thrown a hoolihan into different strings from time to time, while growing up and chasing the brush-wise wild cattle that ran in the shadows of ancient Indian ruins. Southern Utah is an old country where pot shards are as common as cow pies, and if you drew wages punching cows, you earned every dime.

Pete, along with Dale Tunnell, Ken Kleiber, Lee Crump, Malcolm Burdett, and I, thinking we'd see some of this country, had packed our war-bags, loaded our trailers, and headed for Pete's old stomping grounds. We had been in Dark Canyon a week, and every night was spent by the fire serving up big slices of Puncher Pie.

I poked the fire with a stick I had picked up from the wood-pile and then leaned back with my back wedged against my high-backed saddle. Everyone else was moving around, putting up the supper plates, filling coffee cups, and finding his seat around the fire.

I watched Pete chipping at some flint with a deer horn. He's able to chip out an arrowhead while sitting around the fire, and it'll be better than the ones made by those who originally used them every day.

His rough exterior conceals his talent. Pete possesses the ability to hitch a horsehair hatband like a man who's spent time in prison. And rawhide is his friend, yielding to the easy direction of his nimble fingers. Just as leather in his hands finds its natural beauty as braided hobbles, bosals, or quirts, horses naturally respond to the touch of his rough hands. He's worked hard all his life, has felt the burn of the rope, and has smelled the singe of the hair. Pete Steele is a real cowboy, an old-time cowboy.

At these sessions by the light of the campfire Pete would flake arrowheads and speak of the old wild cow outfits. At one point, his hands stopped their work; he put the emerging arrowhead in his lap, pushed back his hat, and in a low voice began telling of a young cowboy who learned that the SS Cattle Company didn't give you a paycheck—you earned it. Pete tells it like this:

In the early days of the SS Cattle Company, Harv Williams was the general manager and foreman. The Navajos called Harv "Nasja," meaning Hoot Owl. The nickname was inspired by the way Harv sat his horse every morning, high on the mesa, waiting for the sun to come up. His shoulders would be hiked up around his ears and only his head moved, like an old hoot owl.

Harv was notorious for getting his crew up and around early. Then he'd lead the string of cowboys out to wherever they'd be working, and they'd sit their horses for hours waiting for sunrise and the beginning of their workday. Harv preached that your breakfast would poison you if you ate it after the sun was up, so every morning around three o'clock he'd roll his cowboys out, ringing on the triangle. In his way of thinking, they'd then have plenty of time to feed the horses, cook breakfast, eat, clean up, throw a saddle on their mounts, and ride out to some distant mesa to wait two hours for the sun to swallow the darkness.

Most said Harv worked his cowboys hard because he was so tight, able to squeeze a penny until tears ran down Abe's face. This quality made him a good foreman for a ranch like the SS but an exception to the unwritten cowboy rule of riding nice rigs because Harv was tight with his own funds as well. He never bought a new saddle—never. He made do with what he had no matter how well heeled his bank account happened to be.

If Harv was trying to dab a line on some old horned she-devil on a far-off mesa and a rock ripped a fender off his saddle, he'd sew it back on with rawhide rather than take his hack to the saddle shop or buy a new fender and put it on himself. He had patched his old, worn-out chaps so often they had taken on the look of a leather quilt.

One spring, in the late forties, a long-legged kid with the strange name of Homadue showed up at the SS seriously looking for work. No one knew if Homadue was his first name, last name, or even his name at all, and no one ever felt pressed to ask. Homadue, after asking around for the foreman, located Harv working a band of colts in the pen behind the house and hit him up for a job. Harv thought the big kid was too wet behind the ears to be working on his outfit and voiced his concerns straight up. Homadue just looked him straight in the eye and seemed deaf to the word "no."

"Mister, all I'm asking for is steady work," the kid said, forcefully pleading his case. "No favors. No slack. Just full-time, old-fashioned, get dirty, break your back, sitting all day in the saddle, puncher labor."

Harv studied the way the kid was dressed and the kid's rig and decided he looked punchy enough, so he gave him a whirl.

Now, Harv was not only tight, but real persnickety about the way things were done around his cow outfit. For example, when Harv grained his saddle horse he liked to stand in the breeze, slowly pouring the oats into a bucket, thus allowing the wind to blow away any dust or chaff that might colic his pony. And also Harv liked his stove wood cut twelve inches long and two inches across. Anything less or more would not do at all. Homadue was a savvy kid and took note to watch his boss, and he quickly picked up on every odd quirk and trick that Harv felt was very consequential to an orderly lifestyle. In no time, Homadue was pulling much more than his share of the weight around the ranch. Harv quickly became very pleased with himself for hiring this new puncher. At times, when Harv was climbing one of his cowboys, he would say, "Watch Homadue. He knows what he's doing." Because Harv wasn't the easiest of men to get along with, you could stand proud when he liked you, and Harv liked Homadue.

Homadue worked all summer and well into the fall. He worked hard, taking any job no one else wanted and, by Harv's estimation, always doing right by it. That next summer, the SS bought out a ranch to the north and took range delivery on 200 head of cattle that had never seen a man up close or felt the burn of a rope. Homadue seemed to always have a knack for catching the ones that got away from the rest of the crew. To his credit, the kid never talked big and always put his skill off to just dumb luck or accident. Even the older cowboys he'd show up now and then liked him. The other cowboys called Homadue a "hand," and a hand always pleased the boss of a cow outfit.

One frosty fall morning, Harv walked out to the bunkhouse with the cold biting at his ears, and as he readied to ring the triangle he found Homadue tying his war-bag up behind his saddle.

"I'm glad you're here, Harv," the kid said, pulling the cinch tighter on his gray. "I'd like to draw my pay and then I'll be moving on."

Harv was taken back. In the moonlight the kid didn't look like the top hand he had proven himself to be, he just looked like a sleepy kid.

"What's the problem," Harv snorted, holding his lantern up higher to get a better look at the kid.

"It's time I move on," the kid said.

"What's eating you, kid?" Harv snapped.

"I'd just like to draw my pay."

"You want to leave just like that?"

"Yes sir."

"Look kid, I hired you over my better judgement," Harv said with anger in his voice. "So what's eating on you?"

"If you got to know, it's like this, Harv," the kid sighed as he leaned on his horse and ducked his head. "At three in the morning you roll us out banging on that darn triangle, just like you're about to do now. We cut stove wood. We feed the milk cows and milk them. We feed and curry the horses, we cook breakfast, we wash the dishes, we saddle up and ride twelve miles to wait two hours for the sun to throw enough light to start to work. After we work hard all day, with no lunch and work well into the dark, we ride back twelve miles to the ranch house where we unsaddle, feed, water, and brush the horses. Then we feed and milk the cows, feed the chickens, cut more stove wood, cook supper, eat, wash dishes and put them away. We shoe horses, repair our tack, and get ready for the next day by lamplight. We're up until 11:00 or 12:00 every night. Then the next morning at 3:00 A.M. you're at that triangle, banging away to start it all over. We do that seven days a week, Harv."

"Well, I guess you got just what you came around here with your hat in your hand asking for," Harv furiously shot back. "I was right. You're too young and soft for a man's job. Well, boy, you asked for the work and I gave it to you."

"No sir," Homadue said in an exhausted voice, pointing his finger in Harv's face. "I said I wanted steady work, full-time work, and that's what you promised me. But that ain't what you delivered."

"What in tarnation are you talking about, boy?" Harv asked, stepping back. "You got full-time work."

"Well, I ain't got nothing to do between 11:30 at night and 3:00 in the morning but sleep. If you call that full-time, you ain't much of a foreman. So I guess I'll just draw my pay if you don't mind."

Pete stood up, threw me the perfect arrowhead he had finished as he ended his story, and said, "If that ain't the truth, that ain't a real arrowhead."

The Accident

 I studied the arrowhead that Pete had thrown in my lap. It was nice—real nice. Maybe Pete's story was the truth—this was sure a real arrowhead.

 I had a good story dancing around in my mind but didn't want to jump into the nightly Cowboy Corporate meeting of the "The First Liar's Club" with my good stuff, so I held back and waited to see who was brave or foolish enough to follow that one. I should have known it would be my friend Malcolm Burdett. He had no fear and didn't have a problem with starting the music to the Bull Ball. Malcolm looked over his coffee cup like he was about to enter a courtroom and tell the truth, the whole truth, and nothing but the truth, and we all knew better than that.

 "That was a good one, Pete," Malcolm said in his best 'you can believe me because this is a true story' tone, "but this one **really** *happened."*

 "Tuck your pants in, boys," Ken said, "it's about to get deep around here."

 Malcolm pretended he never heard Ken and started in with his story.

"Yes sir, I was a grease paint matador once," he said with pride, as he limped across the room. He had a bad leg, and his movement was slow, deliberate, but without complaint. Tip Tucker leaned against the wall while he fished through the old cluttered file cabinet. "I was the best rodeo clown in the entire business," he laughed. "Well, until the accident reduced me to selling tractors to you broke bronc riders."

"I was good, real good," he said. "Anyone who rodeoed in them days will tell you. When a cowboy hit the ground I'd jump in with moves that would make a cat jealous. I could step in front of a cowboy who was kissing the arena floor, lay my hand between that bull's eyes, and dance that Texas ton of tornado to the other side of the arena. I'd wrap that snorting, snot slinging ball of hair up so tight he'd nearly turn himself inside out. He'd be chasing his tail while the cowboy set on the fence waving his hat at the girls. That's how I got the nickname Tip. I had one bull wrapped up so tight, so hard, he tipped over."

Tip pulled the paperwork he had been searching for from the file, then limped back to his desk. He eased himself down into his chair with a brow-furrowing grimace and stretched his stiff bad leg out in front of him.

"It's my own fault," he said, "but if it hadn't been for the accident, I'd still be tipping them over."

"That's awful high for a tractor," I protested as I studied the invoice Tip had handed me.

"Well, Malcolm, that's the one you need, and that's the price you're going to have to pay," Tip said. "Right here's what I paid for it, and right here's what you'll pay for it. It's the best deal I can give you and still feed my dog."

I never questioned Tip's honesty, and I never asked to see his cost. I'd only commented that the price was a mite high, and it was. That's what I liked about Tip; he was straightforward and honest.

"I have to make something," he said, rubbing his leg. "As bad as I wish I could, I can't fall back on the rodeo like the old days."

Although I appeared to be studying the invoice, I was, in fact, calculating how many calves I'd have to run into a trailer to make the payment.

"I miss the rodeo," Tip said. "I really miss it."

"There ought to be something you could do that would get you back in the game," I said, putting the invoice down on the desk.

"I've been gone too long," he sighed. "And besides I'm way too old to be starting something new like that."

I'd heard the story a dozen times from Dad about Tip's accident, of how his career had ended at a Saturday night performance in front of a standing-room-only crowd.

Tip hadn't been at the top of his game that night. In the afternoon show, he had taken a horn while diving between a pair of clown stabbers to save a hung-up cowboy. The bull had thrown his head up just as the cowboy had been whipped down over his rope. The cowboy had been knocked colder than the heart of his ex-wife's lawyer. Unconscious, the cowboy had absorbed two more blows from the bull's horns and was being stepped on when Tip ran up and dove in. Tip had grabbed the tail of the bull rope and yanked. The cowboy had dropped faster than this year's cattle prices, and Tip had been launched into a colorful arching cartwheel that ended on the top rail of the fence. He had bounced off the rail into the lap of a rather large, wide-eyed woman from New Jersey wearing a three-dollar, purple cowboy hat, attending her first and last rodeo.

Tip's limp body slithered from the screaming woman's lap and into the beer, bubble gum, and popcorn covering the concrete floor at her feet. He lay motionless, fighting to fill his lungs as the hazy image of the immense woman seemed to dance and scream in front of his watering eyes.

Tip's partner helped the flying clown from the arena and back to his trailer where Tip laid on his bunk, bruised from his broken rib to his wrenched, swollen knee. Later he would tell himself it was because of the pain that he had pulled the cork and started drinking. He had been banged up before and knew full well that pain was no excuse, especially before a big Saturday night performance, but it was all the justification he needed at the time.

That evening, with the aid of a fistful of aspirin and regular doses of Jack, Tip made it through the first section of bull riding. During the break, just before the barrel racing, Tip put on his first animal act. He strapped his spider monkey, Vaquero, into a tiny saddle on the back of his Border collie, Buckey. Buckey darted about, herding sheep at Tip's command as Vaquero, dressed in his little cowboy suit, maintained a white knuckled death grip on the saddle horn. The crowd loved the act—the monkey hated it—the dog could care less.

After the steer wrestling, just before the second section of bull riding, Tip put on his second animal act. He pulled a large cannon out to the middle of the arena, where he and the announcer engaged in inane dialogue concerning Tip's actions. At the same time, a crew of local boys pulled a miniature wooden castle to one end of the arena.

Out of the side door of the castle came running a large Rhode Island Red chicken wearing a red, white, and blue cape over a blue shirt emblazoned with the letters "SC." The bird wore what looked like a tiny World War II flight helmet and goggles. On cue, the chicken ran across the arena, made two turns around Tip, and then jumped up and posed on top of the cannon. Tip placed a handful of corn in the cannon barrel, and the chicken remembered its attraction to corn but, because chickens don't have much sense, forgot what happened the last time it slid down into the barrel. This, of course, was Tip's plan. Then Tip described to the crowd how "Super Chicken" would be shot from the large cannon and land impressively on top of the castle located at the far end of the arena.

The crowd always grew attentive, the kids would slide to the edge of their seats in anticipation, and with a loud pop from the cannon, the now-deaf chicken would catapult out of the cannon, spread his wings, flap two or three times with the cape flying out behind him, and come to roost on top of the castle.

This particular night however, as "Super Chicken" ran across the arena, jumped up on the cannon, and slid down the barrel exactly as he had been taught, someone should have realized that Tip was not in tip-top form.

In mid-conversation with the announcer, Tip stumbled backward, prematurely pulling the lanyard of the cannon, thus producing an unexpected deafening roar. The Super Chicken projectile, with its wings pinned against its blue shirt, neck stretched out, goggles flattened against its bulging eyes, and cape aflame, left a vapor trail resembling an F-15. The spike of flame from the cannon chased the caped capon across the length of the arena, illuminating the delighted faces of the trusting children.

In contrast, the parents in the audience noticed that the blast had blown the cannon barrel completely apart, leaving the end looking like an exploding cigar. And the announcer, who had seen this act three or four dozen times, realized that Tip, in his drunken stupor, had used too much powder—way too much powder.

In the meantime, SC completed his farewell flight, ricocheted off the miniature castle, and struck the far wall of the arena in the same manner a flaming arrow hits the side of the fort in a "B" western. He hung there for a split second, cartoon like, for all to contemplate (*during which Tip mustered up a useless ray of hope*) and then fell to the arena floor, accompanied by a perfectly timed crescendo, compliments of the rodeo band. TAH-D-TAH!

Cowboys who had been perched on the fence raced to the clown's aid to beat down flames that were consuming his baggy pants and threatening his orange shirt and purple wig. Tip stood beside the burning cannon, slack-jawed at the sight of the black smoke rising from the lifeless carcass of Super Chicken, unaware that he too was on fire.

As the happy crowd realized this was not part of the scheduled act, the cheers, whistles, and shouts of joy quickly transformed into boos and hisses from the angry mob. The crowd didn't buy the announcer's lame explanation that it was not Super Chicken burning in a black melted heap at the far end of the arena but a rubber dummy.

"Let's see Super Chicken," the angry mob shouted. "We want Super Chicken." But they were never to see Super Chicken or his brave performance again.

After a small, heart-wrenching Sunday morning service, Tip buried Super Chicken out behind the horse pens. The clown never recovered from that accident and never went back to the rodeo. The flaming chicken act, as it soon became known, was Tip's last performance. He now sells tractors and raises chickens on his place north of town. His chicken operation grows with the passing of each year because he hasn't the heart to sell any of them.

I held the tractor paperwork up in front of me, and my mind was on the flaming chicken when Tip broke into my thoughts. "Let's go have lunch and we can put a pencil to those payments."

"Today's special is fried chicken," I said without thinking.

Tip wrinkled up his nose, "I'll have the Caesar salad."

"What happened to your leg?" I asked, as Tip limped toward the pickup.

"I had to get up during the night and didn't turn the light on," Tip snorted. "I tripped over Buckey."

The Stampede

After hearing Malcolm's lame story, I felt like it was my duty to these boys to liven up the party a bit.

"Malcolm, I would be the last man on this earth to doubt your word," I said, "but I know this story to be true because I heard it from the puncher's mouth that it happened to."

"I believe it's true," Dale laughed, raising his right hand as if taking an oath. "But I also watched the O.J. trial, and I believed his story."

"You need a life," I said.

"I've got a life," Dale said, "it just isn't a very exciting one."

"If all you had to do was sit around for a year and watch the O.J. trial, I'm sure it's not," Malcolm laughed. "And if you believed his story, we could just tell you that you have an exciting life, and you'd be convinced that you did."

"This is the way it happened, boys," I said, starting my story and giving poor Dale a break.

Scrappy was on a dead run, being pulled along by the flood of stampeding cattle. The night was black, and the cattle could not be seen until the sky filled with jagged lightning, revealing the white terror in their wide eyes. Running wildly through the night, they turned south and headed down the side of the mountain, turning together in one mass like water running down the hill.

Lifting his head to look from under his rain-soaked hat, Roland could see only those cattle that ran next to him. Visible only during the lightning flashes were their shiny wet horns and the dark outlines of their steamy backs as the cool rain pelted their hot bodies. For an instant it was as though the sun exploded in the sky, blinding him, as lightning struck a tree just a few yards from the turmoil of running cattle. As quickly as the light had come, the blackness returned and felt even closer with the cattle pressing his boots on either side as they ran. The smell of hot cattle and the sound of the clicking and rustling horns and rushing hoofs beating the mud filled the span of darkness. The blowing, driving rain felt like knives cutting his cheeks and caused him to duck back under his beaver hat and take a death grip on the saddle.

Sure-footed, Scrappy, Roland's 1,100-pound mare, didn't miss a step under him. Rolling her weight back, she slipped down the muddy, slick mountain on her hocks. He felt her grunt, and she sprang forward through a gnarled cedar that stood head-high in her path. The limbs nearly unseated him, and he gripped the horse tighter with his knees and leaned forward over her neck. Roland's fingers were already bloody from pulling saddle leather endeavoring to keep his seat.

And why not? he thought. *To stay in the saddle in the middle of a mess like this was as much as a fella could hope for.*

It was almost more than could be hoped for. As the stampede of wild cattle plunged down the mountain, Roland caught a pine branch across the chest, nearly clearing his saddle for the fourth time since this run started—but he hung on again. He was riding deep, and all the pine branch took was his left stirrup as the limb brought him around and halfway off his running horse.

Roland's already painful and bloody grip on the saddle got even tighter when Scrappy, still on a run, without warning plunged out into the empty darkness of space. Landing, after what seemed like minutes of falling, in the rushing water of the creek below, he knew they had hit the very bottom of the mountain. The creek wasn't wide, but it was swollen and running hard, bank full. Lightning flashed, and all that could be seen in the muddy, churning water was wet hair and horns of the swimming and fighting cattle.

Scrappy, who had always been a good swimmer, still had her problems. A steer, struggling and in a panic to keep his head above the brown water, was trying to climb into the saddle with him, but Roland wouldn't give an inch. Despite the rider's boot in his face, pushing him away, the steer continued to fight for higher ground and was nearly on the horse's back. The steer had no sooner gotten one of his front legs over Scrappy's neck when the mare hit the bank on the other side and fought for her footing, standing up out of the water. When she scrambled to her feet, the steer was flipped over backwards and rolled off her back, landing upside down in the water to be pushed back under by the other animals fighting to get to the bank.

Scrappy battled to keep her feet under her in the deep, slick mud as she pulled herself and the rider up the side of the bank. She made one final, hard lunge forward in an attempt to put herself on top of the grade. She hit the bank, and it forced her front feet under her, sending her to her belly in the mud. This put Roland where he didn't care to be, eye level with the big steers, which were still on their feet fighting the slick incline. This was a new look at his cattle—an unappreciated look. The yellow mare scrambled to her feet and with a snort, her muscles tightened and she lunged forward again, this time pulling herself up the bank and to her feet. Once on top, there was no time to rest because horse and rider were swept along with the rush of terrified cattle.

The stampede charged, in the dark, up another knoll, then followed a draw that ran down toward the Little River. The Little River was overflowing, and Roland could see every time the lightning lit the sky, that the river was rushing downstream, full of trash and uprooted trees from the storm. Roland was relieved when the cattle turned to take a westward course, rather than running off into the river, and they ran blind along the bank. Half a mile downstream, the cattle broke out of the timber and poured into a large clearing. Seeing his chance, Roland welded himself to the horse's neck and hung his Mexican spurs to Scrappy's side. They raced past the tiring cattle to the front of the herd. Yelling and slapping his wet chaps with his hat, he started turning the cattle, trying to put them into a mill. The lead steers began to turn into the center of the herd, and the rest followed, like Roland had hoped they would. This put them in a mill, and the cattle just circled and began to slow their run. Once this happened, Roland's life started to take on some semblance of order.

By the time the sun showed its face over the top of the mountain, the lightning had quit and the storm was blowing itself out over the mountains to the west. It was still gray, but the knife-like, pounding rain lessened to a light sprinkle. The sky began to clear in the east. Roland had no idea where the rest of the herd and the other men were. After the cattle had settled down, Roland pushed his bunch back up river toward the spot where this chaos had originated. It was not much of a chore to start the cattle in the right direction. They started back easily because Roland had never let them completely stop moving. All he had to do was point them in the right direction, and they moved out of the clearing and down the Little River Valley. He kept them moving in a slow walk until he hit the rut-filled Honobia road, west of the old schoolhouse. The cattle wandered aimlessly through the schoolyard, and since it was so wet, they churned up the ground real bad, but there was nothing he could do about it, so he just kept the cattle moving. Roland pushed them up the road to the trail that crossed the mountain before he turned them and pointed them north.

The sun was high and getting hot when Roland and his small herd of about eighty head topped out on the mountain at the camp, or what was left of it. Pots and pans were strewn about the ground, and the wagon was laying on its side. Not from the cattle turning it over, like the movies would have you believe, but from the panicked cook turning the wagon too sharp.

The first person Roland saw was Poke Warren, a Kansas cattle buyer who had bought his herd and was helping to drive them over the mountains to the railhead at Albion, Oklahoma. Poke had been with him last night just before the cattle decided to stampede for their night's run. Down on one knee with his face pressed to the wet ground blowing into the embers, he was trying to get a fire restarted. He had a mound of pitch pine piled up over the embers about three feet high.

It's a good thing the woods are wet, Roland thought to himself; *if that pine ever catches fire, the whole place could be in flames.*

As tinder, Poke was using a pocketful of blank checks from a Kansas bank, meant for buying cattle. Poke had an angry look on his face as he struck his next match; he couldn't get his matches to light. Poke's clothes were still wet, and his muddy hat lay on the ground upside down beside him. He looked a mess.

"Looks like ya was rode hard and put up wet," Roland said, drawing rein beside Poke and stepping to the ground. Dropping a ground tie on Scrappy, he sat down on his heels. "Where's Jake and Cutter?"

"Saw 'em an hour ago to the north in a bunch of brush that I didn't think I wanted to tangle with. They had the dogs with 'em and had gathered about sixty head. Rest are scattered all over this country. Told 'em I was goin' back to camp to make coffee," Poke said without looking up, still working on his fire. "I don't know about you, but I'm beat to the ground."

Roland looked around for a dry place to sit and take off his boots. Being full of water, he knew once he got them off it would be a fight to get them back on. "You and that Arbuckle coffee of yours. Guess ya'd build a fire every mornin' for coffee even if ya was in a rowboat." He sat down on a stump to pull his boots off.

"Reckon we all got our mornin' habits, but mine's safe. I've noticed every mornin' you saddle that ol' hammer-headed mare, and every mornin' you have to buck her out," Poke said, about to give up on the idea of morning coffee when his last match caught fire to the checks. "And I know you don't always ride her down. I seen you in the dust with her buckin' the stirrups over her back. What is that all about? You ought to get a better horse."

"You've never seen a better horse than Scrappy. After she gets her mornin' buckin' and bitin' worked out of her system, she's solid and shore worth the money. That's why I call her Scrappy. You have to scrap with her every mornin', but once that ride's over, she'll take care of you the rest of the day, and you don't have to worry about her again. Well, that is until the next day," Roland said, pouring the water out of his boots. "Now, if I can just figure out some way to get these boots back on, I'll be in fine shape."

"Here, put some of this flour in 'em. They'll go on easier," Poke said, throwing Roland the small sack of white flour. "Just as well use it like that, we ain't goin' to have time to do no cookin' nohow."

Before Roland could get his boots on, Jake and Cutter came back to camp, driving cattle. "Well, if it ain't Roland Tidwell," Jake yelled, with a big smile on his face. "The last time I seen you, ya was runnin' with a bunch of big-eyed cattle toward Texas. I meant to tell ya not to be runnin' your hoss so...it makes the cattle wild."

Roland didn't answer. He just stuck his finger through a hole he couldn't explain in the front of his shirt.

"Got more than Bar R Bar cattle here," Jake said, stepping down from his gray. He rolled up his slicker and tied it behind the saddle. "Fact is, we gathered everything that wore a brand. We got cattle in this bunch that got their hair burned down Nashoba way."

"We'll just trail 'em to town with the rest. There ain't time to cut 'em out. Keep a tally of the brands and we'll pay for 'em when we get home," Roland said, picking up his reins and stepping back into the saddle. "Get your ropes, boys. We're goin' to be doin' some brush poppin'. Let's go for the stragglers 'fore we run out of daylight."

The rest of the day was spent spinning ropes and watching the dogs heeling the cattle out of the brush. Only a few hours before, they had cussed and swore that if it never rained again it was alright because they'd already had enough. But now the sun was high and burned down on the cowboys as they worked, making them long for the clouds that brought rain.

Headed toward camp that evening, Cutter turned in his saddle to complain to the other riders, "I've had a case of the TOO's ever since I came to this country, and I've lived here all my life."

"Not yet you haven't," Jake said to him.

"You got me there," Cutter said. "But there's always been too much."

"What are you goin' on about?" Jake asked, wiping his hatband with a bandana then pulling it back into place.

"I'm either too hot, too cold, too wet, too dry, or too tired," Cutter told them.

"If you're that darned unhappy, why don't ya just pull up stakes and move out then?" Jake yelled back.

Cutter turned to face Jake and smiled, "Too broke."

The men rode back talking about cattle prices, politics, and horse races. When they got back to the mountain, they made camp where they had tried to camp the night before.

"Hope tonight is a bit more quiet than last night proved to be," Jake mumbled.

"Just look at it as good entertainment," Roland said.

Jake didn't answer; he was already snoring loud enough to start the cattle stampeding again.

The next day Poke was up before the sun, cooking breakfast along with his usual pot of too strong coffee. After a bite to eat the men saddled up, threw the cattle on the trail, and pushed them toward the Albion train yards. The day was a long one but without major problems, and they hit town with a few hours of daylight left.

After counting the cattle as they pushed them into the pens, they made camp in the wagon yard, cleaned up, and then all the drovers gathered at the cafe for supper. Poke didn't camp at the wagon yard with the rest of the boys, and before he could pay Roland for the herd, he went to his hotel room to get more blank checks. The flames took all of the ones he carried. When he returned to the cafe he had a friend with him, a city-looking fella with a round, pale face and wearing a dark pin-striped suit.

"Supper's on me, boys," Poke said as he and his friend pulled up a chair. "What'll ya have, Roland?"

"Steak," Roland said, pushing his hat back. "Reckon we need to support them boys tryin' to stick it out in the cattle business. I've also been eyeing some of that homemade pie."

During supper it was learned that the pale-faced man owned a slaughterhouse just outside Oklahoma City. He was quite interested in the cattle business and asked the cowboys around the table question after question. Their lives were far from anything he had ever seen, and he was fascinated by their talk. They even dressed different and wore their hats while they ate. Why, he never before had heard spurs jingle at the dinner table. He himself sat up straight in his suit with a white napkin tucked into the front of his starched shirt to protect his silk tie.

Finally, he asked the question that had been bothering him all evening. "Mr. Tidwell, I have heard that you drive cattle to market because there isn't a road over the mountain. Mr. Warren also related to me the trouble you had on the trail. Sir, this is almost 1940. What I do not understand is why you do it. Why not move to town? Most everyone else has. It would be a much easier life."

"Well, I thought of that," Roland said, pushing himself back from the table. "Guess I could sell out and move to Dallas, Fort Worth, or even Oklahoma City. If I played my cards right, I might even get a job in your packin' plant."

"We can never get too much good help," the man said, wiping his mouth on his napkin. "I'm sure we could find a place for you if you'd care to join us."

"That's nice of you," Roland said. "But then I got to thinkin' about it. When ya live in town ya work to make enough money to buy a car, so ya can drive that car to get you to work. You work so ya can make enough money to buy another car to drive to work. Sounds like it becomes a big circle to me."

"I guess I see your point," the man said.

Reaching for the door, Roland stopped and turned on his heels, looked down at the pale-faced man, and winked. "No sir, that ain't no kind of life for me. I like my life just like I've got it right now. I raise cattle and trail 'em to market. That way I can make enough money to buy a better hoss ... to trail my cattle to market to make enough money to buy a better hoss to trail my cattle." With that he pulled his hat down, shook his head, and smiled, "I'll just stay in the puncher circle. About the only thing different I can see is that it's just more crowded in town."

Grandpa's Christmas Gift

Malcolm shuddered with a chill, then got up and walked over to the pickup and pulled out his jacket.

"Throw me my coat," I yelled to Malcolm. "I'm not as tough as the rest of these cowboys."

"That chill just bores right through me these days," Pete said, pulling on his coat. "I don't guess none of us are as tough as when we were kids."

"That's the most truth I've heard since I set down around this fire," Lee said, already wearing his coat.

"Lee, where did you get that coat you're wearing?" Malcolm asked. "It looks warm enough."

"It was my Grandpa's," Lee said, stretching out his arms so we could all look at his coat.

"He didn't like it either?" Ken laughed.

"Yeah, he liked it," Lee said. "Grandma gave it to me after Grandpa passed away."

"He must not have liked it much," Ken shot back. "It looks like he didn't wear it much." Lee paid no attention to Ken and went on with his thought. "That reminds of something that happened when I was a kid."

"I knew it would remind someone of something," Pete smirked.

I settled in against my saddle, thinking I should have put the jacket on thirty minutes ago. Lee took a long drink of coffee and paused to push his Wyatt Earp away from his mouth to stall a beat for effect.

"Tell the story," Ken said. "I'd like to hear it before I get too old and my hearing goes out completely on me."

Lee shot Ken a glance that should have froze the coffee he was holding and went into his story.

It was Christmas Eve and I was bone tired. My hat slipped through my fingers and fell to the floor as I sank deeper into the high backed chair. From where I sat I could see the spurred boots standing in the corner. One lay on its side as if to protest the years of abuse and punishment they had endured. The other stood straight upright, proud. Dried mud caked around the heels and spurs, muting the jingle of the Mexican rowels when I pulled them off and dropped them to the floor, as I did every evening after a hard day's work.

I had just finished serving a holiday spread to two hundred head of crossbred cattle. Grass hay was overpriced this year due to a shortage of rain last summer. But feeding the high dollar grass doesn't wear on me like chopping the ice each day so they can water.

With every painful swing of the double-bitted ax, the memory of Grandpa's runaway team flashed through my mind like a series of slow motion movie frames. Being young and unknowing, I had managed to get myself hurt for an ugly situation that was well under control.

But this day was done, and I could enjoy my overstuffed chair as I did quite often. Christmas was always a time for thinking back, and if I remembered correctly, this old chair was a present from Grandma to Grandpa. It never failed to give me hours of evening comfort, just as it had my Grandpa.

All around me, my eyes rested on the things that once belonged to my Grandpa, bringing back all the good memories of him and Grandma. I even still referred to this old place, my home, as "Grandpa's house" when talking about it, which was only right. He built it, and almost everything in it used to be his and Grandma's. Even though he passed away years ago and I've lived here most of my life, it's still Grandpa's house and always will be.

The house has not been changed much since his death. The Indian blankets still hang over the upstairs balcony railing, and Western paintings adorn the thick, rock walls. The house was in order according to his taste, and he was a cowboy. Although everyone said I was just like him, I wasn't. No matter how I longed to be or how hard I tried, I'd never be the man my Grandpa was. However, our tastes in decor were the same, and I saw no need to change the house even one little bit. Besides, I liked it the way it was, the way he had it. It was home.

There were times after his death that I would swear I heard him moving around in the bedroom. I would hold my breath, halfway expecting to see him come through the door with his glasses in his hand, as he had for years, and sit in this very chair with one of his books, Twain or O. Henry. And for years, every night without exception, he would ask, "Son, you feed those horses yet?" I could feel him in this house, his house.

The old man taught me everything I know about cattle and gave me most everything I ever had in this life. What we shared was special, more than slick cattle and fast horses. More than the rough exterior he showed the world, he had a heart as big as a Shaker's barn. We weren't just a grandfather and his grandson. We were friends, good friends. And though I was just a big kid when he died.... God, I loved that old man.

I still have a team of gray thoroughbreds he broke to the harness for Grandma's Christmas present one year. He had traded a couple of nice cow/calf pairs and an old rifle for them when they were just green colts. I thought he was in them too deep, but he knew how badly Grandma wanted a nice rig to drive to church. I wanted to tell him he was too old to be breaking colts, but he wouldn't have listened. So, in secret, he fixed up an old buggy that had sat unused in the barn for over ten years.

When I tried to talk him out of breaking the colts, using the excuse that I felt he was too old, he'd say, "Son, that woman stood by me when I was as useless as whiskey in the preacher's cupboard. Now, at this stage in life, I think she ought to have something she can be proud of."

One evening, never admitting he was too old for such foolishness as breaking colts and not really caring, Grandpa slipped the two grays out of the back corral, where he had hidden them from Grandma, and hitched them to an old wagon that we had for work. Both those colts were white-eyed with fear and prancing side to side, like the ground under them was on fire. I'll never forget how Grandpa calmly and with purpose tied a big cotton rope around one of the horse's hind legs and ran it up over the collar. Then he handed it to me.

"Give her a yank, Son, if they get to acting a fool," he said, rubbing his chin as he studied the details of the situation.

"What'll it do, Grandpa?" I asked.

"It ought to pull his feet out from under him and take him to the ground if he starts to run away," Grandpa replied.

"Will it work?"

"It's never failed me yet, Son," he said with a grin, "however, this is the first time I've tried it. I'm a game rooster if you are."

The old man climbed into the wagon, released the brake, and shifted his weight into the seat. "Untie them, Son," he said pointing his chin at the colts. "We're fixin' to see if it works or not. Now, run alongside us and give her a yank when I tell you to. I can see already these young fools are going to act up."

I pulled loose the slipknot that tied the colts to the hitching post. As the outside colt felt the slack on his bridle, he reared up. It seemed to be a signal for both of them to bolt into a dead run toward the open door.

"Yank 'em down, boy!" Grandpa yelled.

With all my young strength, I jerked on the big cotton rope around the big colt's leg, trying to throw him to the ground. For my effort, I was thrown to the ground with a teeth-loosening jolt, ate three or four yards of dirt, and wrenched my shoulder.

I got myself gathered up barely in time to see the runaway team rounding the corner of the fence into the county road. Not quite clearing the turn, the wagon hooked the great corner post of the fence, pulling it, along with about thirty feet of barbed wire, behind it. I remember the scene as one of boiling dust and pounding hoofs as Grandpa bounced in the wagon like a little rag doll. At least he wasn't laying in the road or impaled on the top of a fence post.

The team ran straight as string for about a quarter of a mile before turning off the dirt road and into the pasture at the bottom of the hill. It scared me to death when the wagon tilted up on two wheels as it made the turn. The out-of-control wagon turned just feet before crashing through the bar ditch alongside the road. Those colts stretched out into a hard run across the pasture, towing the wagon and Grandpa in it. They were about to get into the trees along the creek when the team made its final turn back toward the house. It was none too soon because the creek bank dropped off some twenty feet or so into a bunch of rocks.

Scared for Grandpa, I ducked my head and ran for the back of the house to try to cut the wagon off. Here they came, and I could see Grandpa, rigid stiff in the seat, holding on as the wagon vaulted along, out of control. By the time the wagon came thundering past the back door, I had elected to leap onto the horses' backs as they passed me and pull them to a stop. In my mind, a noble plan at the time.

The colts were well lathered and their nostrils flared as they pulled at the ground for all they were worth, in my direction. As the wagon rumbled past I made a grab for the collar of the near animal. I missed, but I did manage to get a hand hold on the tailgate of the wagon, which for a moment dragged me along behind, with the toes of my boots being wore off by the rocks and cactus. My bleeding hands ached from the grip I had on those rough boards. I couldn't turn loose for if I did, my old Grandpa might be killed. Mustering all reserves of energy, I got an elbow over the crudely built tailgate, pulled myself up, and rolled heavily into the back of the bouncing wagon. I watched with fear as my Grandpa stood up in front of the seat, reins in hand, almost ready to jump.

"Don't jump, Grandpa," I yelled over the rumble of the wagon. "I'm here to save you."

Grandpa turned and looked down on me with gritted teeth. "Thank goodness you're here, Son," he said, reaching out to me. "Hand me that whip. They're wanting to slow down. I'll give them a taste of it and maybe next time they won't be so damned apt to run away."

That Christmas morning Grandpa and I got up early to cut a nice cedar tree for Grandma to decorate. We pulled up in front of the house with the tree in the wagon and two big red ribbons tied to the necks of the grays. Grandma came out on the porch, and I remember her brushing away a few tears that found their way to her cheeks. I remember it as the best Christmas we had ever had. And for many years after, those big grays were the best team on this place . . . well, once they got their run out.

Every Christmas I think of the grays running off with Grandpa. Even though I was just a button when it happened, it still embarrasses me to think that I couldn't see how tough that old man really was. It's a wonder that rough old cowboy could love a big dumb kid like me so much.

As the back door flew open and the snow blew halfway across the room, I understood what was in the old man's heart when he looked at me.

"Dad, I got the truck stuck in the back pasture again." My son stood in a puddle of mud he had tracked into the kitchen, with his head hung low, wringing his hat out in his hands.

I yanked my hat back on and lifted myself up out of Grandpa's old chair. I eased up behind my wife, who was at the sink pretending to be busy and silently biting her lower lip, fighting the overpowering urge to jump the boy about tracking up her freshly moped kitchen. I kissed her on the back of the neck and whispered into her ear, "Don't be mad—I've done worse."

"I know," she said, spinning and punching my arm. "I just finished moping up the mess you tracked in here, and if I didn't love you both, I'd have killed you both years ago."

I slowly turned to my son and flashed him a smile. Then turned back and kissed his mama again. "Let that old truck be. Let's hook up the old grays and go cut your mama a Christmas tree, and maybe we can stay in her good graces."

I walked over and pulled my muddy boots back on and reached for my coat. "Son, you feed those horses yet?"

The Good Old Days

Pete took a drink of the coffee he'd been nursing for the last part of Lee's story and threw the rest in the fire and sat his cup down. I guess he needed both hands for this one.

"If you were to check the burial records of that Texas county, you'll find their ledger reads, Death by Drowning, April 23, 1885, Legless, Bar Y Cowboy."

"That's how you can check to see that I'm telling you the truth just as it happened, but if it didn't happen that way it should have, because it makes for a better damn story. That's the way Grandpa started the story when he told it to Perkey and me, so I'll tell it just as he did."

It was one of those nice Texas spring days where everything was green, including me and the boys. Wes, Ty, Garland, Roman, Bob, Shorty, Doc, and I all had our horses in a ground-eating lope through the long grass. We were in a hurry to get washed up and head off to town. We were going to a dance, and it was the prospect of having our buckles polished by the local gals that brought our lathered mounts to a hock sliding stop at the bunkhouse door and us stepping off, rather than putting them up like we should have.

The bunkhouse was within pistol shot of the white house, which is what we all called the main house. The boss liked the bunkhouse close. We leaned to the wild side, and he liked being able to keep a close eye on us. The boss and his wife had gone to Fort Worth. He was buying cattle and she was just buying, so the boss left Roman in charge. As the man in charge, Roman made his first big decision. He felt since we had just gotten paid and we had been working so hard, we should attend the big dance being held in town that night. Roman felt it would help us get our minds back on cows, and the money we would spend would help the local economy, but we all knew the real reason. He just wanted to see Bonnie Keton.

We were sporting clean shirts with our hair slicked down and were throwing our saddles on our fresh, curried, go-to-town horses when a wagon rattled to a stop in front of the bunk-house. A big, fat gent with a bald head stepped down and knocked the dust from his pants with his hat. He was driving a big freight wagon topped off with every kind of household goods imaginable.

"Hello," the man shouted at me as I pulled the latigo.

"What can I do for you?" I questioned, dropping the stirrup back down.

"I need to hire some fine men of your caliber," the man said with a big, toothy grin.

Garland pursed his lips, shoving the match he always carried there straight out, as though he hoped a bird might land on it. He had a funny habit of pushing his lips out like that when he was thinking on a tough problem. He always had a match in his mouth, his explanation being, "You can whittle them down when you need a toothpick, and you never know when you might need a fire." I can't remember Garland being awake and not sucking on a match.

I didn't put as much thought in the matter as Garland did. "We got a job," I proclaimed politely. "Don't reckon we need another."

The gent never broke stride. He eased into a long-winded yarn of his woes and troubles so the boys just naturally gathered around to hear his tale. He told us his name was Bill Parker and he was a poet, mule skinner, and freight driver. At the moment his occupation was that of freight driver, and he had run into some sour times. He said he had been pulling the hill out of Cow Creek when a barrel of whiskey fell off the wagon. It rolled down the road and came to rest in the ditch. Parker said that if some of us cowboys would throw a rope on the barrel and pull it up to the top of the hill, he would pay us a tidy sum. With a stick he drew little pictures in the dirt describing how he could pull his wagon down below the barrel and use boards to roll the barrel up into his rig. He told us he would stop back after he made his delivery in town and pick up his whiskey. He let us know the small deed would pay ten silver dollars.

We all put our heads together and decided we were headed to town anyway and would be going right by the wreck. It would be the least we could do to help a traveler in need. I'm not saying the ten dollars didn't sway us any. So we told Parker we'd look into the job. He said after he collected his pay in town he would stop back by the ranch and pay us for our services. We all nodded our agreement to the deal.

We were smelling of soap and toilet water, ready for the dance, when we topped out on the hill and started back down toward Cow Creek. It was Garland who first saw it and yelled, "There it is, boys." He was pointing at a big, wooden barrel sitting up proud in the ditch beside the road.

Wes rode up, dropped a loop on the barrel, and dallied off, putting his Mexican spurs to the gray he was riding, and snaked the barrel up to the top of the hill. It wasn't a chore at all and sure not a ten-dollar one at that. Roman stepped off beside the barrel and sat down on the heels of his freshly shined boots.

"It sure is a nice-looking barrel," he sighed, staring up at the rest of us.

"It sure is a nice barrel," Garland assured him, rolling the match around in his mouth.

"I was just thinking," Roman announced, pulling his hat off and running his fingers through his thinning hair. "Well, it just seems a shame to leave this nice barrel here in the road. Someone might come along and steal it. Times are bad, you know."

"They're bad at that," Ty agreed, licking his lips. "You might have a point."

"We was gonna make ten dollars," Shorty said, trying to poke some better judgement into the conversation.

"We'd spend twice that for half that much whiskey," Garland said, pointing at Roman with his match, "I'm with the boss."

I had no opinion on the matter, but I knew which way the boys were leaning.

"I say we take it back to the ranch for safekeeping," Ty said, leaning out over his saddle horn. "That way we'll know it won't get stolen by a bunch of no account, shameless hooligans."

We took a vote, because that's how it's done in a democracy. With only one vote against, that being Shorty, we agreed to keep the barrel at the bunkhouse. Once he saw how the vote came out, he fell right in line. We took turns snaking the barrel up the road to the ranch. When we got to the door of the bunkhouse we stepped down and rolled it on in; there we studied the barrel for a few minutes without a word. Roman was right, it was a nice barrel and big.

"You reckon she's full of whiskey?" Roman asked the rest of us.

"How should we know?" Ty snapped. "We don't know any more than you do about this matter."

We all drew in close to the barrel. Ty sniffed at it, Doc was scratching his chin as Garland picked his teeth with his match; we were all trying to decide what to do next. Wes walked around the barrel and examined it closely. He ran his hand up the side and then all the way around it.

"We ought to open it up to make sure we got the right barrel," Wes said, still feeling the side of the barrel. "This might not be the right one."

"Boys, he's right," Garland said, stroking his chin with the match, "might not be the right one."

"Did you see another barrel out there?" Shorty snorted, shaking his head.

"That ain't the point," Ty told him. "We took this job, and if a job is worth doing, it's worth doing right."

Wes studied the barrel and declared he saw a problem. He didn't think it was whiskey in the barrel because there wasn't any bung hole in the side.

"You ever see a whiskey barrel without a bung hole to tap it?" Wes questioned with one eye closed.

He had a point, none of us had. Fact was, none of us had all that much experience with whiskey much less whiskey by the barrel. But we were all sure a whiskey barrel would have a bung hole. We must have gotten the wrong barrel.

"There ain't but one way to tell," Roman said. "Give me that hammer, Ty."

Roman took the hammer from Ty and then very carefully tapped around the top of the barrel. He did it slowly, working his way around the barrel, so as to not damage anything that might be inside. He tapped, tapped, and tapped on the top until Wes impatiently wrenched the hammer from his hand and smashed in the lid.

"My grandma ain't that darn slow," Wes snapped.

We stood slack jawed, looking at the brown liquid that filled the barrel. Nobody said a word, until Doc broke the silence. "It looks like whiskey," he said softly.

"It's hard to say," Garland told him. "You're the boss, Roman. What do you think?"

"I ain't sure. Guess we ought to taste it," Roman proclaimed. "That way we'll know if it's the barrel Parker sent us after."

Roman got a gourd dipper from a nail that hung above the water bucket and dipped out some of the brown liquid. He tasted and tilted his head. He handed the dipper to Wes who also tasted. In turn, the dipper was refilled and passed around to all of us.

"Well?" Ty questioned, looking at the rest of us.

"Well," Roman said, putting the dipper to his lips for another taste. "It tastes like whiskey, I guess. It's still hard to say. Either it's some of that real good stuff I ain't used to, or it's something else."

"Let me see that," Wes said, pulling the dipper from Roman's hand.

Again the dipper was refilled and passed around to all of us in turn to taste and give our best opinion on what the liquid might be. After three or four rounds, it was decided that it was whiskey. Not the kind we were used to drinking, but the good stuff, the kind we had never tasted before.

"I'm thinking," Shorty said. (That was a statement that surprised us all for Shorty never thought about anything.) "This is found property. How do we know it even belongs to Parker?"

"I hate to say it, but Shorty has a point," Roman said, nodding his head thoughtfully. "Parker was going to pay us ten dollars to pull this barrel out of the ditch. How do we know it was his in the first place. He could have found it himself."

"Besides, we couldn't buy this much whiskey with just ten dollars," Shorty said proudly, changing his position on the matter. "We had just as well keep it."

With another quick vote, this time with all in agreement, it was decided that we would keep the whiskey until the rightful owner came along and claimed it. Until then we would drink a little as a fee for fishing it out of the ditch and storing it in a safe place.

We drank up to recover our wages for pulling the barrel back to the ranch. Possibly we charged too much because the next thing I remember was Wes shaking me and crying. I came around, and Wes let go of my arm and started to shake Ty. I must have passed out. I tried to focus, but my eyes were swimming in a whiskey induced fog. The first thing I saw was Roman sitting on the floor holding his head.

"He's dead," Wes sobbed. "He's dead!"

"Quit yelling," Ty snapped, holding his head.

"It's Shorty," Wes pointed. "He's dead."

Every eye went to the barrel. Shorty was draped over it and had his head down in the whiskey. Roman jumped to his feet, pulled Shorty's head out of the barrel, and eased him to the floor. He was dead. We had all passed out, and Shorty must have lost the dipper and stuck his head in the barrel where he passed out and drowned.

"Do something, Doc," Wes yelled.

"I ain't no Doc," Doc said. "They just call me Doc. It stands for Dumb Old Cowboy."

Panick-stricken eyes searched each other's faces in hopes someone would know what to do. No one did. Shorty was gone. We all sat with an unbelieving gaze on poor Shorty's body, laying on the floor at the foot of the barrel. He looked so peaceful and rested. He seemed to have a smile on his face. He left this earth a happy cowboy. He was never broke up bad, rode a good horse, and was working with us, some of the best cowboys in the country, or that was how we saw it. Could a man ask for more out of this life?

"There's nothing we can do for him now," Roman said, taking charge like he was paid to do. "We'd best bury old Shorty."

Roman led us all to the barn where we started looking for something that would make a good coffin; that was the least we could do for our friend we called Shorty. All we could find was an old door that used to hang between the saddle room and the barn, and the tailgate of a wrecked wagon. We looked at the lumber we were about to make the coffin out of, and it just broke us up to think about putting Shorty in the ground. It was a hang dog day for sure.

"Boys, this is a tough one," Roman said. "We ought to get braced up for it."

So we all shuffled back into the bunkhouse and drank a little of the contents of the barrel. It helped some, but all we could do was think of Shorty. We started talking about how good a cowboy he was, and it was tough to lose him.

"We best get to it," Roman said, swaying to his feet. "Ty, pour the water out of that bucket and fill it with some of that bracer in the barrel. We may need it. We got a tough job ahead of us, boys."

We weren't much at building, so it took us most of the day to hammer the coffin together, using all the wood we had. Finished, we stepped back and looked at our handiwork.

"It ain't long enough," I told the rest of the boys.

"Why, it's big enough," Garland said, moving his match in small circles in his mouth. "Why do you think we called him Shorty. He ain't very big."

"It ain't big enough," I said again.

We all went in the bunkhouse, lifted Shorty up, and carried him out to the barn to try on his new coffin.

"I told you it wasn't long enough," I said as we laid Shorty down in the hay beside the coffin.

We all sat down to study the problem. It was a fix we were in, and nobody had any ideas about what to do. We had used every piece of wood in that barn, and the coffin we had been working on for hours wasn't long enough for the friend we called Shorty.

We sat and drank from the bucket of whiskey until Ty came up with a plan.

"We'll cut his legs off," he said proudly, like it was the best idea he had ever hatched.

"Even drunk that don't sound good to me. I don't think we ought to be cutting Shorty's legs off," Roman told Ty. "Shorty always hated being short as he was. Cutting his legs off will make it even worse."

"He ain't going to be standing up," Ty said. "If it was me, I'd be happy you boys went to all that work to make me a fine coffin, like you did. Why, it wouldn't bother me a bit to lay there with my legs cut off so I'd fit."

We all thought about it for a few minutes, passing the gourd, thinking, and drinking. Roman stood up and looked at Shorty laying in the hay like he was asleep.

"You may be right," Roman said. "You boys cut Shorty's legs down to fit the coffin and I'll go up by the white house and pick some flowers for him. I'm sure the boss' wife won't mind. Bring him on out when you get finished."

Roman started out of the barn, then turned on his heels to tell Ty, "Fill that bucket before you come, we may need something to get us through this deal."

After we cut the legs off Shorty and laid them beside him nice and neat, we hammered the lid on and carried him out into the yard where Roman stood with a handful of flowers he had just picked from the boss' flower bed. The dirt was still clinging to the roots. I looked to the house and could see where Roman had pulled a handful, leaving a big bare spot. Roman laid the flowers on the coffin.

"I been thinking," Roman said. "We don't have a good place to bury old Shorty here on the ranch. We ought to take him to town and have him put in the ground proper."

We hooked up the wagon, and Ty drove it around so we could lift Shorty in. We all sat down around the wagon and passed the gourd, feeling sorry for Shorty.

"You know, Shorty once told me he was in the army," Ty said. "We ought to send him off right, just like the army would, with a twenty-one-gun salute."

"Shorty would like that," I threw in.

"Well, there is seven of us," Wes said, kneeling down in the dirt with a stick to do his figures. Anytime there was figuring to be done, we all looked to Wes. "We will each have to shoot three times."

We all got around the wagon and stood at attention, pulled our pistols, and on command from Roman, we fired. The horses pulling the wagon bolted and ran like we'd shot them. We all busted for the corral and started throwing saddles toward our mounts. Garland was the first one saddled, and with his match clenched in his teeth he spurred out the gate. It took him better than a mile to catch the wagon and jerk the horses to a stop. It was a noble effort, but too late, the wagon had hit a rock and thrown Shorty's coffin out. It busted open, scattering broken boards and legs everywhere.

Bob and Doc were too drunk to ride and ran into each other leaving the corral. It was a good thing they were drunk or they might have hurt themselves.

We gathered up the wagon, the broken coffin, Bob, Doc, Shorty, and Shorty's legs and headed to town with Bob and Doc on the wagon and the rest of us riding our horses. It took us a while to make town because Bob was driving the wagon. He was good and drunk and sawed on the reins, wandering everywhere. When we did get to the undertaker, we took up a collection among the seven of us and gave him two months' pay for a real coffin to give old Shorty a good funeral.

We said our tearful good-byes to Shorty and headed back to the ranch. All the way back we talked of what a good cowboy Shorty was, and how we would all miss him. We had about drained the bucket when Bob ran the wagon off in the ditch at Cow Creek, the same ditch where the whole thing started. We pulled the wagon out with our ropes and drove back to the ranch.

It was starting to get dark when we rolled into the ranch, and Garland, Doc, Ty, Bob, Wes, and I all headed to the bunkhouse to see to our barrel. We fell a few times before we made it to the door. We were laying in our bunks, feeling sorry for

Shorty and knowing we had missed the dance, when Roman came busting through the door.

"*Boys we're in an awful wreck!*" Roman was yelling.

He was walking around, holding his head and crying. We had never seen Roman in such a state.

"Shorty, even dead, is going to come out of this better than any of us," Roman was saying.

"What is it?" I asked.

"Get up to the white house."

We all walked, the best we could, to the house, and as we approached, we could see the problem. Someone had shot the front window out. It must have happened when we gave old Shorty his twenty-one-gun salute, someone had thrown a stray bullet into the house.

"We can go get some new glass and put it in before the boss and his wife get back," I suggested.

"That ain't the bad part. Look where the bullet went after it broke the glass." Roman had his head down and was pointing.

The stray bullet had gone though the glass and right into the boss' baby grand piano that sat in front of the window. Now this was a wreck. Even good and drunk this didn't look good.

"Oh, now what?" Roman sat in the yard holding his head. "We'll never come out of this one."

It was then we heard Garland laughing one of those good down-deep belly laughs. He was laughing so hard he had tears making paths in the dirt as they ran down his face.

"What's so darn funny?" Roman was mad and red as a beet.

"You are looking at the only man in this county who knows how to fix that piano so no one will ever know it happened." Garland was nodding his head. "I bet you're glad you got me around now."

"You can fix the piano to where they won't know?" Roman asked.

Garland pushed his lips out, shoving his match out proudly and nodded.

"You're pretty darn drunk," Roman warned.

"I ain't drunk enough that I can't pull us out of this fix," Garland said, pointing with his match. "I can fix it before the boss gets back. You boys just go back to the bunkhouse and draw me a good stout drink out of our barrel and I'll be along real quick, it won't take me long to fix these bullet holes."

We all stumbled to the bunkhouse feeling better, leaving Garland to his work. We didn't know he was handy with wood, but it was a comfort to know he was going to fix the holes so the boss wouldn't see them.

I had just laid down on my bunk, nursing my spinning head and missing Shorty, when Roman walked over to the barrel and started hammering the lid back on.

"This thing is still half full," he said. "Maybe Parker will give us five dollars for it. I think we need to get rid of it. If Garland hadn't known how to fix the piano, we would have been in a big wreck with the boss for sure. I wonder how he is planning to fix it?"

I rolled over in my bunk to see the evening glow reflecting off of Ty's face.

"He used his match," Ty said.

"A match ain't going to fix that hole," Roman chuckled. "We was shooting .45's. He'd have to stuff a whole handful of matches in that hole to fill it."

"He only used one," Ty said, laying his head down on the table that sat in front of the window. "He just set the white house on fire."

When Grandpa told Perkey and me that story we sat big-eyed and wished we could live such adventures of the Old West.

"What did you do then, Grandpa?" Perkey asked wide-eyed, sitting on the edge of his seat.

"Boy," Grandpa smiled and shook his head. "We hunted new work is what we did."

Cowboy Banking

"Have you known Perkey since you was kids?" Dale asked.

"Known him all my life," Pete responded.

"Not yet, you haven't," Dale said.

"Yeah, I guess you're right."

"Boys, those puncher stories are the best," Dale said, sitting up straight like we would be more apt to believe him if he demonstrated good posture, "but let me tell you one that you won't forget. Funny, but this one involved old Perkey also. You know it's the truth 'cause old Perkey wouldn't lie."

"Perkey ain't telling the story," Lee said dryly as he looked up from under his old, faded hat.

"Hell, I tell it better than Perkey ever did anyway," Dale said, rather proud of himself. "He was always in some good jackpots that make for good stories, but he never was much of a storyteller."

Dale leaned forward like he was about to tell us he was the real D.B. Cooper and was willing to split the money with us but instead launched into his story.

The door of the Catch Pen Cafe swung open wide, and the bite of an icy wind blew a skiff of snow across the floor, causing shoulders to rise and heads to turn toward the man standing in the doorway.

"Somebody nail that door shut," yelled a spurred puncher who was hunched over a chipped cup of hot coffee.

Perkey pushed the door closed with the toe of his worn boot and took a long look around. Dub Williams, the pear-shaped banker, caught his eye, waving from his normal watering hole, the very back booth.

"I saved you a seat, Perkey," Dub yelled, sitting back down.

"I couldn't get within two blocks of this place for all the trucks and stock trailers," Perkey said, knocking the snow from his hat before replacing it over a crisp crew cut. "They giving away breakfast in here or what?"

Dub didn't answer. He only resumed his lecture aimed at two out-of-work cowboys, giving them his layman's spin on the strength of the U.S. dollar compared to the waning Mexican peso. Perkey pulled a faded and worn red bandana from the pocket of his Carhart and wiped his nose before sitting down to some coffee Bette had slid in front of him. He squeezed the cup, feeling its warmth, and eavesdropped on the end of Dub's impromptu financial seminar to the two punchers who knew all they needed to know about the U.S. dollar—that there weren't near enough to go around. Dub, long-winded as ever, began to wind down on his lecture and then turned his attention to Perkey who sat across from him.

"Man, you even got ice in your mustache," Dub laughed and shuddered like it made him cold to look at the ice. "Where you been, Perk?"

"I been feeding horses, breaking ice, changing a flat tire on the old pickup," Perkey said, rubbing the ice out of his mustache. "You know, all that ranch romance them folks in Santa Fe or Dallas would pay big money to experience."

"It ain't even eight o'clock yet," Dub snorted. "Are you nuts?"

"That's up for discussion, besides I guess the wall clock in the barn is broke. I'd better buy them ponies a watch," Perkey said into his coffee.

Dub shook his head. "How old are you now, Perkey?"

"What kind of question is that?" Perkey snorted and stopped short of taking a drink of his coffee. "We went to school together. I guess because you sit around on your ever-widening-banker-butt all day, and I'm forced to work outside within earshot of that old sage Pete Steele that I suddenly grew older than you? I'm the same age as you are, you old fool. Or did you forget in your old age?"

"Perkey, we may have gone to school together, but I guess I'm the only one who learned anything while we were there," Dub said, still shaking his head in disdain. "Just look at the life I have. After I eat my breakfast, I'll go to work in a nice warm office over at the bank. You, on the other hand, will be out in that nasty weather and lucky if you don't catch your death. My friend, that doesn't sound like the good life to me."

"Can't argue that point with you, Dub."

Perkey pulled off his brush scarred jacket and dropped it in a heap on the floor. The snow had already began to melt and form water on the tile.

"I can't figure out how to make a profit in the ranch business sitting behind a desk." Perkey pulled off his hat and dropped it on top of his wet coat. "I'm running behind now. I need to get back to work before I lose the little toehold that took me the last forty years to get."

"You're making my point for me, Perk." Dub pushed out his chest as he boasted and hooked his chubby thumbs in the pockets of his vest. "I, on the other hand, have learned to make a living in the ranch business from behind a desk. That is what I've done for the past forty years while you were out in the cold and busting your back."

"Dub, you're all hat, no cow. The only horse you've got on that forty acres of rocks is a retired sway-backed hammer-head you keep to babysit your grandkids when they come out from Dallas." Perkey looked up to see the other cowboys trying to stifle their amusement. "So how do you figure you're making money ranching from behind your desk?"

"You might think it's funny, boys, but listen up and learn something," Dub said to the two cowboys who were hoping Dub would be giving them a rest on the never ending subject of his all knowing finance wisdom. "Bankers not only own but run this old world. We make money when there isn't any money to be made. We can make money ranching by loaning our money to you ranchers and charging you interest. Perkey, you and Pete raise some of the best quarter horses in this country, that's a given. Then, every year or so you come up against a hard year, and you two come in and ask a banker if you could borrow money to keep the outfit afloat. Boys, you'll have to admit, as much as it hurts you, that if it weren't for bankers, guys like you and Pete would be out of the ranching business tomorrow."

Perkey sat quiet for a few seconds, nodding his head.

"I guess you'd have to say we depend on each other," Perkey said. "So Dub, as bad as you hate to admit it, you depend on us also."

"Perk, what you don't know about horses and cattle Pete does, that's a fact," Dub said, pointing his double chin out. "But having an eye for a good horse don't give you a foot up when it comes to matters of money, and it's money that makes the world go round. It's money that greases the skids. That's true even in the cowboy's little world. Knowing horses don't help you in the cutthroat world of high pressure finance, a world that would have your life's blood running across the floor in no time, a world that we bankers deal in every single day."

"Well, I can't argue that point either, Dub," Perkey said, fishing through his pockets. "I don't know about my life's blood, but the cutthroat world of finance has me in at least an embarrassing spot right now. You see, I don't even have enough money on me to pay for my breakfast."

Dub let out a loud belly laugh and waved to the waitress. "See what I told you, boys. It's a cutthroat world."

Dub turned and made a big show of talking to the waitress, "Bette, put poor Perkey's breakfast on my bill. Will ya, hon?"

"No sir," Perkey protested with both hands extended toward Dub. "I don't like owing anyone as savvy as one of you world financing, cutthroat bankers."

"It's no problem," Dub said. "I understand how it is out there in the cold world for you cowboys."

Perkey pulled a folded paper from his shirt pocket and pushed it across the oilcloth in front of Dub. Dub unfolded the paper and studied it.

"What's this?" Dub questioned, still examining the paper in his hand.

"I need a loan," Perkey said.

"Perk, this is a ten thousand dollar certificate of deposit."

"I guess you do know about money matters," Perkey laughed and picked up the menu to study it. "Well, Dub, can a cutthroat banker like you give me a loan against it?"

Dub studied the CD again and pushed it back to Perkey. "Come on by the bank after you eat your breakfast, and I'll loan you whatever you need up to ten thousand dollars."

Perkey refolded the CD and handed it back to Dub. "Loan me three dollars against it, so I can get some eggs."

Dub pushed the CD away. "I can't loan you three dollars against a ten thousand dollar CD."

"You just said you'd loan me whatever I needed up to ten thousand dollars," Perkey said, pushing the certificate back across the table. "I need three bucks, or was that just a bunch of big-banker blow?"

Dub smiled, picked up the CD, and put it into his tailored suit pocket. He reached into his wallet and ceremoniously dropped three one-dollar bills on the table beside Perkey.

"Come on by the bank when you finish your eggs, and we'll draw up the proper paperwork on this big-time financial transaction. The interest is twelve and a half percent."

He turned on his heels to leave, stopped, and turned toward the two cowboys sitting beside Perkey at the table. "See boys, that's why bankers will always own and run this old world."

Dub started to leave but thought better of it and stopped to give Perkey one more tiny tidbit of information from a banker's point of view. "Remember, Perk, if you default on that big three-dollar loan, you will lose the entire ten thousand dollar CD. I think you'd better stick to ranching, because you know absolutely nothing of money matters."

Dub chuckled and walked away quite satisfied with himself. Perkey waved at the banker when Dub stopped and turned back smiling just before he walked out the door. The banker started to say something but stopped short, unusual for Dub. He only shook his head, waved, and quickly ducked into the snow.

It was almost a year to the day before Perkey stood in front of Dub's large and impressive oak desk wringing his hat in his hands. "I need to pay off that note you're holding against my CD."

With a smile Dub went to his old file that sat in the corner of his office, extracted a dog-eared file, and returned with the paperwork that had Perkey's CD stapled to the inside of the folder. With a very well manicured thumbnail the bloated banker removed the staple.

"Sign this and I need three dollars plus the twelve and a half percent interest," Dub said as he quickly stroked the keys of his calculator. "That comes to a whopping three dollars and thirty-seven cents. You got that kind of cash on you, cowboy?"

Without a word, Perkey reached into his wallet and withdrew three crisp one-dollar bills and laid them, one at a time, in front of the banker. The cowboy then shoved his hand deep into his jeans and came out with a fistful of change. He opened his hand and carefully counted out thirty-seven cents to the penny. He pushed the pile of change alongside the three one-dollar bills on the desk. Perkey laid his hat in the chair upside down and leaned over the desk, took up the banker's pen, and signed the paper that had been pushed in front of him. Dub handed Perkey the CD, which Perkey quickly folded up and tucked inside his coat.

"Thanks, Dub," Perkey said, pulling his hat on and turning to leave.

"Perk." Dub stood up behind his desk. "I don't guess I'll ever understand you cowboy types. I just made thirty-seven cents, and all I did was throw a piece of paper in a drawer. You could have lost that ten thousand dollar CD, you know."

Dub shot Perkey that superior smile he had honed since high school.

"I know," Perkey said. "Thanks again."

"Oh! One more thing," Dub said before Perkey could get out the door. "I need to buy my grandkids a horse. That old one I had up and died on me."

"What was he, a hundred, hundred and five?" Perkey said with a grin.

"Close," Dub said with a smile. "You think you can sell me something safe that won't run off with them kids? And if he does, get me one that will keep on running. They are getting old enough that they have turned into a real pain."

"Sure, Dub," Perkey nodded.

"I hope you're a better horse trader than a money manager," the fat banker laughed. "You may be paying me to take the horse off your place."

Dub graced Perkey with that smile again. Perkey turned and walked toward the door but stopped short of going out. It must have been that smug smirk that stopped him and prompted the cowboy to reveal to the banker the truth of the private matter he and the two cowboys had laughed about after Dub had left the cafe a year ago, a matter that Dub had forgotten to factor in during their breakfast loan agreement.

"Remember last year when you loaned me that three bucks for breakfast?" Perkey said with his back turned to the banker.

Dub smiled and nodded to Perkey's back.

The cowboy turned and looked the banker in the eyes. "I was in town to get a safety deposit box at your bank."

"Yes," the banker said, still smiling.

"I needed somewhere safe to keep my CD," Perkey smiled back. "You know how them boys are at the ranch. They'd never steal it, but they might burn the place to the ground or something like that."

"I know how ranch hands are," Dub said, still smiling.

"Well, when I got to the bank, they told me it was going to cost me twenty-four dollars to rent a safety deposit box," Perkey said. "I thought since I had been banking here for the past forty years there would be no charge."

"That's not how we stay in business," Dub said politely.

"I thought that was a mite too high," Perkey said, shaking his head. "Then you came along and solved my problem. I figured it was just good financial sense to pay you thirty-seven cents rather than twenty-four dollars just to hold a piece of paper. But I don't need to explain that to an old cutthroat banker like you, Dub."

Dub stood slack-jawed.

"Come on out to the ranch after you've finished banking," Perkey said, tipping his hat. "The sun will do you good. You're looking a little pale. I've got a nice quarter mare just built for them kids. I feel lucky today, Dub; maybe I can make that thirty-seven cents back on this horse deal."

The Dance

With no introduction and as soon as Dale had finished his story, Pete said, "When Perkey and I was kids we worked at every ranch in this country. We was always trying to make enough money to go to town and court the gals."

The last days of June found Perkey and me building a corral, down by the river, for the Rocking S Land and Cattle Company. The river ran through the back side of the outfit, and it took most of one day to ride out there from headquarters. So we had camped in the rundown shack at the big pasture the night before and was up early cutting corral posts by daybreak the next morning. Perkey and I both were trying to earn enough walking around money to take a girl to the 4th of July dance. The rub was we wanted to take the same girl—she was the pettiest thing in three counties.

Perkey was real hard on the eyes in my way of thinking, but the one thing I can say for him is he had an eye for horses and women, and he had a nice horse. Sara Mae was a looker, but she was going to be *my* looker, and I had let Perkey know it straight up. I aimed to make enough money to court her, and Perkey, thinking that I shouldn't have an unfair advantage when it came to the game of love, went to work also to do the same. He didn't care much for the work but wouldn't quit, knowing that I had my head set on making a run on Sara Mae and I'd soon have the money in my pocket to do just that.

"This ain't fittin' work for a cowboy," Perkey complained, swinging his double-bladed ax like he was mad at the post.

"What in tarnation would you know about cowboys?" I laughed, keeping up with his pace. "You think 'cause you wear a big buzzard wing hat that you're a cowboy, or because you haven't fallen off that hammer-headed horse of yours yet today?"

"I just hope none of my friends see me cutting post," Perkey said in time with his fevered ax swinging, "It'd be hard for me to hold my head up in town if that happened."

"I wouldn't worry much about that ruining your life if I were you," I shot back. "I'm the only friend you got, and I'm right here doing the same work."

That only brought a grunt from him when his ax hit its mark and chunks of wood flew.

We cut post until noon, without much more talk, and then broke for lunch. I walked over to where the horses were hobbled with their heads down in knee high grass and sat down on the ground beside the saddles. I fished around in my saddlebags until I snagged my lunch, three biscuits and a can of peaches. I cut an X in the top of the can, stabbed a floating peach with my folding knife, and passed the can on over to Perkey. He took a long drink from the sweet juice that the peaches floated in.

"You're going to have to chop faster if you're going to keep up with a worker like me," Perkey boasted after swallowing the juice. "I'm cutting two post to every one of yours."

I looked up from under my sweat soaked hat to see Perkey's pile of post did in fact seem to be slightly bigger than the one I had been working on, but on further inspection I noticed he had been cutting only small trees. He could do it with little effort, and as a result his post pile was growing twice as fast as mine.

"You're cheatin'," I snorted, pointing at his pile of post with my knife that had a sliver of peach impaled on its end. "Look how puny and sorry-lookin' that pile of post is that you have been working on all morning. Did you slip off for a nap while I was busy working?"

"What are you, some post inspector now? There ain't no uniform standard size on ranch corral post. The government hasn't poked its nose in the ranch-post business yet," Perkey mumbled around a mouthful of biscuit. "We're building ranch holding pens, not government housing for the elderly."

"If I was cuttin' those little post," I said, shaking my head, wrenching the peach can from his fist and stabbing another peach, "I'd sure have a bigger pile than that. If that was my pile of post I'd be ashamed of myself and worry about the boss riding up thinking I was some kind of loafer. I'm workin' twice as hard as you. But that's not a new development is it?"

"Pete, if you'd use your head and not your back, you'd fare better in this old cold world." I hated it when he turned cowboy philosopher on me—and he did it all the time. "I'll bet you at the end of the day I'll have more post than you and you can cut any darn size you want."

"I doubt it," I scoffed, eating the last peach. I held out the empty can to him, "want another peach?"

He took the can and saw that it was empty and threw it back into my saddlebag, letting the juice run down on the only pair of clean socks I owned. I didn't try to pull the can out of the bag because it would have given him the satisfaction that it bothered me.

"I'll bet you fifty cents I can cut more post by the end of the day than you can," he said.

"Fifty cents? You'd have to borrow the money from me to pay off the bet," I laughed, eating my last biscuit.

"Well, I've got an idea," Perkey said, putting his finger to his chin. "The winner takes Sara Mae to the dance." He smiled a devilish smile. "What do you think, Paul Bunyan, you want to bet now? That way I won't need to borrow any money from you if I have a heart attack and drop over dead in the next five minutes and you chop all day and beat me by one post."

Neither one of us had asked Sara Mae to the dance, but Perkey and I had been fighting for a month over who was going to ask Sara Mae to the dance. Neither one of us wanted to ask her and then look stupid when we didn't have enough money to get us in the door. So that is how we found ourselves cutting post—trying to earn the money. We thought it was going to get down to who had the fastest horse and could come sliding up to her door first with the money in our pockets. Perkey and I always tried to work things out the best we could because we were friends, but there didn't seem to be an answer to this problem; we both wanted to take her to the dance in the worst way. The deal with this gal was putting us both in a bad bind with the other. It looked like it would test our friendship for sure, and this looked like as good an answer to the problem as any.

We jumped to our feet and ran for the axes. Perkey grabbed my ax, thinking it was sharper—he wanted any advantage. Soon it was raining wood chips on our hats. I was swinging for all I was worth, and every time I looked up, Perkey had his head down with chips flying. I never saw him work that hard, ever. His pile of post seemed to grow at twice the rate of mine.

I have to work harder, I thought, fighting for air and swinging the ax.

I was standing over those oak logs with that double-bitted ax, swinging like the devil. If it got down to who had sweat the most, I would have won hands down, but there was no question he was better with an ax.

I must have been cutting too fast or got careless, I don't know which, but the ax slid off the log and hit my boot. It cut my spur strap right in two and cut my boot wide open. At first I thought I was alright as I didn't feel any pain. I took a few more swings and then the pain-train screamed its arrival into the station. I nearly fell to the ground with the pain but managed to keep it together. Blood ran out of the gash in my boot and out over the toe. I knew better than to stop and take my boot off because I would never get it back on. All I knew to do was keep on working as best I could, but I had slowed down a great deal; the pain was yelling in my head so loud that I thought Perkey would be able to hear it crying out.

It wasn't long before Perkey came over and was leaning on his ax watching me sweat and work. He pulled off his hat and wiped his brow.

"You know Sara Mae likes cowboys. She told me once I look good sitting that big gray of mine." He put his hat on crooked, like he thought he was some kind of a strutting peacock, and he taunted me with that silly grin he had perfected over the years to drive me nuts. "You can quit working so hard. She'd rather go with a real puncher, on a big gray horse. Anyway, I've noticed your post-pile ain't growing very fast, and you ain't never going to catch up. Have you been throwing your post on my pile by mistake?" He threw his head back and gave a big laugh.

"What happened?" he asked, pointing his ax handle at my bloody boot when he noticed I was bleeding.

"Cut myself," I snapped, not looking up because I was embarrassed.

"Don't look good," he said, putting down his ax, "we best have a look."

I could hardly walk and had to use my ax as a cane to hobble over to a fallen tree where I plopped down hard. When I pulled off what was left of my old boot and sock, the blood flowed free. I guess the tight boot had stopped some of the bleeding. It did look bad but not as bad as I thought it was going to look. For that I was thankful.

"You need to get that looked at," Perkey said. "You're going to get lockjaw. Let's get to the shack and doctor it up and head to town to see the doc."

Perkey saddled our horses and we rode back to the shack where, in head-numbing pain, I got down and limped inside. I fell hard on the bunk and Perkey looked for something to put on the cut so we could make it to the doctor. Perkey was rattling and pushing things around in the cupboard. He came out with an armload of things and threw them down on the bunk beside me. On the bunk was a pint bottle of Old Crow with just a little dancing in the bottom, a bottle of turpentine, and an old dirty shirt.

"I'm telling you, you're going to get lockjaw," Perkey said. "That might not be all bad. I don't guess you could ask Sara Mae to the dance then, and it would save you all the shame when she turned you down to go with me. I guess you could write her a note, but I've seen your writing; she couldn't read it anyway. So I guess it's decided who's going to take Sara Mae to the dance."

I saw no humor in the situation. I picked up the Old Crow and uncorked it. Just as I was about to pour it on the cut Perkey wrenched it out of my hand.

"What are you doing?" he shouted. "Are you nuts?"

He took a good hard pull on the bottle, finishing it off, and put the cork back in, then threw the empty bottle in the corner.

"I need to steady my nerves if I'm going to be doctoring on you," he said.

I shook my head and laid back.

"This turpentine will keep you from dropping over dead until I can get you to the doctor," he said, pouring the foul smelling contents of the bottle over my foot. "No need of wasting good whiskey."

"*YhhhOOOOOOOOO!*" I screamed as the liquid fire burned its way down deep into my open cut. "You're killing me!"

"It's working already," he chuckled, throwing his head back proudly. "And if anybody is killing you, it's you killing you. I didn't cut your foot."

Perkey then ripped the old dirty shirt up into long strips and started to wrap it around my foot.

"What are you doing?" I yelled.

"Putting a bandage on your peg leg," he snorted. "What do you want me to do?"

"I want you to go out in my saddlebag and get my clean socks to bandage my foot," I shot back. "Did that one drink make you drunk?"

"I was going to take care to put the clean part of the rag on your foot," he said.

"Look at it and show me the clean part of that grease rag."

"Alright, alright," he said, standing up and heading to the door. "You're getting too darn cranky, and if it keeps up you'll have to find you another doctor."

"Maybe I'll get one that ain't likely to try to kill me to steal my gal!"

Perkey grunted and left to get my clean socks—clean before he let the peach juice drip all over them. He returned and cut the socks and made a bandage for my foot. My foot felt twice its size and throbbed with a pulse of its own. When he finished he stood up, nodding like he was real pleased with his work.

"We'd better get you to a real doc," he said. "But remember, a real doc ain't going to stand for your sass."

"A real doc ain't going to be bent on killing me."

Perkey helped me up onto my horse and then climbed back up on his gray, and we rode toward town. My foot was hurting something awful; it felt the size of a rain barrel. I wasn't sure I was going to make town. We rode for a few hours until we hit the road. Just as I was about to give up and lay down and die, we topped out on the road and saw Jake Turner sitting in his truck. Well, he wasn't sitting up in his truck; he was laying down in the seat with his boots sticking out the window. We just figured it was Jake because it was his truck. I was sure glad to see him; my foot was hurting bad.

"Hello, Jake," Perkey said, pulling his horse up beside the man sleeping in the cab of the truck. "What's going on?"

Jake jumped like he'd been shot. He sat up and rubbed his face, shook his head to wake up, and looked at us like we had two heads.

"Oh! Hi, boys," he said, straightening his hair by running his fingers through it. "Sorry. I guess you caught me sleeping. What're you up to?"

"Pete here tried to cut his foot off," Perkey said proudly, pointing at me with his chin. "I was forced to save his life again. Can you give him a lift to town so the doc can tell the fool he can't dance?"

"I would, but my rig just quit me," Jake said.

"I guess that would explain why you're asleep in the middle of the road," Perkey said, leaning over his saddle horn.

"Yeah, I'm waiting for someone to come by to give me a lift." Jake stepped out of the pickup and the door groaned, asking for grease. "Get down and let me see how bad your foot is, son."

I could barely get off my horse for the pain but refused to let them see it was hurting me. I stepped down off the horse and stepped to the tailgate without hitting the ground. We pulled off the bandage and the smell of my foot in the boot all day mixed with the turpentine was the worst I had ever smelled in my life.

"What in the world have you got all over it, a dead rat?" Jake asked, leaning away from the smell.

"Perkey put some turpentine on it to keep me from getting lockjaw," I said.

"Perkey, I don't know how to break this to you, but that won't help," he said, shaking his head. "Perkey must have dropped out of medical school before they covered the lockjaw chapter."

"You know I saved your sorry life," Perkey said to me.

Jake hunted in the cab of his truck, throwing empty RC bottles out into the road and moving giant mounds of papers from the dash. He came to the back of the truck and put a can of axle grease down.

"Now what?" I questioned.

"Here, this'll help," he said, smearing the black goo on my wound. "It's all I got."

"You were there for the lockjaw chapter?" Perkey asked.

Jake put the grease on real thick and wrapped my foot back up with some old shirt he had pulled from under his seat. It wasn't one you'd wear to church, but the chances of Jake landing in church were slim to none and it was cleaner than the rag Perkey had tried to bandage my foot with that morning. The only difference I could tell was that I could smell the foot even through the shirt-bandage. The grease had a sour smell to it, something like milk that had gone bad the week before with a dead rat floating in it. My foot still hurt bad, but the smell took my mind off some of the pain.

"You boys just as well wait for someone to come along to give Pete a ride," Jake said.

Jake went back to the truck cab and reached into the glove box and pulled out a fresh bottle of Old Grandad, broke the seal, and uncorked it with his teeth. When he spit the cork in the road I knew he wasn't planning on leaving any whiskey in the bottom of that bottle. He took a long pull and handed it to me. I was feeling a little green from the pain and the smell and didn't want to start pushing my luck by drinking, so I pushed it away. Perkey reached across me, took the bottle from Jake, and threw it back, letting a good bit of it run down his throat. I sat waiting for someone to come by to give me a ride to town, while Perkey and Jake drank and told lies. My foot was throbbing to a point I could hear every heartbeat now. I propped my foot up on a red toolbox that Jake had in the back of his truck and laid back, closing my eyes to wait. When Jake and Perkey had finished off the bottle and Perkey had run out of rope tricks to show Jake, Perkey jumped to his feet, falling against the side of the truck.

"Hell, there ain't nobody coming down this road," he said. "We'll be here till next Christmas. Let's hit the leather and ride on into town, Pete. Your foot will fall off and you damn sure will get lockjaw before anyone comes along this road."

Without complaint, I pulled myself back up into the saddle with Jake's help, trying not to put any weight on my aching foot. Perkey grabbed for the saddle horn and missed, falling under his horse. His old gray horse was gentle and just stood still—he'd seen Perkey drunk before and was used to this sort of thing. Jake grabbed Perkey by the collar and yanked him out and up from under his horse.

"Give me a hand up, Jake," Perkey said, weaving until he steadied himself against his big horse. "Did this old horse get taller since I got off?"

Perkey was as drunk as I had ever seen him, and I'd seen him good and drunk before. He stood swaying back and forth with his hand on the gray's rump. I thought he was going to do a header in the dust any second, but he kept his feet, to my surprise.

"Pete, I've been thinking. Your foot looks real bad," Perkey said, slurring his words. "I don't think you ought to be dancing on it. All it's going to do is hurt it more, my friend."

"I'll be able to dance by the Fourth," I told him, "and not only will I be dancing but I'll be dancing with fair Sara Mae."

Man, my foot hurt!

"Like hell you will," he snorted. "You can't even walk. Why would she want to go with you when she could go with a great horseman and real cowboy? Help me up on this horse, Jake."

Perkey didn't realize he was pulling his horse's head around as he was trying to throw his leg over. His horse spun around twice before Perkey shot off the far side like he'd been launched.

He hit the ground hard and bounced with a thud that sounded like someone dropped a watermelon from the back of a wagon. He rolled over, sat right up, and grinned, with his hat pulled down around his ears, then fell over backwards in the road, spread eagle.

"I think he's dead," Jake said with little concern.

"If he is, I'm taking the gray," I said through gritted teeth. "It's the only thing he's got that he doesn't owe money on or that's worth a nickel."

I climbed down, even though my foot was throbbing with pain, to give Jake a hand in getting Perkey back up on his horse. Blood ran out from under Perkey's hat and was dripping off his nose and down to his chin, then onto his already dirty shirt. Jake pried Perkey's hat off and found his head busted open from his right eye to his hairline.

"We could start a hospital right here," Jake hooted. "If you boys got any friends, it just might pay for me to go to medical school."

Perkey shot us an I'm-not-home kind of grin. I could see he was feeling no pain, or anything for that matter. It was good he was as drunk as he was or he would be hurting as bad as I was.

We were sitting there looking sorry and bleeding when we heard a rig rattling up the road. They had to stop or run over us because we had our horses, Jake's truck, and Perkey scattered all over the road. The red truck of Buster McDonald came to a brake-squealing stop in front of us and Buster stepped out.

"If this don't look like a good wreck I ain't seen one," Buster said as he walked toward us.

"Buster, can you give us a ride to town?" Jake asked. "Pete's tried to cut his foot off, Perkey's breaking rocks with his head, and my rig just quit me. We're sure in a fix."

Buster had just taken some calves to the sale and had his trailer on the back of his rig. He gathered our horses and loaded them as we, the injured and drunk, sat on the back of Jake's truck and watched through glazed eyes. Buster helped me into the cab of the truck and the two drunks, Perkey and Jake, tumbled into the back. In spite of the rough and rocky road, Perkey and Jake were asleep when Buster's truck came to another brake-squealing stop in front of the doctor's office. Buster unloaded our horses and just turned them loose. They walked over to the freshly manicured lawn in front of the doctor's office and stuck their noses into the grass. Buster then, one at a time, helped Perkey and me inside and sat us down in the waiting room. He waved good-by and drove off with Jake yelling, "just drop me off at the cafe, I need something to eat."

"What in the world happened to you two?" the doctor asked after taking one look at the mess sitting in his waiting room. "And what's that smell?"

"It's his foot," Perkey said, straightening up and pointing at me with an accusing finger.

The doctor helped us to another room where he cleaned my foot and asked twice what all the stuff was I had smeared all over it. He only shook his head when I told him my story.

"Well, I'll just clean this foot and wrap this little package back up," the doctor said. "It'll be alright, but Perkey, you'll need some stitches for sure. That's a nasty cut on your head. You do that with an ax?"

"It was a bronc accident," Perkey said drunkenly.

After forty minutes of cleaning, patching, wrapping, and sewing we left the doctor's office, owing him any money we had ever hoped to make last week. I had a cane and five or six yards of bandage wrapped around my foot. I had my cut boot tied around my neck with a string the doctor had given me. With a bulky turban that sat his hat up high and off to one side, Perkey looked like he ought to be riding a camel rather than a big gray horse.

We were riding slow through town, in some serious pain, because the painkiller the doctor shot us full of was wearing off. We were slowly making our way back to the Rocking S head-quarters when a pickup pulled up beside us.

"Hi," we heard the sweet raspy voice of Sara Mae say. "My word, what happened to you two?"

I would imagine we were a sight—my foot sticking out in the air with a bandage bigger than the Navajo blanket I put under my saddle, and Perkey slumped over in the saddle holding his aching bandaged head. We both set up straight, pulling ourselves together when we heard Sara Mae's voice.

She was wearing a soft, flowered summer dress that made her eyes look as blue as I'd ever seen. Perkey and I threw a quick glance at one another and knew just what was on the other's mind. At the same time, we jerked toward the pickup where Sara Mae was smiling up at us.

"Would you go to the dance with me?" we both blurted out in unison.

"Oh, yes," she said, melting us with her smile from the passenger side of the truck. "I sure wish I could, but Monty Adams has already asked me. I'm sorry. It would have been great fun to go with the both of you."

Sara Mae's mama leaned over and waved at the two of us and said, "You boys come see us. We'll make some ice cream."

With that she ground on the truck's transmission until she found first gear, popped the clutch, and left us sitting our horses in the dust. Perkey and I both slumped back down in our saddles. Perkey turned and looked at me from under his turban with what was fast becoming two black eyes.

"Monty Adams?" he said with a pained look on his face. "Is he that little skinny boy who lives in the yellow house down over there by the tracks?"

"I think so," I said, watching Sara Mae disappear as her mama drove her out of my life.

"Hell, he ain't even got a horse," Perkey snapped.

I looked down at my foot.

"Or a bandage on his foot the size of a blanket," I said sadly.

Perkey turned and looked dejectedly at me.

I looked at Perkey and then my eye wandered up over his shoulder. I could see our reflections in the plate glass of the hardware store. We looked like victims of war rather than cowboys. The sight tickled me and made me forget my pain. I started to laugh. Perkey looked at me, and it was contagious; he started to chuckle and then it grew into a loud laugh.

"You boys get on down the road."

We turned to see Sam Watkins who owned the hardware store waving us off. "You're scaring my good customers."

Perkey caught sight of us in the reflection of Mr. Watkins' window and started to laugh again.

The laugh made Perkey grimace and put his hand to his head. "Not only does he not have a horse but I bet that skinny Adams kid ain't got a fine turban either. And I know he doesn't have a good friend like Pete Steele who would never let a gal get between him and his pards."

"Let's get back to the ranch and see if we have been fired yet," I said, urging my horse forward. "If we see that Adams kid on the way, you get off and whip him—I don't think I can get down off the horse."

The Making of a Hero

"I was just out of the Navy when I first met Perkey," Malcolm said. "Just before I went to law school he and I had a little ranch, and there were some strange things that happened around that deal."

"You went to law school?" Lee laughed.

"Yeah, I went to law school."

"Let me get this straight," Lee mocked. "You have a law degree and you just didn't feel like being a lawyer?"

"You're right about one thing," Malcolm said, "I just didn't feel like being a lawyer. I knew I couldn't look my family in the eye if I'd sold out and become a lawyer. But I didn't say I had a law degree, what I said was that I went to law school. There's a big difference between going to law school and being a lawyer."

"You went to law school?" Lee pressed. "Come on. How come I didn't know about this great achievement of your adult life?"

"It might be hard for you to believe, but maybe you don't know everything there is to know," Malcolm said.

"Wait a minute," Lee said. "I just can't believe that . . . . "

"Lee, quit busting the man's chops," Dale said, holding up his hand to cut off Lee's question. "I want to hear about this law school detour in the Honorable Mr. Burdett's life."

"You guys never let up," Malcolm said, shaking his head. "Well, here's the story. I got accepted to law school. I arrived and unpacked and attended class for two days."

"Two days?" Lee hooted.

"Please, let the man speak," Dale said in a calm voice that meant we're-giving-you-the-benefit-of-the-doubt, but with a grin that uttered then-we'll-all-jump-on-you-at-once.

"Two days, that was about as long as it took me to see I was in the wrong place," Malcolm continued. "After two days of seeing a bunch of those little pencil-necked geeks, I figured out that

I was not cut from the attorney cloth. So I ended my short but memorable law career."

"Two days?" Lee threw his head back and laughed loud. "Two days, I'd say that was a short career."

"Some people spend twenty, thirty years before they figure out that they should have done something else with their life," Malcolm said in his own defense. *"I, on the other hand, am a quick study."*

"You just decided that you were not cut out to be a lawyer by attending two days of class?" Lee shook his head in total disbelief.

"Well, it wasn't that simple."

"How simple was it?" Lee asked.

"If you need to hear about it," Malcolm said, *"it was like this. I needed to go to the bank one day to send some money home to my mother. She had called and I needed to get the money there quick. So I skipped class. I just thought I'd get Mom her money, wire it to her, then get back to class, but it wasn't that easy. As I was headed toward my car this little annoying professor caught me in the hall and told me to get into class. I tried to tell him I had to go to the bank to wire some money home. He didn't care much for my mother's problem and told me so in no uncertain terms. He then pushed me with his little, skinny index finger to ensure he got his point across. Like I said, I'd just got out of the Navy and wasn't used to that kind of rude treatment. I realized right then and there that I wasn't cut out for school. So I left."*

"You mean you told him right where he could go and the school was about to throw you out on your ear," Lee said. "Knowing some other old Navy salts, I'd say that's closer to the truth."

"No, that is not at all what happened," Malcolm said as if he felt he needed to defend himself. *"What really happened was, I grabbed that bony finger he was poking me with, stuck it in his long nose, and threw his skinny carcass straight out the window."*

"Out the window?" *Pete choked in surprise, spitting coffee into the fire. Malcolm wasn't a violent man, and his confession took Pete totally by surprise.*

"Well, in fact, it wasn't that big of a deal," Malcolm said. "We were on the first floor. But the incident brought it to my attention that I needed to re-examine my life and find a suitable career—being a lawyer wasn't it."

"I'd say that was a good move on your part," Lee agreed. "Finding something else to do, I mean, not throwing the geek out the window."

"Let me get back to my story," Malcolm said.

"If it's better than the flying professor story, it might be something worth listening to," Pete said, wiping coffee from his mouth.

"It's funny that you would call him the flying professor," Malcolm chuckled. "The little finger-poker's name was James Nutt. After I launched him on his maiden voyage out the window, everyone in the school started calling him Wing-nut. The name stuck, and needless to say, he hated it. I heard through the grapevine that Wing-nut took all the ribbing he could swallow and left the school. He told someone one night over a few beers that I ruined his entire life."

"If one little flight out a window can ruin your life, you don't have much of a life working for you in the first place," Lee said. "Now, if you'd launched him out of the tenth floor, I can see how he would feel that way, but the first floor, come on."

"Too many rules at law school," Dale mocked. "A man ought to have the right to pitch a finger-poker out the window. It's only right. What's this world coming to? I don't blame you one bit, Malcolm, I'd have left too."

Malcolm shrugged, knowing he should have never brought up the law school professor pitching incident; this bunch would never give him a break. So he just settled into his story.

It was one of those warm spring days that caught Perkey and I enjoying the shade along the river, sitting our horses and talking about Ronni's pretty green eyes and strawberry blond hair. At birth, she may have had the mean awful bad luck of having a boy's name hung on her, but no one confused her for a boy these days.

You would think that any girl with the stop-traffic beauty Ronni had would have a steady boyfriend, but she didn't. Not only did she not have a steady boyfriend but she didn't date much at all. Me and Perkey, along with anyone else possessing enough gray matter to fear a painful and premature death, were afraid of Ronni's dad. He was a big brute, with arms like tree trunks, who felt anyone taking more than a second look at his daughter needed a good old 1957 butt-beatin'. He stood firm on his unwavering opinion that no one was good enough for his daughter. The problem, as I saw it, was that once you laid eyes on her you soon began to think he could be right. She could be described as "take your breath away" beautiful. In spite of my well-advised fear of her dad, I had choked it back and I was talking big. I was telling Perkey that I was thinking of asking her to the dance this next weekend.

He just laughed.

I was all puffed up and blowing a big boast about how the crisp sleeve of my new white shirt was surely going to be wrinkled from Ronni hanging on my arm at the dance this weekend. I was sitting loose in the saddle, with my hat cocked to one side for effect, when the sky exploded and my horse nearly jumped out from under me.

My pony lunged forward, hit the ground, reared up, and spun. I hung my big Mexican spur to him, putting him back on the ground ready to run, then checked him up. When I got him under rein I saw that Perkey was a quarter of a mile down the river, without his hat, working on a little runaway of his own. After control was gained—Perkey recovered his hat, and we got ourselves together enough to look like the punchers we professed to be—Perkey trotted back up to me.

"*WHAT IN THE WORLD WAS THAT*?" Perkey yelled, doing a very poor job of choking off his panic.

"I'm not sure it *was* of this world," I replied, doing just a slightly better job of hiding my fear. "I've got no clue what it was—but it was cooking."

"You think it was a rocket?" Perkey asked, standing up in his stirrups, stretching to see where the unidentified roaring object had disappeared to over the trees. "It could have been a space-ship!"

"Whatever it was, it sounded like I was under a train. I think it hit the mesa," I said, pointing over the trees. "Smoke!"

We struck a long lope up the river, straightened out a cow-trail that wandered through the breaks, then gave our horses their heads through the sage. We pulled our horses back into a long, ground-eating lope, jumping downed trees, and then we hit a hard, horse-draining run across the breaks. We were leaning over our horse's necks, spurring and pushing the reins. Perkey led the way, spurring his big buckskin out in front. I was doing some serious riding just to keep up—Perkey was better mounted. We were not talking, but my mind was running faster than my mount.

I'd only caught a quick glimpse of the rocket, or whatever it was, as it thundered treetop high overhead in an ear splitting, ground shaking, roar. We had been riding loose, up the river, moving some dry heifers to the summer pasture and talking about girls. I had just stood up in my stirrups and leaned forward to stretch the kinks out of my legs—it nearly cost me my seat. I had my feet behind me, telling Perkey how "I wasn't afraid of Ronni's old man," when from nowhere the thing shot overhead, scaring our horses, to say nothing of taking ten years off my young and tender life. I thought Ronni's dad had a hold of me at first. It scared me bad, and I was sure it would curb all future bold talk about his daughter.

I'd felt the searing heat and teeth-numbing roar at the same time, followed on its heels by an awful explosion. If my horse Rascal hadn't jumped forward, throwing me back into the saddle before he'd reared, I'd have been afoot.

Perkey and I hit the foot of the mesa and reined in our lathered horses. Our ponies' sides were heaving and they were pumped from the hard run. We were pumped by the unbelievable sight of an ink-black column of smoke clinging to the ground as it crawled and rolled up the side of the mesa like a great wave being fed by the roaring fire. A long ugly trench had been gouged out of the earth, ending in a large crater with the ground pushed up into a large mound on the other side. We didn't know what had roared over our heads, but whatever it was had hit the ground with great force. For three hundred feet on either side of the crater, what sage wasn't aflame was blackened and smoldering.

"Nothing lived through that," Perkey said, squinting as he scanned the destruction scattered out before us. "If there was anyone flying that thing. What was it?"

"It wasn't a rocket," I said. "Or it wasn't like any rocket I've ever seen."

"Are you some kind of cowboy-rocket expert now?" Perkey asked, turning in his saddle. "Just how many rockets have you seen?"

"Counting this one?"

"Yeah."

"One."

"Just as I thought," Perkey grunted.

"I've never seen a rocket with windows," I said.

"You just said that you've never seen a rocket," Perkey smirked, shaking his head.

"I've darn sure seen pictures of them, and I've never seen a picture of one with a window."

"Window?" Perkey looked at me with a furrowed brow. "What are you talking about?"

"Yeah, when the thing came thundering over I was thrown back in the saddle and my head was cracked back like a whip. That's when I saw the sun hit a window," I said. "If it hadn't been for my great riding ability and horsemanship, I would have been on the ground for sure."

"I'd buy a rocket with a window before I buy your great riding ability," Perkey said. "This thing could have been a spaceship."

"A what?"

"A spaceship," Perkey said. "You know, a flying saucer, a UFO, something from another planet."

"Oh, something from your old neighborhood," I said. "Sometimes I wonder what planet you're from."

"Then what was it, Rocket-man?" he said, turning in the saddle to face me and shading his eyes from the sun.

"No clue. But the one thing I do know is the thing wasn't shaped like a rocket," I told Perkey.

"What do you mean?"

"I mean it wasn't long and round like a rocket," I told him. "It was short, boxy, with a long flame shooting out the back. It looked black, and I think there was a cockpit in the front of the craft."

"I'm telling you it was a UFO!" Perkey said, pulling his hat off and rubbing his head. "We just as well get some help out here. With everything on fire we can't do anything about it now no matter what it was. Maybe we can keep it from burning down the whole ranch."

Forty minutes after our first phone call, the county sheriff rattled up our dirt road in a worn-out patrol car that, obvious to everyone with the exception of himself, should have been retired three to four years before. Two hours behind the sheriff, the United States Air Force was pulling through the front gate of our ranch. The situation went downhill faster than what had come across out heads just hours before.

As soon as the government showed up, marshal law was enforced on our little ranch. Even though it was our ranch, well, ours and the bank's, the Air Force sealed off the mesa and we couldn't get any closer than a quarter of a mile to the crash site. Even at that distance, we could see they were putting things onto their trucks. It looked like something out of a bad sci-fi movie, with men in protective white hooded suits. Armed and very serious looking guards made sure that we would not get underfoot of the men working. The guards, although very polite, with every sentence containing the word "sir," made it clear that their word was the final law. When the sun went down the lights went up. These guys were prepared.

"I'm telling you this is a UFO," Perkey whispered so the sheriff couldn't hear.

"We don't know what it is," I whispered back.

"That's the United States Air Force up there," Perkey whispered and pointed with his chin. "Not the local Boy Scout troop 418. They brought guns, big guns. This is big-time stuff. This is the same thing that happened in Roswell."

"What are you talking about," I scoffed, turning to him.

"Roswell, Roswell," Perkey snorted, trying to keep his voice down. "Around World War II in New Mexico, a UFO crashed on some cowboy's ranch. His name was Max something or other. Anyway, the Air Force jumped in, sealed off the ranch, and took all the evidence. They first said that a UFO had crashed, then they came out with the lame story that it was a weather balloon; they just covered the whole thing up."

"Whatever."

"I'm telling you the same thing is going on here," Perkey said. "It's going to happen."

"What's going to happen?"

"The cover-up," he said. "The government blanket will go over it. It always happens in deals like this."

"What kind of deal?"

"When a UFO crashes," he snapped.

"We don't know if it's a UFO," I said.

"Then why the boys in blue?" he questioned again, pointing up toward the mesa.

I had no answer for that one. It was strange that the United States government would take such an interest in something like this if it wasn't some kind of UFO.

We watched, waiting for someone to tell us what was going on, but we played out about 11:30 that night, so we rode on down, unsaddled, and went on to bed. The next morning, just about sunup, I was nursing my second cup of coffee when someone started pounding on the front door like the place was on fire. I knew it was a government type because the knock even sounded official, three crisp, loud knocks. Perkey let the guy in and offered him some coffee that he politely turned down.

"I'm Major Mark Burns," the man said with a big smile, extending his hand. "Gentlemen, we have a situation here."

"Situation?" I questioned over the top of my coffee.

"This is a little touchy," Major Burns said. "The United States government is going to ask you to help us out by not mentioning what happened here. We don't want to start any kind of commotion in the community. You understand?"

"I guess I don't understand," I said.

"In blunt terms, this is a situation that needs to be forgotten, gentlemen," the major said. "Your government is asking you to forget it. It's the best thing for you and your country."

"It was a spaceship, wasn't it?" Perkey questioned.

"What it is, sir, is a classified project," the major responded.

"Project?" Perkey shot back. "Your so-called project ripped over our heads and nearly killed us."

"Gentlemen, I think you can understand that I can't talk about this project, and your government is asking you not to talk of it either," the major said, standing with feet apart and his hands folded behind his back. He looked like an Air Force recruitment poster. "There are matters that you cannot possibly understand, there are issues that I cannot share with you on this."

"The thing was flying. It wasn't a rocket, it wasn't a plane, it wasn't a big bird, cow, or horse, it wasn't our chicken coop that a tornado picked up and chucked up on that mesa, or anything else that came off this ranch," Perkey said, leaning into the major's space. "Since it was an object, it was flying, and I could not tell you what it was, then it must mean it was an unidentified flying object, a UFO. Why else would you guys show up with all the trucks, space suits, and guns? Why would you want us to keep our mouths shut if that's not the case?"

"Again, I cannot talk about this," the major said, remaining cool.

"You can tell us what it was up there," Perkey said.

"I *cannot* talk about this," the major repeated firmly.

"I can," Perkey said, shooting me a look.

"Look, I don't want to have to lock you cowboys up," the major said. "But I will."

"What?" Perkey snapped, red-faced.

"Your government wants to keep this under wraps," the major said. "I have the power to take you into custody. You, your ranch, your horses, cows, chickens, that rusted old pickup truck out front, and your mama if she gets in my face on this. It would be looked at as a national security issue."

"You want me to believe that national security would be in jeopardy when a rocket lands on some cowboy's ranch?" Perkey pushed. "I'm not buying any of this."

"I CAN'T talk about it."

"I knew it was a UFO!" Perkey shouted, pointing his finger at me. "I told you."

I rolled my eyes. The major raised his hand, and two of the armed airmen stepped into the kitchen.

"Lock their mama up if she shows up," the major said to the two airmen.

The two airmen stepped forward and one grabbed Perkey's right arm as he reached to his belt for his handcuffs.

"I don't think that silence, to help our government, is asking too much," Perkey said, eyeing the two armed airmen and for the first time seeing that the major had the sense of humor of a hungry, wet bulldog.

"I knew your government could count on you," the major said smiling, waving the two airmen off. "If we have an understanding on this matter, I'll thank you and get off your place."

Perkey snapped off one of those mocking salutes that made the major want to slap him, but he restrained himself.

The Air Force left the ranch, and Perkey called the radio station.

I had visions of the Air Force showing back up and Perkey and I never being heard of again. I was sure all anyone would ever say about us would be something like "whatever happened to those two cowboys?" I was also sure the only reply would be something in the order of, "don't know," then the issue would be dropped forever, never to be thought of again.

The day Perkey called the radio station, the ranch road in front of our place looked like we were holding the state fair. We were up on the mesa when the first cars started showing up.

There wasn't a piece of the spacecraft bigger than a quarter; the Air Force had removed it all. The entire area was burned and blackened. It was impossible to tell anything other than something crashed at this location. I did locate what looked like a small piece of glass, but it could have been a bottle that we broke up there before the crash.

An hour and a half after the first car showed up, Perkey was selling lemonade. They came until dark and some hung around until it was past my bedtime. The next day, just after dawn, there were more cars. That day was a repeat of the first. Perkey drove to town and bought sodas to sell. He showed up with a horse trough full of ice and somewhere in the neighborhood of thirty-seven cases of soda. By the end of the day he had three cans left, which we drank, and a pocket full of money.

The word spread that a UFO had crashed on our place, and there was no turning back. Someone in town was even selling maps to the crash site, that just happened to be our ranch, and the people kept coming. There was nothing to see but a crater and burned sage, but they came just the same. We thought if we charged people to see the crash site, we could stop the flow of people to the ranch; it didn't stop them. Fact is, our traffic just picked up.

As the word spread, TV stations from New York were calling, wanting us to go on all the morning programs. We turned them down. Not that it was too early for us, but because we didn't want to go to New York. The producers kept calling until it was decided that they would send a crew out and we would not have to make the trip. We sat our horses with our backs to the crash site, which was only a blackened, gaping hole in the side of the mesa, and told of the day we were pushing heifers up the river and the "aliens" crashed. *People Magazine* came out. Our picture showed up in a two-page spread where the writer called us by name one time and then we were called the "cowboys," or the "ranchers." *CNN, NBC, CBS,* and *ABC* nightly news sent crews out to interview us. We were on every news magazine show that was out there—however, we passed on *Nightline*; we saw no need to stay up that late.

All the stories looked about the same, with Perkey and I peering out from under our hats and talking about the day the UFO flew over our heads and crashed into the mesa. We told the story over and over and over again. We got better every time, learning when to pause for effect, and by the end of it we had our hand gestures down pat, something that non-showbiz people don't think about.

The reporters would ask things like, "What did you feel when the craft roared over your head?"

"Like I was about to get bucked off," was my answer the first time the question was asked. Then Perkey came up with the line, "I felt we were on the threshold of making the contact of the ages." I wasn't sure what it meant, and Perkey was not that prophetic. In fact it was the local newspaper editor who made the statement the first time, but it was Perkey who figured out it made for a good sound-bite that would show up on every network. For three days, on every news program on the air, you could see Perkey staring out from under the shadow of his black hat, talking about making the "contact of the ages" and then spitting a line of brown tobacco juice to the ground.

After three months of this, Perkey came up with the idea that we should open a bar on the ranch. It was not a bad idea as we were making money on selling tickets to the crash site and selling sodas and barbecue sandwiches. We had all but quit ranching.

We sold the rest of our cattle and took that money to build a big open building with a bar at one end. We bought a state liquor license and opened up the first day to an enormous crowd. The Rocket Ranch Roadhouse was born, and we used the Triple R as our brand. We had "RRR" burned on everything: the front doors, bathroom doors, the bar, and tables. We had our brand printed on cups, plates, T-shirts, and baseball caps that we sold over the bar. Our best-selling T-shirt was a picture of an alien sitting a horse with the RRR brand on him. The Triple R quickly turned into the "in" place.

We hired a local band, and they played to bigger and bigger crowds every night. The deal worked out for everyone. The motels in town were booked all the time. Gas stations had to put on extra people and stayed open all night, and cafes turned into restaurants, allowing them to charge more for a meal. The whole town was experiencing a boom.

The Triple R made more money in one month than we made in an entire year ranching. Times were good—the best. We had our ranch nearly paid off and had made the last payment on the big note we had against the bar the day the Air Force showed up.

I was behind the bar drying glasses with a wet towel when I looked up and saw Major Burns framed by the light coming through the front door. He did not appear to be a happy customer of ours and was motioning for me to come to him. He had the sheriff standing behind him. The sheriff had his hat pushed back on his head giving him that "I'm here on a social call" kind of look—a trick quickly adopted by elected people who want to stay in office. However, Major Burns had the "I'm here to lock your sorry soul up" look on his face, a look issued when he came on the job, I'm sure. It was Burn's game face that worried me. The two intimidating armed airmen standing behind the sheriff didn't give me any relief to my worry.

I punched Perkey with my elbow. His face drained white. After telling the girl behind the bar to take over, we approached the major.

"I knew it was too good to last," Perkey whispered to me as we walked what seemed like the three miles across the dance floor to the front door.

"I'm shocked that it lasted this long," I shot back.

"I thought we had an agreement," Major Burns said as we came closer and he leaned into our space. "I think we need to step outside and talk."

"I like it right here," I said, feeling like my feet were nailed to the floor.

I had visions of the two armed airmen grabbing me and Perkey up and off to some top-secret base in Nevada that officially does not exist. There we would become subjects of some weird and twisted test to see why we were disturbed enough to pull this stunt after the Air Force told us to keep it under wraps.

"I think we need to step outside," the major said again with the crooked smile of a demented man.

"I like it right...," I choked.

"Boys, let's go outside," the sheriff said, stepping around the major. "I think you need to talk to these guys. It'll be OK. Old Buck wouldn't lie to ya."

"It ain't Old Buck I'm worried about," Perkey said.

"It'll be OK, boys," Buck said. "I think it would be in your best interest to talk to the major."

We all stepped outside and took the long walk over to the house. As we stepped in, I looked around, sure that I would never see the place again. Perkey put on a pot of coffee. He always put on coffee when he was worried or needed to think. In this case he was thinking about things that worried him, causing him to make the coffee extra strong.

"What is it?" I asked the major.

He sat down this time and dropped his hat to the floor.

"In fact, I'm not sure if it was your appearance on *CNN*, *Good Morning America*, *People Magazine*, *Larry King Live*, or the *National Enquirer* that did it," the major said without so much as a hint of a smile.

"Oh," was my timid response.

"Oh...OH? The best you can do is OH!" The major had a vein in his neck that I was sure was going to pop. I noticed that he had dropped the "sir" in his remarks this trip, giving me little doubt that he was not happy.

Perkey pitched his hat into a chair next to the major and eyed the coffee that I was sure we would never drink. The next coffee we drank was going to be government issue.

"Boys, I have Washington crawling my frame over your stunts," the red-faced major said. "I don't like it. This is going to stop."

"Or what?" Perkey snorted in a low voice.

Perkey, shut up, I thought, trying to telepathically send him a message.

"Or what," the major said in a calm voice. "Or what? I lock you up is or what."

"It will never stick," Perkey shot back with much confidence.

My telepathic messages were not getting through to Perkey, so I slapped him in the head, opting for a more straightforward approach to get him to shut his flapping mouth.

"What?" Perkey whined, ducking and throwing me a nasty look.

"Let the man talk," I said softly, smiling at the major.

"You may be right, cowboy. I may not get anything to stick," the major said, leaning into Perkey. "But by the time your attorney discovers where we have you locked up, your grandchildren will have grandchildren."

"Ha, I don't have grandchildren. I don't even have children," Perkey mocked. "And I'll tell you one more thing . . . ."

Perkey's thought was interrupted with another one of my well-placed swift swats to the back of the head.

"Quit it," Perkey snapped, waving his arms like a madman.

"Please excuse us, major," I said, snatching Perkey out of the chair by his ear. "My friend and I have a small matter we need to discuss before we continue. We'll be just a minute." I drug Perkey to the back porch, him whining.

"If you don't keep that mouth of yours shut, my boot will be in it." I shook him by the shirt and swatted him in the head again. "We're in deep here, real deep, and you're not helping any."

"That bloated lump wearing a uniform isn't going to tell me what to do," Perkey whimpered, rubbing his head. "That hurt."

"You're not going to have to worry about anyone telling you what to do," I said, pulling him close and getting in his face. "I am going to kill you! Do you understand? I'm going into the bedroom and load my Colt and shoot you if your mouth flops open one more time. I'm thinking that the major and the sheriff might just turn their heads if I was to shoot you."

"I'm not going to . . . ."

"What you're going to do is shut up and listen to the man," I said. "I am not going to be thrown under some secret government jail in Way-Too-Cold, Alaska, just because you want to let your stupid mouth run wild and unchecked. So go in there, sit down, shut up, and let me handle this. I mean it," I said, pointing my finger in his face. "I'll shoot you deader than yesterday's beer."

We walked back in, both of us smiling. Perkey's smile was not as good as mine, but he didn't get the seriousness of the situation.

"I'm very sorry," I said to the major. "Please continue."

The sheriff leaned on the table and spoke to the major. "Give me a minute with the boys, and I'll get them to understand what is going on here. I speak cowboy, and I can make them understand what we need here."

The major stood up, shaking his head, and he and the two armed airmen walked out into the yard where they lit up cigarettes.

"I don't like covering this up, Buck," Perkey said.

"You don't even know what you're covering up," the sheriff said. "Sometimes it's best for everyone."

"Do you know what is going on here?" I asked.

Buck shook his head, telling me he did.

"Then why can't they tell us?" Perkey snapped. "I'm not covering anything up until I know what I'm covering up."

"That's what I told the major," Buck said.

"I bet they don't know what it was that crashed up on that mesa," Perkey snorted.

"They know," the sheriff said. "But they'd like to keep it quiet."

"I knew it," Perkey said, hitting his fist into his hand. "It was a UFO."

"They've identified it," the sheriff said. "They can tell you everything about it. They know where it was built, who built it, what year, and who was in the thing when it crashed."

Perkey's mouth gaped open. "They've known since the Roswell crash." Perkey turned and grabbed me, shaking me. "I knew it, I knew it. It was a spaceship. I just can't believe they could know that much about it. Our government must have been working with the aliens all along. No wonder they don't want us to know. This is big, real big."

"Here is the whole story, boys." Buck slid a file in front of me that had CONFIDENTIAL stamped across its face in red letters. "Read it."

I studied the cover, thinking that I wasn't sure I wanted to open the file. I opened the front cover to find a number of reports. The first one was a report by the United States Air Force. I leafed through the paperwork that was about an inch thick. As I read the reports it soon became clear what had crashed on our ranch. It was shocking, and I couldn't believe it.

"I can't stand it, Buck," Perkey said. "I can't wait to read all that mess. You said you knew what year it was made and all, is that true?"

"1952."

"They have known this since 1952?" Perkey said, jumping to his feet in disbelief. "Who was in it?"

"Clive Rogers."

"Clive Rogers!" Perkey threw his head back and laughed. "They are using names like us. What did he look like?"

"If you saw him on the street you wouldn't be able to pick him out," the sheriff said.

"I knew it, they have been living among us," Perkey said. "This is great. What did . . . ."

"Just let him tell you the story," I snapped at Perkey, sick of his endless questions. "Just sit down and listen to the story and stop jumping around like the floor is on fire."

Perkey sat back down and waited for Buck to tell him the story. As Buck started the story, I could picture it all in my mind.

Even the Air Force had seen a problem coming. They just didn't know how it was going to manifest itself. Clive Rogers was not an alien, he was an American citizen, born in the United States—Arkansas if you need to pin it down. He had joined the Air Force five years earlier. Even though Clive was a redneck from the backwoods of Arkansas, he was one of those guys the Air Force should have loved. He was born with a talent. He could build about anything from scratch. He seemed to just be able to see how anything should work. He was no good with math, but in his words, "pictures of how something should work would just come into my head." There wasn't much about a jet that he didn't know. He could rewire an F-16 from wire he picked up at K-Mart, but couldn't tell you if it was raining. He was always coming up with this or that to improve something in the airplane, but he couldn't balance a checkbook. The Air Force didn't care one way or the other if he could balance his checkbook, they just didn't like him tinkering with the planes and doing things they had not tested first.

On the other hand, the Air Force liked the additive that Clive Rogers invented one late night as the rest of the base slept. His invention had the ability to give jet fuel a punch and pull more power out of the thrust. They just didn't like it that he forgot to tell the F-16 driver his plane was carrying the additive. Clive's downfall came when the driver nearly parked his plane in the tail of another F-16 at 35,000 feet over White Sands in New Mexico.

The Air Force felt they had no recourse but to make Clive a civilian again. A court battle ensued over the ownership of the additive that Clive invented. Clive's lawyer filed a lawsuit demanding 23 million dollars for the invention of the additive, but the courts ruled that since Clive was employed by the government and used all of the government's tools and compounds to make the additive, the invention belonged to the people of the United States as a whole. However, a deal was hammered out between Clive's attorney and the Air Force, allowing Clive to be dismissed without any blot on his record. This allowed him to seek employment in the post office.

Just because Clive was out of the Air Force didn't stop him from doing what he liked to do after work at the post office, and that was tinkering around in his shop out behind the house. He tricked out his Chevy truck. For hours he was welding, cutting, painting, and sanding on his old truck when he wasn't drinking with the boys. You could drive by his house about any hour of the night to see the blue glow from a torch reflecting off his welding helmet as he worked on the Chevy.

For weeks he bragged that he had the fastest truck in the country. That was all he talked about, how fast he was making his pickup. Everyone in the bar heard how he was souping up his truck. One Wednesday he announced that he was going to put on a show of just how fast his truck was, and that anyone watching just might see history made. The next Saturday coolers and barbecue grills were unloaded along the side of a long stretch of blacktop to see just how fast Clive's Chevy truck would run.

Clive was late when he pulled up but it was all forgotten when, to the amazement of his friends, everyone noticed he had made some serious modifications to his Chevy. Pulling, pushing, juggling, and fighting, he slipped the cracked side window back into its track and rolled it down. Clive flashed his pards a crooked, gaping, rotten tooth smile like he had just found the cure to cancer.

"What is that?" one of them asked.

"It's speed," Clive said. "Speed in a bottle. More speed than you have likely seen in your short and sheltered hillbilly life."

During Clive's short Air Force career he had managed to steal a JATO unit. JATO was an acronym for Jet Assisted Take-Off, a solid-fuel rocket that could be attached to heavy transport planes, giving them an extra kick and allowing them to take off on short runways. Clive had mounted the JATO into the back of his 1952 Chevy truck. He had spent months after work welding cross members under the bed, making brackets, bolting it together, wiring, painting, and swilling beer until his truck had a jet engine that looked like it came from the factory that way. His truck had a custom paint job, a classy solid black accented by custom chrome wheels. His rocket-truck looked hot. His friends almost lost it when he pulled up and they saw the jet mounted in the bed.

It was then that Clive Rogers uttered, "Check this out." The last words of many a redneck as they secure their spot in the Bubba Hall of Fame with their unexpected, if only to them, death. With that said, he flipped the butt of his half-smoked Camel to the asphalt like he thought he was James Dean. In what looked like an outtake from the *Dukes of Hazard* he jerked the Chevy truck into gear, raining gravel on his buddies' crop of rusting and primered pickups. He performed a gravel-heaving donut and let loose with what can only be described as a Dixie battle cry. He straightened the truck out and aimed the chipped and bug splattered windshield up the highway, stepping out in front of the cross hairs of the United States Air Force once again.

Burning rubber, Clive raced up the highway a good mile and a half at breakneck speed; the back tires smoked as he hit every gear, leaving his friends wondering why they were out here. The truck was fast but not the big land speed record that Clive had been promising for the past few months in the bar. Clive laid down two perfect strips of rubber as he stood on the brakes, then he spun the wheel, smoking the tires and cutting a donut before coming to a stop facing his friends. Clive Rogers put on his fake look-alike Ray Bans, drained the beer that he had held between his legs, and pitched the bottle onto the road. Clive removed a toothpick from the truck's headliner, put it between his teeth, and smiled at himself in the rearview mirror. As an afterthought he leaned over and set his lunchbox down onto the floor; you can't be too safe.

Clive smiled to himself.

This is something that these hillbillies will never forget, he thought.

Clive gunned the engine twice, causing the two small holes in the muffler to purr. Clive popped the clutch and then caught second gear in a rubber-burning scream of tires. He was in forth gear and doing just over one hundred miles per hour when he roared toward his group of friends. They sat on lawn chairs and coolers, flipping burgers, but every eye was welded to Clive's Chevy as he raced closer.

Clive had his history-making run planned out perfectly, driving it over and over in his head. Just as he reached the flag he had placed along the side of the road, he reached down and hit the red switch that he had installed on the dashboard. The switch touched off what Clive referred to as his "secret weapon," a JATO pack.

There were questions at this point—not the obvious ones like *What was this guy thinking?* but rather, *At what point did this rocket scientist know he was in serious trouble?*

As Buck told the story, I could see Clive Rogers lighting the candle on the JATO. His pulse raced and in a heartbeat his skinny Levis were shoved deep into the new vinyl seat covers with G-forces previously reserved for fighter jocks in full afterburn. The JATO, designed to reach maximum thrust on the low side of five seconds, caused the truck to reach a speed well in excess of 350 mph and, continuing at full power for an additional 20 to 25 seconds, left Clive, the wonder child, a mere insignificant wide-eyed fixture for the remainder of the flight.

Buck explained that the investigation later established from the scorched and melted asphalt that the JATO was ignited approximately four miles from the crash site on the mesa. (Had Clive Rogers survived the flight of the flaming 1952 Chevy pickup truck, the highway patrol would have rightfully sited him for the destruction of the state highway in addition to countless other and more serious moving violations, speed being the lesser of the offences.)

Apparently, Clive Rogers, encased in his Chevy truck, shot straight up the highway for 3.6 miles before the brakes liquefied into a red molten heap that was sprayed onto the highway as the rocket truck attained record speeds, at least on this stretch of roadway. All four tires quickly overheated as well and blew, leaving thick rubber marks and gouges in the road. As the less-than-aerodynamic vehicle became airborne, it performed a surprising corkscrew roll to the right for an additional 1.7 miles, leaving the roadway at the apex of the curve. The Chevy truck impacted the mesa 125 feet from its base, just after it had roared over Perkey and me, scaring our horses. The official Air Force report said that the crash "created a blackened crater in the rock three feet deep."

I visualized the whole thing happening in less than a blink of Clive Rogers' watering eyes. It was somewhere between brake meltdown and where the white-hot wheel rims left the ground that he realized the JATO had a shut-off switch. I wonder if he had time to reflect, as the useless steering wheel bent back into his lap under his white-knuckled grip, that his plan had some flaws?

"What's all this got to do with an alien UFO crashing on our ranch?" Perkey asked.

"It wasn't an alien UFO, you moron," I snapped at him. Sometimes I really wondered what planet Perkey was from.

"What crashed on your ranch was a 1952 Chevy pickup," Buck said. "It was not an alien at the wheel but a hillbilly named Clive Rogers. Are you starting to see the picture?"

"No," Perkey said, looking confused.

"Let's call the major back in here and let him tell you about the problem." The sheriff went to the front door and yelled for the major.

Major Burns and the two armed airmen came back into the kitchen. Burns had gathered himself together and looked much calmer.

"Tell the boys what we need to do to get this thing under control," the sheriff said.

Burns flopped down in a chair and put both elbows on the table, looking more like a rancher than some hard-nosed major.

"Boys, here it is without sugar," Burns said. "The Air Force has lost a jet engine; fact is we didn't even know it was missing until Rogers parked it up on the mesa."

"That sounds like your problem," Perkey shot back.

Major Burns' jaw tightened. I smacked Perkey in the back of the head and pointed a finger at him. He wasn't the sharpest knife in the drawer, but he got the message.

"Since you guys have been on *Leno* and in every magazine and newspaper on this planet, the Air Force has had to assign a team of people to answer the calls from nut cases, UFO clubs, and every blue-haired grandmother with a telephone who reads the *Enquirer.*" Burns dropped his head. "Fact is guys, I'm wore out. Washington is on me like a cheap suit for letting this happen."

Perkey's mouth fell open and I was getting ready to slap him back on track, but for the first time he didn't say anything stupid. "What do we do?"

"The Air Force is proposing this," Major Burns said. "You close this bar, don't let anyone up to the site of the crash, and knock off this circus. You have to stop it."

"We're making money here," Perkey said. "Why should we do this?"

"The Air Force will do this," Major Burns told him. "If you continue to do this and don't knock it off, we will release the reports that the sheriff just showed you to CNN. We will NOT release the part about the JATO being stolen. It will look like you cowboys don't know the difference between a 1952 Chevy pickup and a UFO crashing on your place. You guys will look like idiots. That will not be a hard sell here."

"What if we close the bar?" I asked.

"We, the Air Force, do nothing," Burns said. "We leak a story to some new hotshot in D.C. that a government satellite came to earth and landed on your ranch. There will be a file of dummy reports that say the satellite was critical to some nonexistent program that holds great national security. We will play it off like the government always does for a few weeks and then we will hold a press conference telling the world that you guys are national heroes and you put out this story about the UFO crash to give us time to get a new satellite up, thus saving our nation from certain ruin."

"Who's going to believe a story like that?" Perkey asked.

"Do you forget that you were on *Good Morning America* talking about a UFO crashing in your backyard?" Major Burns laughed.

"Good point," I said, raising an eyebrow.

"Everyone in the world will believe it," Burns said. "I'm starting to believe it already. Ten years from now we will all believe it because by then we will have told it so much it will be part of real history."

Perkey rubbed his head.

"We will turn the whole thing over to SPIN and they will handle the story for us," Major Burns said.

"Spin?" I questioned. "What's a spin?"

"I'll tell you this," the major said, leaning toward Perkey, "we'll tell you everything there is to know about this if you are in. You will be a part of it then. So what's it going to be, boys? Keep up the alien story and we go with the 1952 pickup crash, and you look like just two tobacco spitting hicks who don't know the difference between an old Chevy and a UFO. Or, you can choose to become heroes to a nation. To me the decision doesn't seem like that much to think about."

After a short meeting between Perkey and I, a meeting where I only had to swat Perkey in the head once, I declared, "We're in" to Major Burns.

"Good," the major smiled.

"Now what's with this spin thing?" I asked.

The major smiled and shook his head. "I have been given the option of telling you everything you want to know if in fact you want to work with us on this. SPIN stands for Secret Projects Influencing a Nation. They do just what it sounds like they do, they spin the truth."

"Never heard of them," Perkey said.

"I know," the major smiled. "We do very good work."

"It is hard to believe," I said, agreeing with Perkey for the first time.

"SPIN was created in late June of 1947 . . . ."

"I knew it," Perkey cut the major off. "They did cover up the Roswell deal. Didn't they?"

"I can't talk about that," Burns said with a smile. "But SPIN was born just after the Air Force said that a UFO had crashed in Roswell and just before they came out with the weather balloon story."

"You're saying there was a cover-up on the Roswell deal?" Perkey questioned.

"I'm not saying a thing," Burns said. "Except that SPIN can handle whatever we need."

"What can you talk about?" I asked. "You want us in on this with you, and we have no idea what is going on or what this SPIN outfit can do."

"I can tell you that they did have small parts in a lot of the things you read about in the papers," Burns said.

"Like what?" Perkey questioned.

"I can't tell you what part they played in the events that you know about, but I can assure you they have played a major role in many of the things that you have seen on CNN and will read as history," Burns answered.

"Give us some examples," I pushed.

"The moon landing," Burns said.

"What did they do about the moon landing?" I questioned with disbelief.

"Kennedy overstepped himself a bit by saying we would land a man on the moon by the end of the decade," Burns said. "That's all I can say."

"The moon landing?" Perkey's mind was working overtime.

"The moon landing, Kennedy, Dallas, the Bay of Pigs, Vietnam . . . ."

"Kennedy?" Perkey snorted. "Are you telling us that SPIN shot the President?"

"No! I'm telling you that SPIN controlled the information that came about it," Burns said. "I can't talk about this. I have already told you more than you need to know. The question is are you in or are you out?"

It didn't take us long to hammer out a deal with the Air Force. In the deal we were able to keep the bar open. The Air Force, or SPIN or whoever, leaked the information about the satellite crashing. A rising star with the *Washington Post* broke the story. There was a front page spread, above the fold, with pictures of the satellite that crashed—where that came from I have no idea. The *Post* ran excerpts from official reports "obtained exclusively by the *Washington Post*," and the nightly news picked up the story. The Air Force did just what they had told us they would do and denied the whole story, with a straight face, for fourteen days.

On the fourteenth day, the Air Force called a news conference and came before the cameras. With all the weight that the United States government wields, the Air Force held their head high, telling the American public that they could now, "without fear of compromising our national security," talk about a covert operation the United States had been operating. An Air Force spokesman sporting enough medals to give him unquestionable credibility stood behind a pulpit with the Air Force seal and apologized to the American public for the government's deception in the satellite matter. The spokesman stressed that the government was forced to tell the lie because of national security. He waxed on about how important the satellite was to our nation's security and then he gave Perkey and I official hero status. With a case of industrial strength nerves, we stood beside the spokesman, wearing our best clothes and wringing out our hats.

Our phones started to ring, and we ended up making another round on the talk show circuit, this time with a spokesman of the United States Air Force in tow. We had our fifteen minutes of fame and then the world forgot the whole thing.

"You sure it wasn't you that went out the window, landing on your head, and not the professor?" Lee asked. "I don't remember anything like that being all over the news."

"I told you the world forgot the whole thing," Malcolm grinned.

The Funeral

Lee Crump has a big Wyatt Earp-looking mustache and a sense of humor as dry as a mummified road apple in August. He had been up stretching, been over to Ken's cook table grazing, and then came back to the fire. He squatted down on his spurs beside me and threw me a rare grin.

"I don't mean to bring the mood down," he said, looking at us one at a time. "But I'm going to tell the story just the same."

It looked like rain the day we buried him, just adding to our already depressed mood. There were a lot of low-headed, hat-wringing cowboys standing around that fresh grave, trying to muster the words to say good-bye.

Willy was old, having lived a long life, and at that age death is expected. You'd have thought we could have drawn comfort from looking at the tragedy in that light. However, the only thing anyone could say was, "he died on the range that he loved" and "death came quickly, not causing him a second of suffering." But none of that seemed to ease the sting of our missing him.

We had watched in horror that fateful day when death came for him. There was really nothing we could do—nothing that could be said. Death never asks if you're ready to go or if you're finished on this earth. When it's time there is nothing you or anyone else can say or do to postpone the dark angel's arrival.

At first we thought he was only stunned, possibly with the breath knocked from him, and would jump to his feet. When he didn't, we all drew close and to our disbelief saw that Willy was dead. He could have been asleep, as peaceful and quiet as he appeared, nothing like he was in life. If there was ever a storm or wreck involving a rope, chances were good that Willy would be on one end of it.

On the day of the accident, we had started out early as we always do, striking a long lope toward the breaks along the river, watching the sun paint a little gray in the sky just before it came up. The boss had sent us down to drag home an old bull that wandered over onto the neighbor's range. The task was a common one because the old devil was constantly roaming off. Having done the chore in the past, we knew we were in for trouble. But we were not ready for what came our way.

Trouble erupted when Perkey shook out a loop and made the mistake of spurring his horse when he was pointing in the direction of the stray bull. Perkey ran up and dropped a line on the bull's horns and, with a quick flip of the wrist, rolled the rope over the bull's back and behind his hind legs. Perkey then spurred on past and tripped the animal. Sonny loped up and double-hocked the mad bull that was attempting to gain its feet.

Things were going our way, and it was shaping up to be a short day when Perkey's cinch broke. Suddenly, he took a ride without his horse behind the bull, which had slipped Sonny's rope. Perkey had tied hard and fast and was forced to give the old bull the rope, rig and all. This somewhat irritated Perkey because the saddle the bull was dragging across the river on the end of his new rope was itself only a week old. Perkey also knew he was going to hear a sermon from Wes starting with, "I told you not to put an old cinch on a new saddle."

This old bovine had been ungovernable since I was a kid. Any hand who came upon him would have a story to tell later. One summer that bull kept me up a windmill for the better part of the day and half the night. I'd been riding a green horse and stopped at the windmill for a much needed drink. I had my face stuck in the tank when my horse reared and broke loose. I jerked my head up in time to see the bull approaching like a run-away freight train. He snatched my back pocket as I shinnied up the ladder where I'd still be if not for him losing interest and wandering off.

The next spring, we were working cattle when that same bull hooked Sonny, pinning him up under the bottom rail of the corral fence. He was hooking and pawing Sonny and came close to killing him and would have if Perkey hadn't jumped in to help. This old bull was trouble every time we had any dealings with him—today was no different.

Perkey was cussing when we spurred by him to catch the bull, which was dragging all the tooling off his new saddle. Sonny was in the lead when we hit the river, and his horse, Chicken, was the first to pull up the bank on the other side. Chicken was quick with a lot of bottom, and because of that I was forced to dodge the mud his hind hoofs were throwing at me. The big buckskin put Sonny close enough to mail a loop that settled on the critter's horns. Chicken sat down in a hock-sliding stop that would have been the envy of any reining horse owner, but the bull did an equally good job of applying the brakes. Cat-like, the bull spun and hooked Chicken, putting the white-eyed horse over his head, looking like a hood ornament on a '43 Nash.

Unhurt, Chicken fell over backwards, and Sonny was lucky too that his horse didn't roll over on him. One of the older cowboys who passed me tried to get a rope on the bull but in the commotion discovered he wasn't enough of a hand. In desperation, he jumped from his horse and threw Perkey's saddle around a small pine tree, still tied to the rope looped over the bull's horns. The pine tree held, and Sonny was able to backpedal away from harm.

In repayment, the bull turned on the good Samaritan who had saved Sonny. Running full tilt when he hit the end of the rope, the bull was stretched out, uprooting the small pine tree. The bellowing bull scrambled to his feet and continued the chase. The old cowboy took to the brush attempting to escape, barely staying one step ahead of the bull.

The rope, saddle, and pine tree all ricocheted behind the bull as he gained ground on the sprinting old man. Just as the bull was about to hook his victim, the pine tree hung between two other trees, commuting the doomed man's sentence for a second time. This minor setback only enraged the bull. He abused the rope and what was left of Perkey's new saddle until the rope broke. We were all trying to help but just couldn't seem to get into position.

For all the good it did him, the old cowboy had caught his horse but was unable to mount for the horse was dancing at the end of his rein. The cowpony had his ears back, nostrils flared, and kept backing up, staying at arm's length. The fearful horse had seen the bull charging with his head down, and the horse developed a growing need to be somewhere else.

It was at that very second that death claimed Willy. He just stiffened and fell under the horse. They speculate it was a heart attack that ended his life, possibly from too much excitement for his age. I guess, we'll never be sure. It really doesn't matter what it was that took him. He's gone. Now we were saying farewell to our friend.

"Adios, Willy," Perkey said as he turned sharply on his heels and walked away.

We were leading our horses away from the grave when one of the new hands said, "You say his name was Willy?"

Perkey could only nod.

"Well," Sonny said, throwing a glance at the rest of us. "Nobody called him by his full name, just Willy. His real name was Willy-Hook-U. He threw the best calves ever to suck milk. But anytime you rode up on him, you'd best cowboy up, because a meaner bull never drew a breath."

"We'll sure miss him," Perkey said.

One-Eyed Jacks or Better

Ken had just finished washing and putting away his supper dishes. He walked over, plopped down on the log beside Lee, and handed him one of the apples he was carrying. "Want to hear a good one?"

"That would be something new," Dale said.

"It happened when I was a kid."

"Better write this one down," Malcolm snorted. "If it's from Ken's childhood, he might just name the guy who invented fire in this one or who discovered rocks."

"It was a guy named Wayne," Ken said.

"Wayne?" Malcolm questioned.

"The guy who invented fire," Ken said dryly, "but that doesn't have a thing to do with this story."

"Wayne," Malcolm laughed, "Wayne. The guy who invented fire was named Wayne?"

Ken just nodded his head.

"What was his last name?"

"That is his last name," Ken said. "Unless you know different and can give me a name, I'm telling you his name was Wayne."

"Ken ought to know the guy's name," Lee said. "When Ken was a kid fire was still cold and the rocks were still soft. Now let him get on with his story; as old as Ken is he may not have the time left to tell it."

"Thank you, Lee," Ken said. "I think."

"**One**-eyed Jacks or better to open," was how he began every poker game, but that's not how he got his name. He'd gone by the name One-Eyed Jack since he was twelve, but not because he played cards. Of course Jack enjoyed a good game of cards, maybe better than most anything else in his life, with the exception of drinking beer. When it came to cards it wasn't beginner's luck that put him ahead on the money count at the end of the evening. He was good. There had been times when a slick had seen him drinking and had bought Jack a few extra rounds, just to make the game more interesting. Jack would always be most gracious, thank the man, and drink right up, for even drunk he played cards with an unnatural skill.

"One-eyed Jacks or better to open," he'd say with a charming smile, but that's not how One-Eyed Jack got his name.

Jack Conrad's left eye was good enough with the help of his spectacles. He had no right eye. Where his eye should be, Jack had a ghoulish dark hole that sank way back into his head. From it extended a long scar that wound around his right ear and disappeared into his gray hairline. Jack wouldn't wear an eye patch. "Makes me look like a pirate," he would say. So his empty eye socket was there for the world to see, and One-Eyed Jack didn't care one way or the other what the world thought.

My Uncle Titus told me the story of young Jack on his father's ranch in Texas, across the Red River from what is now Oklahoma. Jack grew up watching Indians cross the river back and forth. They never were much trouble, unless you factor in a missing calf now and then. Jack's father merely saw it as the price of ranching near a nation of poor, starving people.

On one beautiful summer day, Jack and his brother, Samuel, were riding loose, headed for their best fishing hole. They reined up under a live oak, tied off the horses, and took down their poles from behind their saddles. Samuel caught some grasshoppers and Jack dug worms. They were set for an afternoon of fishing.

Jack was asleep when his cork started dancing so Samuel reached over, set the hook, and hauled in a catfish.

"Give me my fish," Jack bellowed, jumping to his feet. "That's my fish!"

"I caught it," Samuel taunted. "I'm the one fishing, you're sleeping."

Jack was yelling and the altercation was about to get up a head of steam when Samuel saw three men coming toward them, on foot. The boys stopped their fighting and stood quiet as the men came closer. It wasn't until they were too close for the boys to run that Samuel and Jack realized they might be in trouble. The three hard men were Indians, with cold eyes that clearly projected their wicked intentions. Samuel, the oldest, just nodded. The stone-faced men made no response at all. Their cold eyes surveyed the boys' camp.

One of the Indians had a rifle, which he held loose and down at his right side, and one wore a pistol stuck in his pants with just the butt and hammer sticking out for the world to see. The third man, bigger than the others, had no weapon the boys could see. It was the third man who walked over to the horses and, as he stroked Samuel's horse, spoke to the others in his own tongue. The others nodded to him in agreement.

Samuel pulled the poles in and began to tie them behind his saddle.

"Gentlemen, we'd best be going," he said, forcing a smile. "Ya'll are welcome to the fish."

"Get in the saddle, Jack," Samuel barked, gathering his reins.

Jack was scared; it was as though he was frozen but managed to ease over and put his hand on his stirrup. One of the Indians said something in a low tone and pointed, like he wanted Jack to move away from the horse. Jack made a quick jump into the saddle. The closest man, the big one, grabbed Samuel's horse by the bridle and reached for Jack but missed as Samuel whipped him hard across the face with the long reins.

"Run!" Samuel screamed. "Run!"

Jack lunged his horse into the big man; the Indian with the rifle shot from the hip, sending a bullet through Samuel's chest and knocking him back against his horse. Both horses broke for home. Jack looked back over his shoulder; he could see his brother Samuel laying at the men's feet, not moving.

Jack welded himself over his horse's neck and spurred him hard. The white-eyed dun was pulling at the ground as fast as he could as bullets kicked up dirt all around them. When Jack turned to steal another look a bullet ripped into the side of his head, throwing him down against his horse's neck. The reins slipped through his loose fingers and fell down under his horse's hooves. The horse stepped on one of the loose reins and stumbled. At the instant Jack knew they were going down, the rein broke, the horse's head came back up, and he took up the race with Samuel's riderless mount, who lead the way.

Jack could see nothing. All he was able to do was wrap his fingers in the horse's mane and cling to his neck. The horse ran as Jack whimpered in pain. The gunfire stopped, but Jack's horse gave no hint of slowing. Jack just hung on in a daze. He could feel his own hot blood running down his arms and onto the horse's neck, making the animal slippery and hard to hold, but letting go of the horse meant letting go of life. Finally, as his horse came to a bouncing stop, Jack was jarred loose. He slipped off the horse's back and into the darkness of unconsciousness at his own doorstep. The last thing he remembered was hearing his mother's scream.

Jack's father and a J Bar T cowboy who worked for him loaded Jack's limp body into the wagon. As the cowboy drove them to town, Jack's mother cleaned him up and prayed that Jack's life would be spared. Jack's father took the rifle down from above the fireplace, caught up Samuel's horse, and went looking for his missing oldest son.

At the river, the trembling father stopped cold at the sight of his son's lifeless body, lying on his back, staring at the disinterested heavens. Samuel had never moved. He had been killed instantly by the Indian's first bullet.

For nearly an hour the father sat in the dirt, crying. The man sobbed, holding his son's head, stroking the boy's matted hair. When the father was able to get himself together he carefully lifted his son onto the horse, sat the boy upright in the saddle, and stepped up behind him. He drew the boy back into his arms and rode home, letting the horse slowly find its own way as he held his dead son tightly.

Samuel's father was sitting in the dark with his son when the J Bar T cowboy and Sheriff Matson came through the back door. The sheriff stopped, giving his eyes a moment to adjust to the darkness, until the form of the boy's body lying on the bed became distinguishable. The man sat in a chair beside the bed, still wearing the shirt bloodstained from embracing his son for the last time.

"Russell, what happened?" the sheriff questioned, putting his hand on the man's shoulder.

Choking, Russell Conrad could only shake his head.

By first light, the sheriff and the J Bar T cowboy, along with a few neighbors, had found where Samuel and Jack had been attacked. The ground still wore the brown stain from Samuel's spilled blood. The sheriff could see where the boy's father had sat, holding his son.

Jack was slow to recover, taking months to heal, regaining his sense of balance and learning to function with only one eye, but Samuel's killers were brought to justice that same day. The Indian who had shot Samuel made the last mistake of his life when he brought his rifle to bear in the direction of the sheriff. The sheriff shot him without ceremony and promptly asked, over the top of his smoking Colt, if the others wanted the same. It is told that the pistol hidden behind the belt of the second man suddenly became red hot. He threw it into the dirt so hard the hammer broke off.

I don't remember if they hung those men. Jack, One-Eyed Jack, never talked about it again.

Although Jack has been gone for some years now, he still jumps to the front of my memory like he was here yesterday. I clearly remember Jack from when Perkey and I was kids loafing around the cigar shop with my dad, watching the men play cards.

One Saturday One-Eyed Jack was in rare form—he couldn't lose a hand. While his luck held, Jack spread his charm like hot butter on fresh baked bread. As I finished my Coke and stood to leave, Perkey asked Jack how he came to lose his eye.

"Well, let me tell ya," I heard Jack say.

That caught my attention. Thinking Jack was going to tell the story, I sat back down.

"I wasn't always this way son," he said, squinting his good eye at his cards. "I was a good-looking lad once, a lot like Ken there."

I could feel my face redden.

"Give me two," he said, throwing two cards on the table.

"I was a devil of a looker and had a soul to match. I was a sinner for sure. Son, I met the Lord in a tent meeting one hot summer afternoon." He stopped as though he was thinking about it and finished off his cold beer.

"I've since strayed off course," he remarked, putting his empty glass back on the table.

"There was a group of us cowboys who saw the error of our ways that Sunday, possibly as a result of the heat and hangovers. Anyway, we certainly regretted the sinful lives we all had been leading up 'til then. After we repented, the preacher decided it would be fitting that we should all be baptized. So we started off, on foot, for the river. It was a long, head throbbing, hot walk. We should have been riding, as any good cowboy would do, but the preacher elected that we should walk. We sang hymns along the way, to keep up the faith." Jack stopped and smiled.

"It was real hot that day, Texas-August-hot. Real hot." He got up from his chair and walked over to the cooler to get another beer. "Yessir, real hot."

"When we finally got to the river, the preacher, who in his eagerness was well ahead of us, stopped dead in his tracks," Jack said, pouring the fresh beer into his mug. "Right there in the river in front of us was a woman bathing, as naked as the day she was born. The preacher yelled for us to cover our eyes. It would be a sin to look upon her in the flesh. I fought that powerful lust and hid my face behind my hat."

Dad caught Jack's good eye and pushed the cards over in front him. "Deal," he said.

Jack deftly shuffled the cards. With nimble fingers he rolled the cards over in his hands, cut them a time or two, and laid them down for Dad to cut. Dad only motioned for him to deal.

"Well, what's that got to do with how you lost your eye?" Perkey pressed.

Jack raised the cards, ready to deal but stopped, appearing to think about the question.

"Well, son," Jack said, "the preacher warned us that if we were to look upon that young, sweet, beautiful, naked woman's flesh we'd be *STRUCK BLIND BY GOD!*"

Jack chuckled. "I chanced only the one eye."

He winked at Dad with his good eye. "One-eyed Jacks or better to open."

Rodeo's a Gamble

"I guess everybody knows Perkey," Pete said. "Dale, I was surprised to hear that you knew him."

"I knew ol' Perk real well," Dale said, spitting into the fire. "We chased many a wild cow together. Not like you sissy cowboys."

I rolled my eyes. I knew this was going to be good one. Knowing Dale like I do, I knew he would weave a story so tight even he'd believe it when it was finished.

It was hotter than a two-dollar pistol shooting uphill. We shaded-up around the water like any wise animal would do in this heat, especially animals carrying sufficient body fat to put the surgeon general's army on full alert. We sought relief in hopes of catching a breeze off the pool at the Ramanda Inn in Del Rio, Texas.

"It's hot enough to drive a man to wearing a short sleeve shirt," Perkey said, fanning himself with his hat.

I didn't answer. I sat quietly cultivating a plan to win back the twenty bucks he had cheated me out of after the Pecos Rodeo last Fourth of July. We had been eating at the cafe when Perkey said, "I'll bet you twenty bucks that if you pick out any cowboy in the place, I can tell you whether he rodeos and in what event."

"Mighty big talk," I shot back around a mouth full of T-bone.

"Better yet," he went on, "you pick a handful of them, and I bet I don't guess wrong once on what event they enter."

"What event?" I said, sliding a crisp Jackson to the middle of the table, "and I do the pickin'?"

"Give it your best shot," Perkey snorted, matching my twenty.

I noticed the steak seemed to taste better since Perkey's twenty was about to pay for it. We had missed the rodeo, and I was sure he didn't know any of these cowboys. This was going to be easy pickin's.

"Them three at the far table," I pointed with my fork, "and the fella in the black hat sitting alone at the counter. Tell me what event they were entered in tonight."

Perkey smiled big, pushed his hat back on his head, and shoved his plate away. "You couldn't do better than that?" he scoffed.

"Let's hear it, Mister Can-I-borrow-some-money-cause-you-got-my-twenty."

"Well, you can see they rodeo," he laughed. "They're covered with dirt and dust. So I've already won half the bet."

"What events?" I pushed him. "And I'm going to check to keep you from crying about losing your money."

"The fella with the black hat at the counter rides saddle broncs," Perkey said, giving me a wink. "The boy with the striped shirt is a steer wrestler. The fella with the brown shirt against the wall rides bareback broncs, and the other one is a roper."

I walked over to the cowboy at the counter who was pushing some spuds on his fork with his bread and asked if he rodeoed. He said he did. Without prod, he launched into a colorful story explaining what had kept him from hitting the Pecos pay window in the saddle broncs event: somebody opened the gate. I thanked him and walked to the table where the three other cowboys sat. In answer to the same question, they told me that one rode bareback, one was a bull dogger, and the other a roper. My mouth hung open in disbelief. Perkey had called every one of them, right down to the man.

"Do you know that fella over there?" I said, pointing at Perkey who sat watching, picking his teeth.

"No," came the reply in unison.

"Is he in the movies?" the saddle bronc rider questioned, leaving me to believe his eyes were as bad as his luck.

I ambled back to the table and flopped down.

"Well?" Perkey asked. "Was I right, or was I right?"

"You were right," I grunted as he scooped the money off the table. "But how did you know?"

"Easy," Perkey said. "Just look at them."

"I did look at them!" I snapped. "How did you know what events they were entered in?"

"The cowboy at the counter," Perkey said, pointing with his toothpick. "He wears that black hat turned up on the sides like the saddle bronc riders like to wear them. His boots are spur marked, and the heels are high and underslung, so they won't go through the stirrups. The big fella in the booth with the striped shirt came in limping, wearing a knee brace and no belt. He had to be a steer wrestler. See the cowboy in the brown shirt?"

I nodded.

"His hat is bent up in the back from laying back and getting western on those bareback broncs. The horse's rump hits him in the back of the head on every buck, which bends his hat. Also, his elbow is wrapped because bareback riders hyperextend it pulling on the rigging. Plus, he holds his neck stiff like it hurts him. You ever see a bareback rider who didn't have a bad neck? The other fella is missing the end of his thumb, and he has talcum powder on his jeans. Unless he was changing a mean baby in the parking lot, I figure him for a roper."

I'll admit I had been impressed on the Fourth of July in the cafe, but now I had him. We were sitting around the pool, and nearly everyone was wearing swimming suits. No under-shod heels, hats bent in the back, or talcum powder to give Perkey a hint of these cowboy's events. This was my chance to win back my twenty and more.

"I bet you can't tell me if these guys are cowboys and what event they're entered in tonight," I said, throwing forty dollars on the table next to Perkey's half drunk iced tea. "You picked four winners last time. I bet you forty bucks I can pick out two people who'll stump you this time."

"This'll be good," Perkey said, fishing forty dollars out of his Wranglers. "You figure your luck has changed?"

I appraised the crowd, paying close attention to stay away from anyone who limped, wore a neck brace, or had a wrapped elbow or even so much as a bandage on their little finger.

"What about him?" I said, pointing out a dark haired kid wearing nothing but a pair of swimming trunks and a baseball cap that read, *Fish Tremble When They Hear My Name.*

"A lover, a fighter, and a wild bull rider," Perkey laughed.

When I called the kid over, he called me "sir." I hate that. With a swelled chest, he declared his expertise to be bull riding. I pushed my hat back and scratched my head. "How?"

"When he first came out to the pool, one of those young gals over there knocked over a chair. The kid took off running with his knees in the breeze, looking over his shoulder. He had to be a bull rider."

I was in trouble and knew it. I had to pick out one more person, and if Perkey could correctly name the event, I was out a total of sixty bucks on this game. I scrutinized the crowd closely. I didn't want to pick one of the girls. Chances were good they were all barrel racers. Too easy. I sipped my tea quietly until I spied a cowboy step through the glass doors behind Perkey. The man wore a black hat, not bent in the back like a bareback rider and not rolled up like a saddle bronc rider. It looked more like a country singer's. He wore a pair of Ropers that looked like he'd worked all summer in them. And no spur marks were on them. He sported a big mustache that Wyatt Earp would have envied. No talcum powder, no braces or limps. No stiff neck or bad elbow, and he looked too big to be a bull rider. This was my man, the money man, the man who would stabilize my bank account.

"There's a cowboy sitting across the pool right behind you," I said, pointing with my chin. "Tell me what he does."

Perkey smiled real big. "Say good-bye to your money."

Perkey slowly stood up, making a show of it. He stretched and turned to face the man who was watching the crowd like he was waiting for someone. Perkey quickly spun back around on his heels. His face was white and his Cheshire cat smile was gone. He jerked his hat down low over his eyes.

"He's an electrician," Perkey said, raking the eighty dollars off the table. "Let's go."

"Now just a minute," I protested, jumping to my feet. "You expect me to believe you just know this guy's an electrician? I don't see any tool belt, any black tape, or any fuses hanging out of his pockets. So what makes you think he's an electrician? I'm calling him over and find out."

"He wired my barn," Perkey snorted. "Now let's go. I still owe him three hundred bucks."

Horse Sense

"Let me tell you about some horses that Perkey has,"
Malcolm said as he unwrapped a cigar.

"You got any more of those?" Pete asked.

"Yeah, didn't anyone ever tell you if you didn't have enough
for the class then don't bring them to school?" Dale said.

Malcolm passed around a handful of cigars. Everyone took
one and the cigar ceremonies began, with cutting the ends, wet-
ting the sides, and lighting.

"What were you saying about Perkey's horses?" Pete asked.

"I was going to tell you a story about them," Malcolm said.
"Something you might need to know if you ever borrowed them
from him."

"Why would I need to use his horse?" Lee laughed. "I feed
enough of my own and sure don't need to be using his."

"It's just information that might come in handy," Malcolm
grunted, and blew a smoke ring into the air.

Dale punched me in the ribs with his bony elbow. "It's
Perkey and he's hauling them two horses."

Dale pointed his chin toward an approaching cloud of dust
chasing Perkey's outfit. Two nice but worried quarter horses, a
stout 16-hand sorrel gelding and a blue-steel roan mare with a
nice head, could be seen through a missing section of Perkey's
stock trailer. (*"Stock trailer" might be a somewhat loose descrip-*
tion of the rig Perkey had in tow. You could stand in it and spit,
and the chances of hitting the floor were as good as not for all the
holes that were worn through Perkey's ancient plywood patches.
The sides were rusted through to daylight and pipe welds and bal-
ing wire kept the uprights upright.) The show-stopping quarter
horses stood splayfooted and white-eyed, heads down, watching the gravel road move beneath them as Perkey's rig rattled to

a brake-squealing stop. He jumped out and began rooting in the bed of the truck before the cloud of dust overtook him and settled over the backs of what could have passed as two AQHA champions if Perkey had ever wanted to show them.

"Had a flat," Perkey snorted, "and stopped to pick up Jasper." Jasper was Perkey's grandson, a strapping but dim fifteen-year-old boy with big ears that stuck out on each side of his head like open doors on an old Hudson.

The spring gathering was about to commence and the rest of the crew had already rolled their ropes, saddled up, and ridden off. Dale and I thought we were the drag until Perkey and his grandson rolled up.

"Watch them two," Perkey warned, gesturing toward us and waving a frayed rope under Jasper's nose. "They're good hands, but if I hear you cussing like them, I'll wear this rope out on you."

"That rope is already wore out," Dale said. "You ain't scaring the boy."

"Mind your own business," Perkey said. "Or I might decide to wear the rope out on you, mister."

The boy only grinned as he worked the trailer gate. Stepping in, he took ahold of the lead rope on the roan, which immediately sullied up. The boy tugged and pulled and waved his hat at the horse, but the mare refused to budge. The horse stood with her head down and feet wide apart.

Dale leaned on his saddle horn and squinted at the ruckus going on in the trailer. "Same old deal."

Dale and I had used Perkey's horses the previous fall and had no problem until we attempted to lead them out of the trailer. Those two horses were the best I had ever had the privilege to straddle, but as I remember, we spent the better part of the morning trying to unload them. They had loaded just fine and had the manners of a preacher on his first visit, but they refused to come out of the trailer when we tried to unload them. After we had tried every trick in our bag we ended up shaking out a rope, tying one end to their halters and the other to a tree, and driving the trailer out from under them. Admittedly not very cowboy like, but a method proven to be effective nonetheless. Remembering that show, Dale and I were naturally interested in how Perkey was going to manage this cowboy chore of unloading his stubborn mounts.

Perkey rummaged and rooted in the back of his truck until he produced two headstalls from under the flat tire. He paid no attention to the boy in the trailer fanning his hat, yelling, pulling, and fighting the horses that continued to stand like stone statues on the courthouse lawn.

Perkey marched toward the rear of the trailer, whistled twice, and yelled real loud, "Here Bud. Come on Bud. Get out here."

The two horses all but knocked the kid down jumping for the gate. It was an unexpected race to see which would hit the

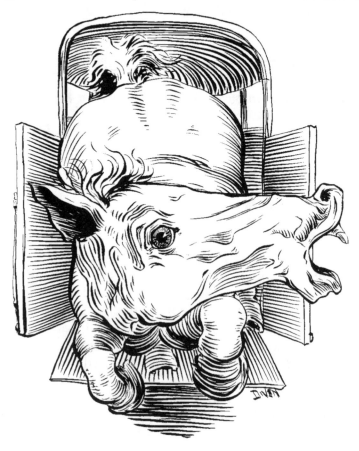

ground first. Both horses rounded the trailer on a run and practically stuck their heads into the headstalls Perkey held.

"Well, I'll be," Dale drawled, slack-jawed.

Even though these two fine animals deserved to be under nice new show saddles, Perkey and Jasper threw two seriously worn work saddles on their backs, and we all struck a long ground-eating lope to catch up with the others.

When we reined into a walk Dale eased his horse up beside Perkey. "You know, Perkey, I've been around horses all my life and I always thought I could get along with about any of them. But last fall when we used Bud and that mare we had some problems."

"Couldn't unload them?" Perkey grinned. "They're real bad about that."

"I guess we just needed to know how to call ol' Bud there," Dale said, pointing at the sorrel with his chin.

"This horse's name is Walter and the blue-steel roan is Pistol," Perkey said. "Nether one is named Bud."

"Pistol and Walter?" Dale wondered aloud, "Who in the heck is Bud then?"

"Bud's my blue heeler," Perkey laughed. "Now he's real handy to have around. Bud opened school for these horses on unloading out of a trailer. He'd start barking and nipping at their heels, making you think the devil himself was under them horses. When Bud took to the trailer them ponies were more than happy to give it up. You'd have thought that trailer was on fire the way they wanted out of it."

Dale laughed and looked back at me. "Malcolm and I thought it was your horses that needed more training, but I guess it's your dog that needs the work."

Perkey frowned. "How's that?"

"We heard you yell for Bud," Dale said, still laughing, "but I noticed he didn't exactly come a-running. So I guess it's the dog that needs the training."

Putting his hand on the rump of Dale's horse, Perkey leaned over and whispered in Dale's ear. "Bud's been dead more than three years, but don't tell these horses."

Perkey's Shortcut

"Perkey always rode some good horses," Pete said.

"I bought a horse from him once," Lee said. "Best horse I ever owned. He could sure put a handle on a pony."

"When we were kids Perkey had a horse named Nip," Pete said. "Smartest horse I ever seen. At times I was sure that Nip was going to talk and if he had it wouldn't have surprised me any."

"I remember that horse," Ken said. "I think he had a drivers license."

"Just a learners permit," Malcolm said. "Everyone knows horses can't have a full blown drivers license. Don't be stupid."

"Let me tell my story," Pete said.

"You been telling stories all night," Lee grunted.

"At least my stories are the truth," Pete said. "Not some bull havin' a heart attack."

"Get on with the story," Lee snorted. "Somebody might drag out a Bible and that will end this deal."

Summer was losing its grip. After the sun went down the cold teeth of fall nipped our ears. We were just big kids at that time, and the cold didn't bother us much at all. We were too puffed up with pride that the boss would send us to do such an important job. The only thing that slowed us down was the fact we couldn't see. There was no moon and the pines blocked any light the night sky might have given up to the trail.

We had moved a bunch of slick, fat cattle off the summer pasture and down into the breaks where we could keep an eye on them. It had been a long, hard day, and our ponies were laboring with every step toward home. We lunged them up out of Salt Creek and up to the top of the hill where we stopped to let them blow. Perkey stepped off and pulled two biscuits from his saddle wallet. He handed me one. It was hard but I was hungry and it tasted good.

"We ought to get off the road and head straight home," he said with an air of disgust. "Them old cowboys had shortcuts all over this ranch."

"Perkey, it sounds good to me," I said, pushing my big hat back on my head. "Only problem is I don't know where any of them shortcuts might be, and it's too dark to be looking for one now."

"They're everywhere," he laughed. "I been with them old brush poppers when it was darker than a tax collector's heart, and they always took the shortcuts. They'd never ride up the road like some dude on a bloated, barn soured oat burner."

I just shook my head and urged my horse Mouse up the road. Perkey pulled up alongside of me, still talking.

"I'm telling you, Pete, I know how to get home from here."

"Straight up the road to the fork, then cut back down off this knob to the river," I said.

"I'm talking about a *shortcut,*" he pressed, leaning forward in his saddle. "We'll be another three hours getting home this way."

"Perkey, it's too dark to see a darn thing," I protested. "It's all we can do to see the road we're on."

We rode for another fifteen minutes with only the sound of our tired horses' hooves between us. We had reached the top of the grade, where the road cuts back down off the knob. Perkey stood up in his saddle, looking like he was trying to get his bearings.

"Look at Mouse," he said, pointing at my horse with his chin. "He's wore out and Nip is about give out hisself. These horses are done in. We ought to be cutting across so they don't have so far to walk. It's only right, Pete. A good cowboy would be thinking of his horse."

"I still say it's way too dark to be cutting across."

"Think about it, Pete," he said, waving his hand out across the dark hills. "The river is right down there. Instead of riding the road all the way to the bottom, then cutting back, we ought to just cut across right here."

He was right. We could hear the river at the bottom of the hill. Cutting across would be a lot closer. I just wasn't sure because it was so dark.

"It's awful dark, Perkey."

"Pete, you shore look like a cowboy," he said laughing. "You can rope and ride, and you know your cows, but you don't think like a cowboy. A real puncher wouldn't make these old tired horses go so far out of their way. Maybe you ain't got what it takes. Don't get me wrong, I'm not saying there's anything wrong with you. I'm just saying maybe you ain't cut out to ride with the sure-enough cowboys."

Looking back on it, I know it was the kid in me that took up Perkey's challenge. If it happened today I'd say, "Reckon you're right," and ride Mouse straight on down the road.

"It's right dark, Perkey," I said. "You sure you know what you're doing?"

"I'm telling you," he said pointing, "we head off down there and it's a shorter way home. Let's take the shortcut."

"All right." I didn't feel good about letting Perkey talk me into the idea. "You lead the way."

"Maybe you'll make a good cowboy after all, Pete-my-boy."

Perkey reined Nip off the road and into the darkness. It was so dark it was hard to see Mouse's ears, much less Nip's rump. Our two horses were gentle and bridle wise so we just let them pick their way along down the hill. The night was crisp and the snow squeaked under the horses' hooves.

I had just started to relax and think that Perkey was right about his shortcut when I heard a god-awful screeching and clacking. It was the most terrible sound I had ever experienced in the dark, terrible because I couldn't begin to see what was making it. It was the unnatural sound of steel and rock being pulled against one another.

SCREEEEEECH, SCREEECH, CLACK, CLACK, CLACK. Then a new sound: *SNAP, SNAP, CRACK,* and a faint "*aHHHa-AAAAAAAHHHHHHHhhh.*" Brush was breaking. Then the screeching and the clacking started again and only stopped with more brush breaking and a final "*GRUNGTH.*" It got quiet. Real quiet. Too quiet.

"Perkey," I yelled as I pulled Mouse's head up and stopped. "Perkey, you OK?"

Nothing.

"Perkey!" I yelled into the darkness. "Perkey, where are you?"

"Pete," I could hear Perkey call from somewhere below me—far below me.

"Perkey," I yelled again. "Where are you?"

"Down here," his faint voice called back. "Down here. Don't follow me down."

Then he stopped talking and I could hear more brush breaking. I sat still and listened, trying to get my bearings. I could hear Perkey cussing and then brush breaking and Perkey cussing again. I stepped off Mouse and led him down through the darkness between the piñon. I had only gone three or four steps when my boot touched a shelf of slick rock that sloped off down the hill, and I fell. Mouse stopped before stepping on me.

"Pete," Perkey yelled. "You ought to find another way down."

"What?" I yelled.

"I said you ought to find . . . *Aaaaaahhhhhhhhh . . . .*"

Perkey's instructions broke off with his scream. I thought he was telling me not to follow him, so I edged Mouse south awhile and then tried to make my way down the steep hill. I took every step slow and easy, feeling my way with the toe of my boot. Then I came to an edge of the world where the hill just fell away into the empty blackness. I kicked some dirt off and could hear it hit bottom just a few feet away, so with much faith I stepped off into the dark, pulling Mouse along behind me. Within a few more steps, I again found the end of the world as the hill dropped off into space. Again, I tested the drop-off with a little dirt, and confident there was solid ground just a few feet away, I stepped off.

I called to Perkey. He yelled back. He was still below me so I lead Mouse on. At yet another drop-off I kicked the dirt again and stepped off the edge. This time I fell through about six feet of air before coming to a momentary stop at the end of my reins. Mouse, being a trusting horse, stepped off behind me. We both hit bottom in a few more feet, and I had the air knocked out of me. I was lucky. When I hit the ground I fell but had the good fortune to have rolled out of the way of Mouse, who landed right beside me. I was flat on my back trying to gather my wind. Mouse stuck his wet warm nose on my neck to see if I was still among the living.

"Are you coming to help me or not?" he yelled.

I couldn't answer him.

"Pete?" I could hear Perkey yelling at me from below me, but I couldn't breathe. "Pete, are you coming to help me?"

"Give me a minute," I croaked, still trying to get my wind. "I can't find my hat."

"I don't need your hat!" Perkey yelled. "Just get down here!"

I groped around for my hat, pulled it on, and limped toward where I could hear Perkey cussing. He never cussed when his pa was around, because he would get a good woodshed beating, but his pa wasn't around, and Perkey took full advantage of this lack of supervision.

"What happened?" I shouted in Perkey's direction.

"Coming down that hill we hit slick rock," Perkey yelled as I got closer. I could still hear the methodical breaking of branches. "Nip sat back on his hocks and we slid right on down that hill like riding a sled. Nip thought about backing up but all he could do was sit down. We came off them two ledges like they was covered with ice. I rode it out in fine style and would have gone clean to the bottom but Nip got hung up. Come here and give me a hand."

I couldn't see Perkey but he was easy to find. I just followed the sound of brush rattling and cussing. When I got to the source I fished in my pocket for a match and lit it. The match head flared to life and the flame threw a light that danced in the brush. I saw a sight that was branded into my memory.

There was Nip, hanging in the fork of a low tree, with all four hooves in the air, and a look of silent resignation in his big brown eyes. Perkey was sitting straight in the saddle like he was waiting for the parade to start or for someone to take his picture.

"Pete, me and Nip are both stuck in these branches," Perkey said. "He's good and gentle so just push his front feet back and he'll slide right out the back of this tree."

"What in the world?" I sighed.

"Just push!"

I tied off Mouse to a nearby piñon and made my way around the tree so I was in front of Nip. I pushed Nip's front feet back until his back ones hit the ground. He slowly reared up and backed out of the tree fork. Nip was a good horse. Perkey never stepped off and stayed with Nip like this was something they did every day of their life.

"Well, I tried to tell you it was too dark to leave the road, but no, you wouldn't listen," I scolded. "No, you insisted this was a better way."

"See, there you go, Pete. You just don't listen." With the help of another match Perkey was busy inspecting a big hole in his shirt. "I called it a shortcut, not a better cut, not an easy cut, a shortcut. It's just shorter. I thought you'd be cowboy enough to make it without a bunch of crying. But I guess I was wrong."

Molly

"I guess that since Perkey isn't here to defend himself we'll just all tell a story on him," Lee said.

"If he was here he'd tell it himself," Pete said.

"It's best you tell it, Lee," Dale said. "I told you Perkey can't tell a decent story. He wants to leave out all the good stuff."

"You mean the lies," Malcolm said.

"I'd call it the color," Lee said.

"Well, give us your colored version," Dale told Lee.

Perkey shouted instructions as I backed the gooseneck into the open space next to the cafe. "Come on back. Come on back. Easy. Cut left, cut left. No, left. Your other left, dammit. Left, left ... your milk hand not your sandwich hand, left. That's the right left. Come on back. More, more, more...."

I heard glass break and the truck stopped. I knew I'd hit something.

"Whoa," Perkey yelled. "That's good."

Perkey's backseat driving habit was as familiar to his friends as his gal-legged spurs and his back-leaning handwriting. It didn't just occur when Perkey was in the cab of the truck with you in heavy traffic. It took place anytime a vehicle near him was moving. He commonly shouted out driving tips as I pulled through gates and backed up to loading chutes. Nor did Perkey restrict his vocal roadway wisdom to just me. He shamelessly delivered his driving tips to anyone who possessed a valid drivers license, something he did not possess. You might think this would become a rather annoying trait, but that was alright because I had developed some irksome habits of my own. One of which was to ignore Perkey completely.

It was between "Cut it back your way" and "Look out, Lee, you're going to run over the sheriff's car," that I saw Buster

McDonald walking along the storefronts. I was shocked, to say the least, as Buster was not one for window shopping. He felt he had gathered, in the past seventy or so years, everything he needed to make it through life in high fashion.

Buster's wardrobe was that of a rancher from the old school. He sported Mexican spurs that he never took off his Bluchers. He wore his canvas britches stuffed into the tops of his boots and no matter the weather, he wore a starched white shirt buttoned to the collar. In his words, "If it'll keep the cold out, I guess it oughta keep the heat out too." He might have had a point because he always seemed to fare better than the rest of us.

This evening Buster walked slow and deliberate, like a man digesting his last meal on his way to the gallows. He didn't get around too well afoot anyway, so he stopped now and then to lean on the side of the buildings. Old Buster had what we call cowboy knees, ones that wanted to bend sideways rather than back and front as God intended. A malady that comes from a lifetime on horseback, chasing wild cattle in the river breaks and over rough country.

I can't think of a dozen times I've seen Buster afoot, and this was the first time I ever saw him in town. If anything was needed at the ranch, Buster would send "the little woman," as he called her. Such occasions gave her the excuse to shop and go to the drugstore to drink a root beer float and get in some "social-gossip-izing" as Buster called it.

With Perkey's expert guidance, I parked the rig with no paint transfer to the sheriff's car but with the taillights on the trailer broken out when he backed me into a telephone pole.

When I hit the pole and my head bounced off the back window, knocking my hat onto the floor, I didn't wait for Perkey to yell "whoa." I turned off the truck and walked out to see Perkey looking through the side of the trailer checking on the horses. None of the broncs had a saddle under them or a leg hung in one of the missing parts of the trailer. Everything was intact, all but the taillights, so Perkey turned without a word, heading toward the cafe.

"Do you think we need to back up any more?" I asked sarcastically.

"No, there's a tree behind the trailer."

"Oh," I said, wondering if he had gone completely mad.

We took our usual table in Bette's section because Perkey and she were dating. It probably wasn't anything of a serious nature, but she was the only single gal in the county near Perkey's tender age of forty-five. I'm not sure Perkey and Bette even liked each other. They sure didn't have anything in common. Bette wanted to move away and see the world, while Perkey was born knowing that anyplace you couldn't see from horseback wasn't worth seeing. Of course, these differences wouldn't stop most folks from tying the knot. Leastwise, such was the advice Perkey heard from the other cowboys as they drug the problems of the world to the campfire each night. As for my feelings on the matter, I always encouraged the relationship. I knew if they ever broke up, Perkey would have me driving up the road another twenty miles every time we had a hankering for pie. It seemed in my best interest to keep love alive.

As Bette finished taking our order and giving Perky his daily "I love you" sermon on how he ought to be eating better, Buster came through the door. He looked real bad, drawn and beat. His normal starched white shirt was wrinkled and looked like he had slept in it. He drew up a chair at our table, pulled off his hat, and let it drop to the floor. He ran his fingers through his thinning gray hair as Perkey yelled, "Bette honey, bring Buster a cup of coffee; he sure looks like he could use it."

We'd looked for Buster at the Bar Y branding earlier that morning. Usually, Buster didn't miss a chance to neighbor up. He made every rodeo, jackpot roping, and branding within a hundred miles. Buster may have been old and crippled when afoot, but sitting on a horse made him younger than men half his age. He roped like he thought it was a root canal that needed to be over quick, and when he threw, he caught. When Buster was dragging them to the fire, you best know how to burn hair—he didn't have time to wait on you.

I was surprised to see him looking so sorry. "Your edges look frayed, Buster," I said. "The little woman let you out looking like that?"

"Molly's bad sick," he said in a choked voice just above a whisper. "I've been up with her all night."

He looked like he was going to cry. I'd never seen Buster like this. She must be bad off.

"The Doc says he's done all he can. Now all we can do is wait," Buster said, rubbing his face. "The Doc ran me off. Said I wouldn't be any good to her in the shape I'm in. Told me to get some supper, but boys, I sure ain't hungry."

Buster wiped his watering eyes on his dirty, wrinkled sleeve, leaving a line of dirt across his cheek. "If she doesn't pull out of this, I don't know what I'll do."

Perkey and I searched for the words that wouldn't come to comfort Buster. Buster and Molly had been together for years, and it wasn't often you saw one without the other. I was thinking Buster was right, I didn't know what he'd do without her.

"I'm sure she'll be fine," I ventured with all the assurance I could muster.

"Lee, she's burning up with fever," Buster said. "I told her the same thing, that it will be alright. But I ain't sure, boys."

Buster gazed out the window through teared eyes at the cool spring evening. He was an old-time rancher and should have seen the spring as a good thing with the coming of the rains, the grass, and new calves—but all he could see was Molly may leave him. It seemed that all the years of fighting fires, floods, storms, droughts, and bankers caught up to Buster right there, and he sagged in his chair.

"You boys should have seen her when she was young. She was beautiful. Big brown eyes that could look right through you, long graceful legs, and a face of an angel," Buster said. "She was a real head-turner. Most men couldn't keep their eyes off of her."

Buster jarred himself back to Molly and jumped to his feet. "I best be going," he said, fishing in his pocket for coffee money. "I can't eat right now. I need to get back to her."

"You go on. I'll get the bill," Perkey said. "If it's alright, Lee and I'll drop by before we head home?"

Buster forced a smile and nodded. His eyes filled with tears again. "I'm ashamed of it boys, but I didn't always treat her right," Buster said. He cleared his throat and ducked his head with shame. "She deserved better than me."

"She loves you," Perkey said sadly.

"Years ago I'd pull a cork on occasion, but she'd always take care of me. She was always there when I needed her and never had a complaint. I sure don't know why."

"It's because she loves you," came a booming voice from behind Buster.

Startled, Perkey and I looked past Buster to a short, bald gentleman dressed in a dapper suit, who had rested his ham-like hand on Buster's shoulder.

"Sir, I don't know you," the man said, sticking his hand out to shake. "I'm the new preacher in town. I didn't mean to eavesdrop, but I was sitting at the next table and it was hard not to. It's clear to me that Molly loves you very much and that you love her. So why don't you go tell her. It'll mean more to her than anything the doctor can do for her."

Buster ducked his head, turned on his heels, and walked out without comment.

"I hope I didn't say anything to upset the old gentleman," the preacher said.

"It's just hard on him, preacher," I assured the man as he watched Buster slowly walk out the door.

"Tomorrow's my first sermon here. I'll see to it the church prays for Molly," the preacher promised. "What's the man's name?"

"Buster McDonald," Perkey replied, standing up and dropping money on the table for the meal.

"Yes, tomorrow in church I shall make a special time of prayer for Molly McDonald," the preacher said, imagining the impression it would make on the congregation. "The whole town will be praying for his wife this time tomorrow. The Lord will listen to the pleas of his children."

Perkey pulled his hat on and looked the preacher square in the eye.

"Buster and Molly ain't married, preacher," he said.

"Oh my, my," the preacher said, shaking his head. "But, now is not the occasion to concern ourselves about such things. The woman needs our prayers. I'll still see to it that prayers are said in her behalf."

"Preacher, it'll tickle Buster to hear that," Perkey said. "We'll tell him."

In the truck I immediately turned to Perkey before he could start his driving instructions and asked, "Why did you say that to the new preacher?"

"I didn't do anything wrong. Hell, everyone knows Buster and Molly ain't married," Perkey grinned. "And it'll tickle Buster that the new preacher will ask for prayer for Molly at his very first church service." Perkey couldn't contain himself any longer and laughed out loud. "It'll tickle him to death. Can't you see that preacher's face when he finds out that Molly is Buster's buckskin mare?"

Worlds Apart

"Any of you boys ever punch in Oklahoma?" Ken asked.

"They got cows in Oklahoma?" Pete asked.

"Just wild ones."

"The kind I like," Pete smiled.

"Well, if you'd quit interrupting me, I'll tell you what great brush poppers Dale, Perkey, and I are," Ken said.

"More lies," Lee laughed. "More lies. You might make some-one believe you're a great puncher, but looking around this fire I don't see the gullible fool."

"After this story you will have your mind changed," Ken said.

"The only thing I'd let you change is my oil," Lee said. "And I'm not sure about letting you do that."

"Forget him, Ken," Malcolm said. "Tell the story before Dale thinks of one and puts us all to sleep."

I'll never forget that day. I'm not good with dates, never have been. That's why I keep the bank's calendar hanging in the kitchen. I mark off each day and write down such things as when I doctor, wean, when my mares foal. I even have Barb's birthday marked in red—keeps me out of trouble—but I didn't mark that day. A hot iron couldn't have burned any deeper into my memory. Half a lifetime has passed. Still I remember.

It was hot and I was sitting a big bay horse with sweat running down my face, burning as it reached the cut below my right eye. The open gash was a medal of a war waged that day among the brush of the Indian Nation in southeastern Oklahoma. I had sought comfort in the shade of a large oak and sat quietly watching the tall grass dance under the warm summer breeze. My big bay deserved the rest.

Those mountains were the last stop for the Choctaw Nation when the United States Cavalry had marched them up the Trail of Tears from Mississippi. The mountains were named when the Choctaws decided they had had enough of the forced march and said, "Kiamichi," which means "go no further."

I stretched in the stirrups and shifted my weight to straighten my rig. This was a rough country with horse-crippling rocks and brush that laid in wait to chew up both horse and rider. We had cattle scattered throughout that man-eating-brush, and they were wise in its use to their advantage.

The cattle weren't really ours. We were just day labor. They belonged to an old preacher. I don't believe he was a real preacher, and I'm not sure why everyone called him that unless it was that he sure liked to talk. In the tall tale department he took second place to nobody. Most of his talk consisted of boasting of his past adventures. I was of the belief that long threads of fiction held those tales together, but who was I to call a preacher a liar.

The preacher always kept a big pistol close even though he wasn't very good with it. To hear him tell it he was a big pistolero and had on one occasion been forced to dispatch two unsavories to the hereafter behind a blue haze of gun smoke. If pressed to demonstrate his highly bragged about skills with the sidearm, he would allow, "that was in my younger days," or "I just cleaned her." Not being a man who took to work, and thinking grass was free, the preacher had gotten into the cattle business. However, the lesson learned was cattle meant nothing but work.

Even though his herd had their heads down in stirrup-deep grass, they were starving. They had been going downhill since he had kicked them out on his range. He had tried everything, and now he reasoned that his cattle were poor because they were wormy. Since he knew that meant a lot of work, he had come, hat in hand, to ask Perkey, Dale, and me for help.

We told him we weren't big on the idea, but he had some strong talk, promising a full evening of entertainment at the end of the job. Since we didn't have anything else going on and since the show he promised sounded to be a good time, we threw in with him.

Before sunup the following day we all met at Mr. Burges' ranch house. Mr. Burges, the fellow who tended the cattle for the preacher, was the worker of the outfit. An old man, Mr. Burges walked on two-inch riding heels that were worn to the outside, giving him the air of a man best suited for horseback. On foot he could hardly get around, but mounted, he was the youngest-looking one among us.

Mr. Burges had been a cook in the army, and proving that he took to his trade, he slid a pile of griddle cakes across the table with a side order of bacon, sorghum, and sweet milk. Talk was short. No one wanted to come up shy on the hotcake count. After breakfast, the sky was starting to show a little light as we struck a long lope toward the river.

Those cattle had been to school, and the dew hadn't burned off the grass before we were in a jackpot. At the first sight of men on horseback, those wild cattle took flight and hit the brush. Quail would have been easier to pen than those brushwise cattle, leaving their social skills in need of polish.

Perkey was a hand with a riata and chased a cantankerous old mosseyhorn into the creek and up the other side. He spurred up on the cow and rolled out a loop, took two spins, and was just about to mail it when she took to the brush. Not hesitating, Perkey tucked the rope under his arm and ducked his head as his horse hit the brush on the heels of the runaway cow.

The progress of the chase could be followed by the sound of breaking brush, bawling cattle, and Perkey's cussing. Perkey's cussing stopped as quickly as it started. I figured an attack of better judgement must have seized him when he remembered he was working for a preacher, but I realized my error when the old cow bolted from the brush chased by a riderless horse.

"He quit his horse," Dale said, reining Pistol, his blue-steel roan up beside me.

We drew up at the edge of the brush and called to Perkey but heard nothing, so we eased our horses into the thicket. The thorns and thick branches clawed at our chaps, and only the big brims on our hats kept our faces from being chewed up. It's a mystery how Perkey had ridden as deep into that brush as he did. It was all we could do to get through it at a walk.

About a hundred yards into the thicket we found Perkey, bloody, laying on his back, eyes staring straight up to heaven. His hat was missing and one boot was pulled off and laying beside him.

I leaned forward in my high-backed saddle. "You all right?" I received no reply.

Dale threw his leg over the roan and stepped off. His bat-wings hung in the brush for just a second, and his Mexican spurs jingled as he walked to the body on the ground.

"You alive?" he asked, fanning Perkey with his hat.

The first sign of life came when Perkey closed his eyes and reopened them. He had had the wind knocked out of him, so in trying to speak, all that emerged was a high-pitched cat-like racket, "*AAAAAAaaaaaAAAAA.*"

Attempting to be polite, Dale ducked his head and held his laughter, but his eyes filled with tears that ran down his face, making little paths in the dirt. Not wanting to display my amusement, I covered my smile with my hand, pretending to brush back my mustache.

"I couldn't believe you jumped your pony headlong into the briar patch," Dale chuckled after Perkey got his wind.

"That hoss stayed with her," Perkey said, plucking his hat from a branch. "I had no say in the matter."

"If I had've made it," he smiled, "it sure would have been pretty."

At noon we broke for lunch with only half the cattle penned. We didn't linger and were quickly back to the job at hand. Dale, Perkey, and I were tracking wild cattle and dragging them out of the brush while Mr. Burges and the preacher worked the corral.

Mr. Burges would worry the cattle up the chute. The preacher would catch them in the head trap and worm them.

Dale glimpsed a motley faced heifer down toward the Mountain Fork River and gave chase. He built what he called a blanket loop, one that would cover anything, and was closing in to make a catch. She was trying to make the river, but Dale felt he had enough horse under him and kept coming. She slid down the bank on her hocks, then leaped to freedom just as Dale's loop dropped around her horns. She stretched out like a dog on a short leash, dragging Dale and the roan into the river. Dale popped up like a cork, still wearing his hat. Pistol climbed out one side and the cow out the other, pulling Dale's rope. Dale was a dally man.

In the meantime, Mr. Burges had been kicked by an unruly beast when he attempted to run a bunch up the chute. He wasn't hurt to speak of, just a few bruises. The ol' preacher came closer to getting hurt when a bent horn she-devil with an attitude turned back on him. She pinned him to the fence with a horn on either side of his bloated belly. Mr. Burges saved the man-of-the-cloth by jumping, waving his arms, and drawing the cow's attention. She turned on Mr. Burges, and the reverend wasted no time getting his fat carcass up the fence.

I received the cut on my face when I made the mistake of roping a big cow while on foot. She was standing in a heavy thicket. I mistakenly thought I could throw a rope on her and then tie her off until I could get some help. The idea sounded workable at the time, so I tied the bay off and eased back into the brush on foot. Cat-like, I slipped from tree to tree. When I got close enough, I stepped out and took a spin with the loop. Who would have thought she would have charged me? I beat her to the tree and dropped the rope on her as she went by. Before I could snub her off, I got a close look at about five acres of brush from the other end of that rope. When I did get the rope around a tree she turned back. That cow and I cleared some brush before I heard Dale yell, "Need some help?"

"No," I panted, hoisting myself up a low limb. "Unless I want out of this tree."

We penned the rest of the cattle just before dark, and the sun set on us as we topped the mountain, riding toward Arkansas. We were tired but looking forward to a full evening of entertainment. The thick trees blocked the moonlight, making it impossible to see the trail so we let our horses have their heads. The big bay stumbled under me as we slid down the side of the mountain. Catching his balance, he lunged forward to make the grade up the other side. We rode without a word, heads down, trusting our mounts.

After we cleared the timber, we hit a road and picked up the pace. With only a mile of road behind us, we crossed the Arkansas line and took the first lane. We drew up in front of a small white house, and by the light of the moon we stripped off the saddles and fed our horses. We knocked the dust off our clothes with our hats and went on into the house. The excitement in the house was laced with the smell of horse sweat and dust. Each of us knew the evening's entertainment would be something that we would not soon forget, something to tell our grandkids.

Taking a seat in a straight-backed wooden chair, I accepted a glass of water from the lady of the house. I hooked a spur over the end of an empty chair and pushed my hat back. Even though it has been years since that night, I've not lost a moment of that event to the passing of time. I remember the way we were dressed, still wearing our hats, boots, spurs, and chaps, how we had ridden up on those tired ponies, and how we sat in the house listening to our horses outside pawing the ground and blowing as they ate. What a funny sight, I thought. We could have graced the cover of an 1885 dime novel. In fact, the date was July 20, 1969, and we were gathered around one of the few television sets in that part of the country to watch Neal Armstrong make history by putting the first human track on the moon.

"You darn liar. That didn't happen to you, it happened to me," I said. "Perkey and Dale weren't there; it was a good friend of mine named Wes Tischer and another long legged cowboy

whose name I can't remember. And what's that about the calen-
dar and Barb's birthday?"

    "It was a good story I heard you tell," Ken laughed. "I just
thought the calendar and Barb's birthday gave it a nice touch."

    "So did I, Ken," Malcolm laughed.

    "Have you no shame?" I asked Ken

    "Yeah, but I left it home," he said. "I didn't think I'd need it
here."

Chicken and the Hero

"I liked the story, and I don't think Steve could have told it as well," Malcolm said, leaning over to pour himself another cup of coffee. "You boys want to hear a real punchy story?"

"It must have happened to someone else," Dale said, "'cause you ain't no puncher."

"As a matter of fact, it was Perkey again."

"Do you think Perkey will live long enough for all this to happen to him?" I asked.

"He is one exciting individual," Pete said.

"I'm still wondering when he finds time to do just the things I've heard here tonight," I said.

"Well, this is a true story," Malcolm said.

Wayne Murphy stared at the distorted reflection of his weather hardened features as they rippled and swayed in the sheets of water that ran down the window.

"Texas' never seen this much water," he said, turning from the rain beaten pane. "We got to do somethin' or I'll lose those cattle."

"I'll have Chicken saddled by first light," Perkey said nervously.

Wayne buttoned up his slicker tight to his neck and tugged his rain-heavy hat into place.

"Thanks, Perkey," he said, stepping out the door. The cold rain ran down the back of his neck as he turned and stuck out his rough hand to shake. "Ya know it could get rough. But I'm in real trouble."

"I wouldn't be much account if I couldn't help out a neighbor in a tight," Perkey said.

Clasping Hector's threadbare old serape around him, Perkey struggled with what the next day held. Through the window he saw the outline of the trees blowing between the flashes of lighting. He tried to sort out his feelings and look at things calmly, without worry. If it would just quit raining, maybe they wouldn't have to go.

Perkey was jerked straight up by an explosion of lighting and thunder that shook the whole house and lit up the room. He shook his head to loosen the cobwebs of the fitful night's sleep. Taking his pocket watch from the nightstand, he waited for another flash of lighting to read the time. Four thirty.

In the dark, buttoning his shirt, he listened to the howling wind and rain beating the paint off his house.

The line of riders first appeared as ghostly shadows in the gray morning light. They rode Indian fashion, one behind the other, up the muddy road. From under his hat, Perkey watched the rhythmic bouncing of the horses' heads as each step brought them closer. Finally, the riders drew rein in front of him.

From the back of his mouse-colored gelding, Wayne threw Perkey a big grin. "Good morning to be by the fire," he said. Turning in his saddle, he pointed his chin at the other riders. "Perkey, you know everybody? Ike Ludlow, Martin Green, and Micky Hudson."

Green looked like a man who didn't get his morning coffee. He leaned over his saddle horn and shook with Perkey.

"Did Wayne fill ya in on our problem?" he questioned.

"We're driving cattle in before the river reaches them."

"It sounds easy," Green said. He pointed a crooked finger. "Yonder a few miles, where the two rivers come together, Wayne's got a bunch of she stuff, or did yesterday. The river is on the rise and now there ain't nothin' down there but an island and it's gettin' smaller with every drop of rain. If we don't throw them on this side, they'll just stand there bawlin' 'til they drown."

"This ain't going to be a Sunday outing," Wayne said. "That water is running hard and it'll pull ya under. The cattle are going to be hard to handle, and watch for snakes."

"Snakes!" Green groaned.

"We need to look out for each other." Wayne cut a piece of tobacco and pushed it into his mouth. "Let's get to it before we drown," he said, touching a spur to the horse.

Fearfully, Perkey fell in behind the riders as they started toward the river. The mud sucked and pulled at the horses' hooves with each step.

The slicker clad men rode into the wind until turning into a large stand of trees. Down the muddy hills, the horses slid and picked their way around the underbrush. They rode for what seemed like hours in the rough country. Up and down, back and forth they rode. The rain never let up.

The horses seemed out of control at times, losing their footing, sliding on their hocks, then breaking into a run to keep from falling. Perkey was about to make himself sick with thoughts of water by the time they spilled out onto the ravaged banks of the river.

Now Perkey's heart jumped into his throat and his stomach coiled into painful knots. Unconsciously, he drew Chicken to a grinding halt. Fighting back panic, he swallowed hard against the taste of fear. His eyes worked frantically in every direction, scanning the turbulent scene ahead. Everywhere his eyes fell was water; muddy, churning, raging water.

"There they are," Wayne shouted, pointing to a small patch of land protruding from the brown rushing water.

The island was a mile away, crowned with dark shadows that Perkey presumed to be cattle. Between the riders and the island was the worst water he had ever seen. The bottom land was flooded with the turbulent waters of creeks and rivers overflowing their banks. Carried along were uprooted trees and other trash caught by the quickly rising flood.

Ike, Martin, and Mickey were pointing out a proposed route over to the cattle when Wayne drew up next to Perkey. "Ever swim a hoss?" he asked in a low voice.

Perkey shook his head and swallowed hard, unable to tear his gaze from the raging scene. Wayne leaned over and whispered, "There ain't much to it. Just put him in the water and give him his head. But if he starts to sink, slide off and grab his tail."

Perkey turned in disbelief. His face was white. "Do what?"

"If he gets in trouble, slide off the saddle and grab his tail," Wayne repeated. "If ya feel like ya need to turn him, use your hands on the side of his neck." Wayne spit a line of brown tobacco juice into the river. "Let him go with the current as much as ya can."

Wayne barely finished his explanation when Ike spurred his sorrel, disappearing into the water with a splash and resurfacing a few feet downstream. Martin and Mickey followed. Wayne and Perkey walked their horses to the bank.

"You'll do fine," Wayne said.

Perkey stared at the water with an open mouth as frightening visions flooded his head. Crawl off the back of the saddle, he thought. The minute I hit the river it's over. My boots will fill with water and drag me straight to the bottom like an anvil. Eventually, I'll end up as part of a buzzard's diet.

Perkey turned to ask Wayne if he should remove his boots but it was too late. Wayne had jumped his horse into the river and was gone. Perkey choked back fear. The possibility of his boots filling with water wasn't all that troubled him. The surging, swirling current tugging and pulling everything along was bad enough. The fact that he couldn't swim made it worse. He had always been afraid of the river.

The rain peppered him. Chicken stood at the edge with his hide twitching and his head down, as though smelling the water. Touching a spur to Chicken was one of the hardest things Perkey had ever done. He urged the horse on. Chicken leaned forward, then reared back. Again, Perkey touched a spur to the horse but with the same result. Perkey looked up. The black clouds held no promise of relief. And Wayne was swimming away.

Perkey's heart pounded in his throat. Pulling his hat down hard, he thrust his spurs into the big horse with authority, sending them bolting into the river below.

Dirty brown water covered them like a grave. As Perkey feared, his boots filled with water, pulling him down. His slicker and clothing choked him. Deeper and deeper into the river they went. Life had dealt him the final blow. What he had feared all his life was coming true. He would drown. Suddenly, they broke the surface and he gulped air. Chicken's eyes showed white and his nostrils flared as he battled the current to keep his head up.

Perkey, a big man with heavy muscles from years of hard work, knew he was too much for Chicken. The horse couldn't stay up. To save them both, Perkey slid back onto the horse's rump, grabbed his tail, and slid off. Again he sank. He strained against the horse's tail to raise his nose above water. Free of the excess weight, Chicken started to swim. Perkey clung tightly as he was dragged along through the water and debris. His hands ached from his white knuckled death grip on the horse's tail. Perkey knew if he lost his grip he would also lose his life.

The riders swam toward the island, occasionally reaching shallows where the horses could walk for short distances before swimming again. A hundred yards from the bank, they met a deer swimming the other way.

"He's got better sense than we do," Perkey mumbled, encouraged by his limited success.

When Chicken reached the island, he wasted no time getting onto dry land, an action Perkey supported completely.

The island was less than twenty acres in size, and soon the cowboys had gathered the small herd. They crowded the cattle into the water and pushed them toward the opposite bank. Perkey slid off his horse's back, once again keeping a death grip on Chicken's tail.

The cattle were driven to safety with only one loss. They had bunched up in the deepest part of the river and a calf was pushed under, never to resurface. Even so, the men felt lucky. And Perkey couldn't believe his good fortune. He had survived the day.

Saturday morning, Wayne was in J.D. Wilson's Drugstore on his round of errands. "Wayne, come on back here. I want to talk," Mr. Wilson shouted from the back room.

"How's business J.D.?"

The old man straightened up from his ledger. "Martin Green was in and tells me you had some cattle trapped by the flooding."

"We got 'em all but one."

"Who helped you gather them?"

"Ike, Martin, Mickey, and Perkey."

The old man took off his glasses and rubbed his eyes. "I couldn't believe it when Martin said Perkey was there."

"Why not?" Wayne asked. "He's a good hand."

"Perkey can't swim," the old man said, pulling a handkerchief out of his vest pocket to clean his glasses.

"That explains his bad color the other morning," Wayne laughed.

"That's not all," the old man said, replacing his glasses. "He's afraid of water. He'd never get close enough to the river to fish, after the accident."

Wayne looked perplexed. "What accident?"

"Well, when Perkey was a kid I worked on his father's ranch, and us cowboys about raised him." The old man paused and looked down at his hands like the story was written in the wrinkles. "He liked to ride with us. It was cold the day of the accident. There wasn't nothing between us and the North Pole but barbed wire.

"I was riding with this old Mexican," J.D. laughed. "His English was as bad as my Spanish. We couldn't talk but we sure had a time.

"Anyway, we were riding along the river and Perkey loped on ahead like a kid will. We rode along for a while until we came upon Perkey in the water. His horse had thrown him. The old Mexican ran ahead and jumped in because the kid was in trouble. I came up and threw them a rope.

"Perkey was near froze," Mr. Wilson said, rubbing his hands again. "I didn't have a blanket so the old man wrapped the boy in his serape. I rode back to the ranch carrying Perkey. The old Mexican's chaps were frozen stiff when we got there. The Mexican caught a chill and passed away a few weeks later.

"I rode with him for two years," Mr. Wilson said. "And I can't even remember his name."

"Hector."

Mr. Wilson and Wayne turned to see Perkey.

"His name was Hector," Perkey repeated.

"Perkey, if I'd known all this, I wouldn't have put you on a spot by asking for your help," Wayne said.

"It's time I was getting over fear of the water," Perkey laughed.

"You should have told me," Wayne said.

"I was raised by some good cow people. Hector was one of them. They taught me a lesson," Perkey said. "If a neighbor needs help, you help him. If Hector hadn't gotten in the water that day I'd have gone under."

"If you hadn't gotten in the water the other day, I'd have gone under," Wayne said. "But you still should have told me about your fear of the river."

"I was going to but then I realized that I didn't know my way home."

"That didn't happen to Perkey," I said, "it happened to Al Grugan and Al passed away five years ago."

"I know," Malcolm said. "I heard the story about ten years ago but I knew Al wouldn't mind if I used his story. It is a good story."

"It was a good story," I said. "But it didn't happen to Perkey."

"I just used Perkey 'cause you all knew him."

"You're as bad as Ken about stealing stories and tacking someone else's name on it," I said.

"It's still a good story," Malcolm laughed.

Retirement

"When Perkey started getting older I remember his boy started talking about him retiring," Lee said. "Perkey didn't think too much of the idea."

"Perkey didn't care much for his boy's ideas in general," Pete said.

"He sure didn't like the kid's idea on retirement." Lee pushed his hat back and folded his arms as he started his story.

Retirement, a concept conceived by some lazy, pimpled-face kid who hadn't lived long enough to ever have a real job, Perkey was sure of it. He didn't like this retirement concept, no matter who thought it up. He saw no need for it and couldn't understand why his boy was so big on the idea. The idea of a man laying around the house all day being retired just wasn't natural. It wasn't by Perkey's design that his cattle were sold, but it came from family pressure. His boy insisted on making those long drives up from the city every weekend just to harp, nag, and plead with his dad to sell the cows and "move in town where life would be easier." How was living in a smog-choked little house and listening to the neighbors fight going to make life easier? Would the pain from his jack-out-of-place shoulder be easier to live with when it rained? He didn't think so, but it was during one of his weaker moments that he told the boy he would retire. What was he thinking?

Now, one wooly range bull was all that stood between him and his golden years of leisure playing bingo with wrinkled, blue-haired women who were just one more husband away from calling it quits. Perkey didn't think much of laying around in town and eating at the city-run center for the old and getting fat. He cared even less for his son's idea of buying an RV, or as Perkey called them a "Lizard Hutch," to drive around the country to see the Grand Canyon with the "newlyweds and the nearly deads." He remembered how Buster McDonald's health was sent into a nose dive last year just after he sold all his cattle. Perkey's boy said that Buster sold out because of his health, but Perkey figured it was the other way around; it was selling his cattle that caused his sudden bout with bad times. Buster just needed more sunshine and wasn't getting it in town.

The old bull holding up Perkey's retirement party should have been on the truck with the rest of the herd, but you don't get to be an old bull by being stupid. He eluded the cowboy's last sweep of the big pasture. So Perkey saddled Cat.

Cat got his name when he was tied in the stall and a barn rat happened to pass through on his last trip to the grain. The young colt kicked the stall down trying to kill that rat. The rat ran from one end of the stall to the other, trying to escape, but the colt chased him like a cat and killed him. So Perkey started calling the horse Cat. Perkey would leave the horse in the barn at night, and his rat population was diminished greatly. Every morning Perkey found dead rats in the barn where the colt had stomped them into the ground. When Perkey went to saddle the horse he would yell, "here kitty, kitty, kitty."

The idea when Perkey saddled Cat was to just hunt the old bull, or that was the plan he had made over his eggs that morning. But plans change as this one had, and now it didn't matter what Perkey had planned, what was happening to him was a storm and bad one at that.

If this is retirement I'm too old for it, he thought.

In all of Perkey's years he couldn't remember it being this hot this early. Maybe it just seemed hotter. After all, he was five rungs up the windmill ladder, his hat was on the ground, and the sun was pounding a baseball-sized blister on his bald spot. Even the water in the tank below was throwing heat back up in his face.

Perkey pulled his bandana from his back pocket and laid it on his blistered head in an attempt to keep his brain from cooking in its own juices—it wasn't working. The second he removed his hand the wind blew the bandana off and he nearly fell to his death reaching to catch the fleeting cloth. Regaining control, he adjusted his grip.

I know I'm way too old for this.

He folded the bandana corner to corner and put it back on his head, tying it under his chin like he had seen Bette do on windy days when she went to town to shop. Unconsciously, he looked around, hoping no one would see how ridiculous he looked. But who would see? Buster was the only one who ever rode out this far. But Buster wouldn't be coming; he had sold his cattle. It made him sick enough he had to move to town.

Perkey's thirst grew as he caught himself studying every ripple the wind stirred on top of the tank just below his reach. Every so often the dry west wind picked up a mist from the flow of water going into the tank below his feet and blew it back up over him. The mist was cooling but it didn't help his thirst, and the sound of the running water was unbearable, turning him into a lunatic.

For the past three hours Perkey had been treed up this windmill ladder by the old bull he had gone out to fetch. He never saw the animal as he stepped off Cat to get a drink. His hat was in his hand and his mouth was an inch from the cool water when Cat reared, pulled the reins away, and left in a high lope, leaving Perkey afoot. The brindle bull was on top of him before Perkey realized it. Perkey was left with nothing to do but climb this ragged old windmill.

Now Perkey could see Cat with his head down at the top of the hill grazing like it was Sunday afternoon.

If I had a rifle, I'd kill you as dead as that rat, Perkey thought as he watched Cat. It wouldn't do any good to call for him—he'd already tried that with no success. "Kitty, kitty, kitty, kitty, here kitty." Cat never moved. He was a good colt, but a colt just the same, and he would be of no help now.

Perkey's problem now was not the colt, it was the bull, which sported an impressive set of horns that rolled out and turned up on the ends, and he seemed determined to demonstrate their usefulness. Perkey had no further desire to see them any closer than from the ladder of the windmill, for whenever he had tried to descend, the beast would paw the ground, duck his head, and blow dust with every breath.

To better study the situation and clear his mind, Perkey pulled a plug of tobacco from his denim work shirt and bit the corner off. He rolled the tobacco around in his mouth, pushing it to the side.

"GET!" Perkey yelled.

Holding onto the rung with one hand, Perkey leaned out from the windmill and spit a line of brown tobacco juice that splattered directly between the bull's eyes. The animal bawled, threw his head up, sending a looping line of saliva over his back, and ran at the base of the windmill. The bull hooked the ladder, backed off, and started bucking in a circle like some animal half his age, then he made another run on the ladder, hooking it and nearly shaking it loose from its base. Perkey's left foot shook loose when the wooden windmill rocked under the angry bull's abuse.

Perkey looked around for somewhere to go, but the nearest cover was a tree about three hundred yards away, and it wasn't big enough to climb. Not that it mattered, for even though Perkey and the bull were both retirement age, Perkey knew he'd never outrun the bull in his boots.

What a laugh, he thought. He'd never outrun that old bull in a pair of those high-dollar pump-up running shoes the kids were wearing, even on his best day with a twenty-yard head start.

Perkey went on up the ladder to continue formulating an escape plan that didn't include becoming a hood ornament for a bull. He grunted as he pulled himself up onto the platform. The platform moved under him and the rotting wood splintered off.

"Everything on this place is old," Perkey shouted down to the bull. "You ought to just get that through your head. You're old too."

Most of the boards on the platform were missing and the remaining ones were secured with only half enough rusty nails. Maybe it was time to hang up his rope and call it quits. Perkey settled down to get comfortable, readjusted the bandana head-scarf, closed his eyes, and tried to think of a way out of this mess.

A sudden loud cawing of a crow that had landed on the fin of the windmill woke Perkey with a jerk. Frantically his arms went out and he grabbed at the rough platform to keep from falling. For his trouble Perkey came up with a handful of splinters.

"Old man on an old windmill because of an old bull," he said, looking at the slivers of wood sticking from his hand. "Now the old man has old wood sticking out of his old hand."

He carefully slid his hand into his pocket, located his bone handled folding knife, and started digging at the splinters.

"I'm not likely to take much more of this," Perkey threatened, not looking up from the crude surgery. "My good nature might just take leave of me any minute." He pointed the knife at the bull. "I'd be thinking about that if I was you."

Perkey's head had blistered like a bad paint job in Phoenix, in spite of his bandana head covering, and if that wasn't enough his legs had gone to sleep. It fact he wasn't sure he'd be able to climb down off the windmill if his brawny jailer were to allow it.

"It's getting late you know. But I don't guess you care much about time," Perkey said, replacing the knife and retrieving his pocket watch. "If you knew about time, you'd know I eat my supper about this time."

Of course, the bull paid no attention. He was shaded up under the windmill with his eyes closed. His breathing had become steady and Perkey was sure he had fallen asleep. Perkey remained still and watched the bull. After several minutes of watching the bull sleeping in the shade, Perkey felt it was time to make good his escape. Slowly he stood up, giving his legs a chance to get the blood circulating. Quietly, he eased down the ladder, carefully watching the beast with every step. Perkey put his right boot on the ground for the first time in more than four hours. He paused at the bottom rung to give his legs time to get the feel of land under them, and just in case he needed to beat it back up the ladder he didn't want to be that far from it. The bull didn't move.

Perkey took three quick cat-like steps and bent to pick up his hat. Looking back between his legs he saw the bull's eyes come open like two spring doors, and he swore the animal smiled. A foot race broke out around the stock tank with the bull gaining on Perkey with each step. Perkey dipped his hat into the water as he rounded the backside of the tank and scrambled up the ladder.

"That does it," Perkey screamed, beating his fist on the ladder as he regained his perch on the platform and sat down.

He wrung the water out of his hat into his mouth. The water was brown from the sweat and dirt on his hat and tasted like a mud pie. It helped, but there wasn't near enough of it. But he wasn't about to complain. He yanked the silly scarf off his head, and pulled his wet hat on. The cool wet hat felt good on his blistered head. As bad as it was, things were looking up, he had his hat back. However, the bull had acquired a trophy, the back pocket of his jeans.

Just then, as though tantalized by a taste of victory, the bull ducked his head and hit the bottom of the windmill again, nearly jarring Perkey off. The windmill shuddered and groaned. The bull hooked the bottom again and then a third time.

"All right, all right," Perkey yelled. "You'd better quit. You and I could both get hurt in this deal. I could fall off and land on you. I ought to do it just to teach you a few manners."

Perkey shifted his weight, trying to find a part of his anatomy that didn't hurt. Pushing his hat back on his sunburned head, he studied the bull.

"What's the problem here?" Perkey questioned in his most convincing voice. "Haven't I always kept feed in front of you on the cold winter days? No matter how deep the snow or how high priced the feed, I never left you wanting. Remember last winter, didn't I almost die when I fell through the ice trying to keep you in water? And even though I was low sick, I came out every day to feed you and chop ice. Remember when the mud was so deep the truck wouldn't move? I hooked the horses to the wagon just so you wouldn't go hungry. And when things got tight, I borrowed money from that thievin' banker Dub to feed you. How do you repay me? You got it good and don't even know it. You got it soft. Maybe if I had cut you, you'd be acting better today," Perkey laughed.

"What do I ask of you?" Perkey continued. "I don't hook you to the wagon or saddle you every morning. I don't ask you to guard the place or be a companion. If you had a job it would be to eat, eat, eat and chase the cows around. For that you keep me treed up this windmill all day."

Perkey stood up and looked around. Cat had grazed closer. The sun would be down soon, and Perkey had no desire to spend the night on this old wore-out windmill.

"Well, so this is a sample of retirement; setting around all day, dozing in the sun, whittling' at splinters, checking the clock. I guess after I sell you that will be that. I've been a cowboy all my life, but with no cattle what is a man? What will I be? If I keep wearing my hat and boots, people will think I'm some country singer or a truck driver."

As Perkey had been talking, he had been climbing down off the windmill. He stopped just out of reach of the bull. He took another look at his horse.

"We're both done," he said to the bull. "We've both outlived our usefulness. We won't neither one be worth anything without cattle. Who will keep an old bull like you? Everyone wants a young one."

Perkey stopped.

"That's the problem," he said. "You ain't ready to quit your way of living."

Perkey stepped off the ladder. The hair on the back of his neck stood on end and every muscle tensed as he and the bull sized each other up. The only thing between them was a light

145

breeze. The old bull dropped his head. Perkey's legs cramped too bad to run.

"I got a plan," Perkey said. "Just go on and I'll keep you out here and get you some cows. We may be old, but we're not ready to retire."

The bull turned and began walking away.

Perkey went weak in the knees and let out a sigh.

Three weeks later Perkey's son called. "Well, Dad, how's retirement?"

"Not bad, not bad at all."

"I've been trying to call you every day, but there was no answer."

"I was out," Perkey said. "This retirement takes more time than I thought it would."

The boy laughed. "What have you been doing with yourself, Dad?"

"You said I needed new friends after I retired," Perkey said. "You were right. I have a new friend."

"Dad, that's wonderful," his boy said. "What do you guys do all day?"

"Water sports was on the card for today," Perkey said.

"Great, Dad," his boy said with a delighted tone. "Tell me what else you've done."

"We have taken nature rides, we've done crafts, leather work, painting...."

"Dad, who is your friend you are doing all this with?"

"Uh...."

"Dad."

"Uh, Buster."

"Buster McDonald?"

"That's him."

"Nature rides. Would that be riding among cattle?"

"Uh...."

"Crafts. Would that be fixing fence? Leather work. That would mean working on saddles and tack? And I guess painting would be the barn? You and Buster went back in the cattle business didn't you Dad?"

"Guess it's all in how you look at it," Perkey said. "Did you know people pay to do this sort of thing we do every day. As a matter of fact Buster ran an ad in the *Western Horseman* and is selling the chance to ride with real cowboys and live the life of a cowboy."

"Ride with real cowboys?" his son asked. "Who would that be?"

"Why, that would be me and Buster, son."

"You really did this?"

"We have seven people who want to be cowboys coming in from Germany next week," Perkey said. "We charge them nine hundred and fifty bucks each."

"And just what are you going to have them doing?" his boy asked.

"Why, punching cows," Perkey said.

"Just what you have been doing all your life?" his son said. "The same thing you just retired from?"

"Retirement is wonderful," Perkey laughed. "Got to run, son. I've got people waiting to see the Wild West, and I've got to run over to Buster's to get some horses for our guests."

Time Riders

"*Seems like all of the old punchers are gone,*" *I said.*

"*There isn't many of them still around,*" *Pete said, poking the fire with a stick.*

"*I did a silly thing once,*" *I said. I knew the minute the words were out of my mouth it was the wrong thing to say.*

"*You did a silly thing? Once?*" *Dale said.*

"*OK, I did a silly thing once that I'll tell you about,*" *I laughed.*

"*If he's saying up front that it's silly,*" *Malcolm said, "then it ought to be silly.*"

I can still see their faces, lit by the campfire, and can hear their voices spinning tales that echo through the canyons of my memory. We shared the little food from our saddle wallets, stretching it into a week. We huddled together, our slickered backs to the pelting rain. Lightning hammered the South Dakota grasslands as we watched our hobbled horses jump in surprise each time the thunder rolled.

The last time I saw them was August of '87. We were from different points on the map, and our rigs spoke of home. We rode high-backed, A-fork saddles, McClelland, or Mexican rigs. Most wore canvas trousers held up by canvas or leather suspenders. Our shirts were boiled, collarless, or homespun shirts, and some wore vests sporting pocket watches. High-top boots with big spurs were in order, and, without exception, each carried a hip-gun. We were each from different walks of life, drawn together for five short days.

I'm saddened that their names and hometowns have faded with the years. It happens in life. You lose track, you move, you become absorbed in the events of the day. Sometimes your best friend is lost to time. Your first girlfriend, whom you swore to love to the grave, is forgotten. Men you were drawn to, who rode with you, who you vowed to keep in touch with, are lost track of.

This story started when Chuck swung his boots off his walnut desk and threw me an issue of the *Western Horseman*. "Read that," he said as I attempted to catch the magazine that landed on the cowhide covered sofa.

Chuck Walker was a practicing attorney in Redondo Beach, California. You'd think a man who lived and worked at the beach would be surfing every morning—not Chuck. He looks more like a Montana rancher. The first time I met him he was driving a Suburban with a license plate that read "COWLAW." His offices bring to mind a Tombstone saloon rather than *L.A. Law*, with red flocked wallpaper, saddles, tack, and other western decor.

"Read what?" I snorted, irritated that I hadn't caught the magazine and more irritated that he had thrown it so poorly. "You throw like a girl," I observed, not that I have anything against the way girls throw—it just popped out.

Chuck pointed out a story of a group of "nuts," as Chuck put it, who were putting together a ride in South Dakota.

"Some Yankee is putting this together," Chuck said. "They're going to wear 1880s clothes, ride period saddles, and eat only the type of food that was around in the 1880s. If it wasn't around in 1887, they won't use it."

The article told of the strangest thing I had encountered in weeks, with the exception of Chuck's Happy Trails Law Office: a posse chasing bad guys. At the time, I was a Los Angeles police officer, and something had to be well within the boundary of strange before I even noticed. This ride landed within that boundary.

To describe what these men were planning, phrases like "experiment in living history" and "authentically re-create the American West of the 1880s" were used.

"It sounds like they're nuts," Chuck laughed. "Just our kind of people. Let's check it out."

We contacted the "Yankee," as Chuck labeled him, and found that he was planning a period ride for the next summer; 1887 was to be the period.

Chuck and I signed up, dispatched our money, and started receiving a newsletter describing their rules and criteria. We soon learned these guys were serious about history. Knowing that we would be on horseback and camping for five days, we started piling our camping equipment on the floor and sorting through it, throwing aside what would not be found in the local emporium in the year 1887. We culled sleeping bags, flashlights, camp stoves, and lanterns, along with all the rest of our equipment. Nothing would do except the matches, and Chuck questioned them. We soon discovered we would need to have our clothes and equipment made, but after months of planning we were finally ready.

Throughout our first night in South Dakota, it stormed like I had never seen before, clearing the next day. After breakfast, Chuck and I went back to our motel to get ready to go to the Shearer Ranch where the ride was to begin. We threw our Wranglers and Ropers to the side, pulled on our canvas trousers and high-top boots, and tucked our trousers into the tops according to the period.

Approaching the ranch, we encountered a man on horseback in a long lope. He reined his horse in and pointed the way to the meeting location. As we topped the hill and headed down toward the Cheyenne River, we threw the truck into a four-wheel-locked-skid, not believing our eyes.

"They may be a little more nuts than we are," Chuck grinned.

It was strange (you know by now I recognize strange) to see an 1887 camp. Scattered along the river were white canvas tents, a chuck wagon set up and cooking, a freight wagon pulled by a span of long-horned oxen, buggies, horses on a picket line, and men with handlebar mustaches that made my police approved 'stach look like a starter kit. My strange meter was pegged.

We had been transported back to 1887. Time travel was possible. No one at the camp spoke of anything post-1887, and they

had the look nailed: the right clothes, guns, and saddles, right down to the labels on their canned goods.

After lunch, the men divided up into two groups: the good guys and the bad. As a cop I was drawn to the posse. However, being an attorney, Chuck was confused. Weighing all his options, he came to the conclusion that there was a possibility of a trial after the capture. The job of defense would no doubt fall to him, the only attorney in the group, and this deal wouldn't be pro bono. He rode with the posse.

The desperados, about six of them, all hard-looking men with attitudes, were given an hour head start. The posse members put their gear together and got ready for the chase. I thought I had too much hanging on my horse and whittled it down to a black slicker, one blanket wrapped in a small ground-tarp, metal canteen, rope, saddlebags of dried food, and a pair of hobbles I carried around my horse's neck. Luckily, Chuck had a big stout horse. Being a courtroom lawyer, he prepared for any happenstance and brought two of everything he might need. He looked like a peddler and sounded like a one-man band. In his defense, he did cowboy up. With all the rattling, his horse humped up a few times, but Chuck never quit him.

An hour later we gave chase, and for days we trailed those bandits over the South Dakota landscape. We learned what it was to travel horseback in 1887—rough. We ate and slept on the ground and shaded up in the trees along the river.

It was pushing dark one evening, and we had our horses hobbled with their heads down in some good buffalo grass. I was leaning on my saddle, eating from a can of peaches, when Chuck punched my ribs. "Who do you think that might be?" he asked.

"Whoever he is, he's a few pages farther back in history than we are," I said, watching the rider come out of the trees.

The bearded, buckskin-clad man rode a nice sorrel and had a flintlock handy across the pommel of his saddle. He had a big paint in tow with his load snagged down with a diamond, like he knew his ropes. My strange meter was acting up again.

The mountain man rode straight up and asked if he could light. He was no sooner on the ground than he spied me eating peaches and asked, "Had supper yet?"

Chuck explained we ate light but invited the rider to share what we had. The man smiled and said maybe he could throw something in the pot.

"We don't have a pot," Chuck said.

"I can fix that too," the man said.

After Dan Deuter introduced himself, he dropped to the ground and built a bird's nest, piled kindling around it, removed a flint and steel from a pouch around his neck, and started striking. It wasn't long before he had a fire going.

"We got matches," Chuck allowed after Dan had his fire going.

The fire burned and we talked until it was down to glowing coals. When his coals were right, Dan pulled from his pack a large bundle of brown butcher paper tied with string. He cut the string and opened the paper to reveal meat.

"We've got matches," Chuck said. "But we don't have meat."

Dan smiled. "You will have, soon."

"I like this guy," Chuck whispered to me.

As Dan placed the meat directly on the coals, he told the story of a buffalo hunt he had joined and of how this cow was killed. The smell held our attention.

During supper, Dan mentioned that he had seen a group of riders just five miles ahead of us. As the moon rose, with that information in mind, four of us rolled out of our blankets and saddled up. We rode to within a mile of where Dan described the camp to be, stepped down, pulled off our spurs, handed our horses off to our lookout, and started off on foot.

We saw their horses grazing first and got low to the ground to crawl up on the camp unseen. The horses' heads came up, and they started to throw a ruckus. We stood up so the horses could see we were just men, and they put their heads back down. When we got up on their horses we unhobbled them and tied a note to the tail of a roan we would leave behind. "We have your mounts." We signed it "Sincerely, the posse" and, doing what any 1887 posse would do, we stole their horses.

The next morning we loafed around the camp until one of their men appeared at the top of the ridge astride the roan, red-faced and grinning, waving a white handkerchief. We gave the horses back so we could resume our fun, but not until after we ate lunch together and bragged on what a great posse we were.

The next day and a half was spent chasing the desperados, catching only glimpses of them from miles away. We came upon a pond, and since it was so hot and we were such a good posse we decided to take a swim. We stripped off our saddles and clothes, letting the horses graze while we floated around wearing nothing but our hats and smiles.

Knowing the posse business, we had put out a guard, who only woke up after the bandits rode through our camp shooting blanks from their pistols and stampeding our horses as they waved our clothes over their heads. One of the bad guys then produced the only non-1887 piece of equipment that was allowed, a 35mm camera, and began snapping our pictures wearing nothing but our hats, hats that were not on our heads. Because our guard, you guessed it, Chuck, thought it so funny, we felt it only right that he too should get the chance to swim. Having two of everything in his saddlebags, he had dry clothes.

After eating our fill of crow served up by the desperados and buying our clothes back with praise of their great desperadoship used like legal tender, we collected our clothes and gathered our horses. The chase continued for the rest of the week in like manner. By this time, my Los Angeles police-issue stress level had fallen out of the red. Chuck had calmed some too; I could tell because he hadn't threatened to sanction any kind of legal action in several days.

After the ride, I was invited to Dan Deuter's house where I met his wife Cat. Dan and Cat are artists, and I was fortunate enough to buy some of their work that still hangs in my home.

Even with the fun Chuck and I had on that silly ride, we've lost track of those guys. I wish I knew where they are now.

"Most of the old punchers are gone," I said, pushing the fire with a stick and then standing.

"You should have invited Chuck with us," Pete said.

"Why don't we just invite everyone we all know," Ken snapped. "I thought we were trying to get away from it all? Besides, I'm not cooking for an army. I do have my limits, you know."

"He's getting cranky in his old age," Lee laughed. "You off your meds?"

"I'm just saying that if we keep inviting everyone and their dog, we could just as well stay home." Ken pulled himself to his feet and walked over to the cookfire and poured himself another cup of coffee.

"Was it OK to bring the dogs?" Malcolm asked Ken.

"Dale always brings his dog," Ken said.

"That's because his dog forgets who he is and bites him when he comes home if he leaves him more than fifteen minutes at a time," Lee said.

"I still think Steve should invite Chuck next year," Pete said. "He sounds like our kind of guy."

"Chuck passed away in '95," I told Pete.

"You're right, all the old punchers are gone," Pete remarked under his breath.

They Call Him a Cowboy

"Old punchers, that reminds me of a story about Warren Harris," Dale said.

"Warren's not that old," I said. "He's about our age."

"I wouldn't say any of us are spring chickens," Lee said. "What makes you think we don't call you old when we are talking about you?"

"Alright, alright," Dale snorted. "I'm just saying that it reminded me of a story. I didn't think we'd get into some long-winded debate about age."

"Maybe you ought to think before you start calling people old," Ken said.

"Maybe you ought to get on with your story before we're all too old to hear you," Lee shot back.

"Steve knows Warren, but I don't guess the rest of you do, and he's not old, he's about our age. We asked him to come along with us on this ride, but he was tied up in court and couldn't get away. Warren's a real hoot. I was hoping . . . ."

"Just get on with the story," Lee said. "I think you're making my hair gray."

"Alright!" Dale said. "Don't get your saddle blanket in a wad."

Taken aback, Warren fell against a table full of dinner salads and desserts, shoving the long table into the wall with a head-turning crash. He was completely oblivious to the head-whipping, brow-furrowing shushing from the crowd obviously upset by the loud and disturbing commotion near the elevator. Rather, Warren was open-mouth stunned and was leaning back, with his left hand in what was once intended to be some poor fool's dinner salad, for balance.

She's beautiful, he thought, righting himself and wiping the honey-mustard salad dressing from his hand with the corner of the white tablecloth.

She had stepped off the elevator with poise and style. She had the biggest brown eyes and the longest lashes that Warren had ever seen. She was staring right at him, and he was certain he'd never seen such unquestionable beauty.

She was being escorted into the room by a young, good-looking man with chiseled features. Her young escort was wearing a high-dollar, custom-made, black, pure beaver hat and dressed in black tie, giving him the air that he had just stepped from the pages of a magazine ad.

Warren wanted her.

They were eye to eye, just inches from each other. She moved on and practically brushed against him as she passed. His hand, on impulse and acting on its own, reached out and lightly touched her as she strolled past him. Without warning, she hesitated and turned to steal a noncommital glance at him before turning back to face the room as if he did not exist.

It was at that very second he made the decision that life truly was much too short and that he would have her. At all cost, he had to have her. It was beyond his control, there was nothing he could do. He had to have her.

He watched as she walked head up and self-possessed into the twelfth floor ballroom. Every eye was on her. Warren knew that nearly everyone in the room was thinking the same thing. They were thinking they wanted her also. It didn't matter. He was going to have her and nothing short of his death tonight would stop him. He would take her home, no matter what the cost. He had to have her, nothing else mattered.

It was that split-second decision, forged with honey-mustard dressing still dripping from his hand, that kick-started Warren's cowboy adventure. From that night he could be called a cowboy, because he bought her. After the bidding was finished Warren owned the finest registered Brangus cow he'd ever seen.

Warren Harris was born and raised in the middle-class, tree lined suburbs of Chicago, Illinois. Kicking around the Windy City as a kid, all he ever wanted to do was be a cowboy. It was not the normal attire for the city, but he wore a cowboy hat since he was old enough to pester his mom to buy him one. She ordered Warren a cheap wool western hat from the back of a dog-eared copy of the Miller Stockman catalog he showed her every chance he got. Thinking it was just a phase the boy was going through, his parents gave him that hat for Christmas, and to their astonishment he never outgrew what they called a "phase." Although Warren ended up in law school and became a lawyer, he never lost the lust to be a cowboy. The first chance he got he packed up and headed west. He landed a job as a prosecutor for Santa Fe County, New Mexico, and married a local girl from northern New Mexico.

Rose was a young, ranch-raised, dark-eyed, Hispanic girl, who took his breath away at first sight. The first time he saw her he knew it was hopeless to try to live a life without her. She was one of those women over which time had no claim. She was wise way beyond her age and possessed a beauty that laughed at the passing years. Warren pursued Rose, like he did everything in life that he really wanted, with an unwavering determination. She loved his bold honesty and the vision and attitude he had toward life, so she married him.

One evening after work, as Warren was sitting in their Santa Fe home reading one of the several cattlemen magazines delivered to his house monthly, he read about a Brangus sale that was going to be held at the Shamrock Hotel in San Antonio. On the twelfth floor in the ballroom no less. The sale was a black tie affair by invitation only. Who'd ever heard of such a thing?

"Those Texas boys know how to throw a party," Warren laughed to Rose.

"What are you talking about?" she questioned from the kitchen.

Warren pulled himself out of his chair and took his magazine to her. "I'd give anything to see something like that," he told her, pointing out the article.

Warren had not been married that long and had little idea how well Rose was connected.

She listened to him bubble about the sale and how exciting it would be to attend. Without telling her husband and hoping to surprise him, she had no problem getting him an invitation to the prominent sale. With one phone call Warren was on the guest list, and three days later he received an impressive gold engraved invitation in the mail to the prestigious sale.

Thrilled and surprised, Warren ran to Rose with the news that he had been invited to the sale. He wasted no time getting to the phone where he called and reserved the last room in the hotel for him and his young and well-connected bride. He bought Rose a new dress and rented a tux. With the excitement of a kid awaiting Santa, they piled in his pickup and headed to San Antonio.

The night of the sale he was in awe, and at every turn something new and delightful found his eye. He had just stepped off the evaluator and was stopped in his tracks by the grand sight of a sale going on in the twelfth floor ballroom. It was then, as he stood in disbelief, that she stepped off the evaluator. The most beautiful Brangus cow he'd ever seen. He knew then that he was going to be in the cattle business.

That night Warren, in a rented tux, stood shoulder to shoulder with the best of them and became the cattle baron, fulfilling a dream he had hauled around with him his entire life. He bought not only that beautiful cow but two of her sisters.

However, that night on the twelfth floor of an San Antonio hotel ballroom, there were two things that failed to register with Warren. As his hand would shoot up in a bidding duel for his prized cattle, he failed to take into account that he didn't own so much as a square foot of land, nor did he have a trailer to move his newly acquired bovines. Being a man able to make a snap decision and not allowing the small and seemingly inconsequential details and problems of life interfere with his destiny, Warren bid himself into the status of a cattleman.

Filled with the moment, he took Rose by the hand for a moonlit stroll, ending up by the side of the swimming pool. Life didn't get any better. With his beautiful wife at his side, added to the moon's reflection off the water of the pool setting the mood, and a bill of sale for three of the finest Brangus cattle he had ever seen in the pocket of his rented jacket, pride choked him.

"Look," Warren said, pointing to the still pool and pulling Rose in even closer. "Isn't it beautiful?"

"There's no question," Rose purred into his ear as she tightened her grip on the love of her life.

Feeling romantic and thinking about stealing a kiss, he stroked her face, pushing her dark hair away from her lips. She lifted her face toward him and her lips came to his. She nuzzled into his neck, and his gaze fell on the romantic setting of the swimming pool.

"This is a wonderful evening," he said. "That pool is so beautiful it makes me want to just jump right in."

"After the bath you just took?" she purred.

Warren had to laugh.

Before they left for home to borrow a trailer, he had to see his herd one last time. Warren fished around under the seat of his truck and came out with a 35mm camera, blew the dust off of it, and then headed toward the pens were the cattle were kept. When he reached the holding pens he climbed the fence to snap some pictures of his "girls," as he had started calling them.

Warren and Rose drove back to New Mexico where they rented a pasture for his new herd and borrowed a stock trailer to bring them home. He and Rose then loaded up Gus, their dog, and headed back to Texas.

After suffering three flat tires on the borrowed trailer, Warren got tired of stopping at every little gas station along the way and waiting for some guy to patch the tires. He jumped off the interstate at Fort Stockton, Texas, and pulled into a tire store, where he slid his Visa card across the counter to pay for a set of four tires for the borrowed trailer. By the time they got the trailer back on the ground, he and Rose were wore out so they got a room at the Holiday Inn. The next morning they got up early, ate breakfast, and pulled back up on the interstate.

Warren glanced at his watch and saw that it was approaching 1:00 P.M. He was feeling the strain of the miles and the hunger that had been nudging at his empty stomach for the past hour. He pulled off the interstate at Kerrville, Texas, and into the parking lot of the Y O Ranch Hilton, because it looked real "cowboy."

"How about some lunch, babe?" he whispered Rose awake.

Warren playfully pulled Rose by her hand out the door behind him and pushed the pickup's door shut with the toe of his boot. They were laughing as they walked across the parking lot, and Rose was running her fingers through her hair. As they approached the hotel's restaurant, Warren noticed a new Ford truck parked in front of the door. The truck looked new, but the roof was pushed down like someone had jumped on it. The truck's windshield was shattered and had spiderweb cracks running from one end to the other. The truck was covered in mud, and the driver's side door was caved in. The rig had a beat-up trailer hanging on the back of it, and it was clear that both truck and trailer had seen better days.

"Now there's a real cowboy rig," Warren laughed as he pointed out the beat-up truck to Rose. "It's brand new and looks like it's already wore out."

"I just hope nothing falls off of it and lands on us," Rose said with her dry humor.

Warren pulled the door open for his wife, took off his hat, and bowed at the waist, "Ma'am, may I?"

She stepped through the door, and Warren tugged his hat back on, sitting it on his head with one side touching his ear and the other nearly on top of his head—the way a man wears his hat when he wants to tell the world, "I feel good."

The jukebox was playing, and Merle was crooning "Mama Tried" when they came through the door. It was cranked up loud enough to make Warren think someone could have rolled the jukebox out of a beer joint and into the restaurant. Warren came up behind Rose, put his hands on her smooth shoulders, and danced her across the floor toward an empty table. Life was good, real good.

They danced past a cowboy sitting alone at a table nursing a cup of coffee. The cowboy's head was down, and he didn't notice them pass. He was wearing a hat which, like the truck parked in front of the door, had seen better days. His silver belly hat was bent out of shape, covered with dirt, and had a hole in the top of the crown. The cowboy's shirt was old and ripped at the shoulder and covered in mud, just like the truck. The only thing clean on the man was his hands. No doubt he had just washed them. He had a bandana as a makeshift bandage wrapped around his right hand, and he had both hands pressed against the coffee cup.

The two lovebirds found a booth and slid in just as the waitress handed them a menu.

"You from around here?" the peroxide blond asked.

"Santa Fe," Warren smiled back at the girl.

"I love Santa Fe," she said, holding her order pad to her breast.

"Everyone loves Santa Fe," Warren laughed. "Unless they live there."

While a battle waged within Warren as to whether to order the chicken-fried steak that he wanted, or the tuna salad that Rose thought was healthier, two more cowboys came through the front door. The first puncher flagged them down with his bandaged hand. He caught their eye, and they serpentined their way through the chairs and tables to his table as they waved off the waitress.

"We're not staying," one of the cowboys said to the waitress.

They both sat down, and after a few minutes of what looked to be a serious meeting of arm waving and napkin drawing, the latecomers stood, shook hands with the first cowboy, and left.

"He must be the foreman," Warren leaned over and whispered in Rose's ear before kissing it.

He was about to make his case for the chicken-fried steak to Rose but cut off his remarks when the waitress suddenly appeared at their table. Deciding to live on the edge, he ordered the chicken-fried steak, and Rose shot him a disapproving look, as he knew she would, but said nothing. She ordered the tuna salad as he also knew she would.

"What?" he asked in a guilty tone. She could always burn a hole in his conscience with that look. The bad part of it was that she knew she had that power.

"Nothing," she said softly. The second part of the guilt trip. "Honey, I just worry about your health."

"That's your job, babe," he laughed, "but you don't have to work every day."

After Warren savored every last bite of his chicken-fried steak and under that loving but burning look from Rose, he wisely passed on the pie offered by the waitress. He didn't want to push his luck to the point of breaking. Warren took the bill from the waitress, counted out enough to cover it and a good tip, and left it on the table. He slid out and stood up holding his hand out to Rose.

"Let's go get the girls," he said, helping Rose from the booth.

As they passed the cowboy, still sitting with his head down and nursing his coffee, Warren pulled up short beside the table as Rose kept walking. They were holding hands and her arm was stretched out to its full length. She was pulled off balance causing her to laugh as she stumbled back toward Warren.

"How you doing?" Warren said, letting go of Rose's hand and extending it to the cowboy.

The cowboy looked up, somewhat surprised, from under his weatherbeaten hat. He took Warren's hand and pumped it.

"Guess I been better," he said with a Texas drawl.

"I was wondering if the Y O Ranch gives tours?" Warren asked, thinking he'd take Rose out to the ranch for the day. Then he and Rose could pick his cattle up tomorrow.

"Don't have a clue," the cowboy said, shaking his head. "I ain't from around here."

"I'm sorry," Warren said. "We saw you talking to those other two cowboys and thought you were the foreman for the ranch. We thought you were giving them their marching orders."

"Nope," the cowboy laughed. "I'd be the last guy they'd be taking orders from about being a cowboy."

"We were on our way to pick up some cattle that I bought at a sale in San Antonio last week," Warren said, pushing his hat back. "I saw you . . . ."

"I hope you fare better than I did with them cattle," the cowboy said, cutting Warren off.

"You bought some cattle at the Shamrock Hotel last week?"

"Just one bull."

"I saw some good ones at that sale," Warren said. "Is he going to work out for you?"

"Nope," the cowboy said without hesitation.

Warren looked confused. The cowboy shook his head, reached into his pocket, and pulled out a Polaroid and slid it across the table to Warren.

"I'm sorry, ma'am," the cowboy said, coming to his feet and taking off his hat. "I didn't even see you standing behind your husband. Here, have a seat."

The cowboy held Rose's chair as she took a seat, and Warren slid into the chair beside her. Warren picked up the Polaroid the cowboy had pushed over in front of him. The picture was one of the man who now sat across from him. The man was wearing the same clothes he had on now but cleaner and newer looking. His hat was new looking, without the mud on it, and had a large feather band on it.

The trademark of a dude or a line dancer, Warren thought.

The man even looked younger in the picture, smiling back at the camera, like he owned the world.

"That was me this morning," the cowboy said, with a hint of fatigue creeping into his voice.

Warren studied the picture again. The man was standing straight and proud, holding a lead rope, and attached to the other end was a large, well-built cross-bred Brahma bull sporting a pair of horns that looked like bicycle handlebars protruding from his large head. The bull didn't seem to care one way or the other if someone was taking his picture, or if he was tethered to the end of a rope. Warren noticed a pickup in the background with a trailer hooked to it. The truck and trailer seemed to be the same ones he had passed in the parking lot, with the exception of the mud, dents, and broken windshield.

"I don't understand," Warren said, wrinkling his brow. "What is this?"

"Let me describe to you my day," the man said, shaking his head. "If you have the time."

"I sure wouldn't want to miss this story," Warren said as he and Rose exchanged glances, not knowing what they were about to hear. "We've got the time."

"I'm not a real cowboy; I don't work cattle for a living. I'm a dentist, and I've got a few acres outside of San Angelo," the cowboy said. "I saw an article for this sale in San Antonio, and I pulled in some favors to get invited to it."

"It sounds like my story," Warren said, smiling at Rose. He reached out and touched Rose on the arm. "Well, fact is, she got me in the door."

The cowboy waved to the waitress and held up his cup. She saw him and hollered, "I'll be right there, honey."

"Would you two like something?" the cowboy asked.

"No, thank you," Rose said. "We just finished eating."

The waitress wiped her hand on her apron and grabbed the coffeepot. The cowboy stopped talking as he watched the young girl come across he room. She poured a cup full of coffee for the cowboy and then vanished behind the counter without a word.

"I should not have even gone to San Antonio to the sale. Beyond doubt, I should not have bought any cattle when I got there, but when I got down there I was impressed. I was impressed with the whole thing. I was so impressed that my judgement went out the window. I whipped out my checkbook and bought this bull," the cowboy said, pointing to the bull in the picture with his index finger. "I just couldn't help it. I don't know, I guess something just came over me. It was like I was possessed—I had to have that bull. I got carried away and got caught up in the bidding. As a result, I paid too much, and the funny thing is I don't even own a trailer."

"That sounds way too familiar," Rose said with a grimaced look. She was talking to Warren more than to the cowboy, and Warren glanced at her. He broke into that boyish grin that Rose loved, and she smiled at him.

"Last night I drove down from San Angelo, checked into a hotel down here, and this morning I showed up to retrieve my prize bull." The cowboy was smiling and must have been conjuring up a vivid picture of that morning. "It was a good morning, and I was having fun. I even posed for that picture. As you can see, I was real proud. I know I look a little silly, but I was proud. After they took my picture some of the cowboys who worked for the ranch loaded my bull for me. Man did I feel like a cowboy."

The cowboy pulled off his hat and ran his fingers through his unruly hair, then dropped his hat to the floor upside down.

"I was tooling up the interstate with Chris LeDoux cranked up," the cowboy laughed. "I was singing loud like some silly fool, when my truck felt like someone lifted it up off the road, and it nearly wrecked right there."

"What in the world happened?" Rose asked with a puzzled look. "Did you hit something?"

"I thought I hit something," the cowboy said. "My new bull decided he had rode in the trailer as long as he needed to ride and jumped straight out of the trailer, is what happened. Well, he didn't get clear out on the first jump."

Warren whistled through his teeth.

"I ran off the road and down into the ditch," the cowboy said, making a motion with his hand to demonstrate the direction of the truck's travel. "I was running about sixty down the ditch. It looked like a motor boat throwing a roster tail of mud up onto the freeway. To make matters worse the bull had himself hung up half in and half out of the trailer."

Warren put his hand on Rose's arm as they listened wide-eyed intently.

"I took a second to glance into my rearview mirror as I fought for control of the truck." The cowboy leaned back in his chair. "I saw that my new bull had jumped out of the top of the trailer somehow. I'll never forget it, he was looking right at me. That big head of his just filled my mirror. I couldn't tell if that bull was afraid, mad, or what. He came out the front of the stock trailer, rolled down the gooseneck, and landed square in the middle of the bed of the truck. At this point I knew he was mad, because he was kicking and fighting. He kicked so hard that he knocked big dents in the side of my new truck. He also kicked out the back window."

Warren hadn't even noticed the back window missing in the Ford.

"I'm just lucky he didn't kick me in the back of the head and kill me right then." The cowboy took another sip of his coffee and wiped his mouth with the back of his hand. He seemed to be reflecting on the thought of how close the bull came to killing him. "The bull came to his feet and lost his footing and fell back into the bed of the truck, just as I got the rolling wreck stopped.

I bailed out, grabbed my rope, and built a quick loop. The bull's head raised up as he attempted to get back to his feet, so I roped his head before he could get back up. At this point, I was thinking I was one pretty good cowboy. I moved around to tie him off to the gooseneck, but I forgot that my rope was tied off to my saddle horn. When I rope, I tie hard and fast; the rope was still tied to the horn. I couldn't get the rope off the saddle and around the gooseneck in time. That gave the nasty beast time to spring to his feet. At first I thought he was going to pounce on me, like some cat on a bug. But with his left hind hoof he stepped right in the middle of my saddle and broke it right in half."

The cowboy stopped, shook his head, and then took another sip of coffee.

"I just bought that saddle," the cowboy continued, with a hint of regret in his voice. "Funny thing is that old bull slipped on the saddle and his feet came out from under him. The saddle saved me. When the bull slipped, the saddle sailed out of the back of the truck. I pulled hard on the rope, and it burned through my fingers like a hot knife through butter. The old bull jumped on top of the cab of my new truck, grinding the top down. I guess you noticed that as you walked in. When the top came down the windshield broke and the bull rolled off onto the hood, denting it, then he rolled off onto the ground."

Warren's mouth was hanging open in disbelief.

"That bull hit the ground on his back, rolled over, came to his feet in a flash, ducked his head, and hooked my headlight, breaking it out," the cowboy said. "He was mad, real mad. He was standing by the door of my truck, shaking like a wet, cold dog. I thought about jumping back into the truck but couldn't with him standing guard right there. Before I could figure out where to go he ducked his head again and charged me. When he fell off the top of the truck the rope that was still attached to his head became entangled around the side mirror of my truck. He hit the end of the rope and snapped off the side mirror. He chased me around the truck, and on the second time around I saw my chance and I threw myself down between the trailer and the truck. This didn't stop him. He hooked at me, nearly tearing the tailgate off my truck. Thinking I needed to be in a safer place, I crawled up under the truck and stayed there. He put his nose low to the ground, and I know he was thinking about how he could crawl under there and get me. He had my tailgate chrome hanging off his right horn. I guess he lost interest after walking around the truck a few times, looking for me, and just walked off. Then it really turned off bad. Like he was some big gentle calf, he wandered off across the interstate. The oncoming traffic was put into a four-wheel locked skid, and my bull caused an accident."

"That's horrible," Rose sighed.

"It gets worse, ma'am," the cowboy told her. "About this time the highway patrol showed up. This big trooper pulled me out from under the truck and told me if I didn't get my bull off the road he was going to have to arrest me. I must say to you jail didn't sound that bad to me at this point. The bull was grazing in the median of the interstate with not a care in the world, still wearing my rope with the saddle attached, and my tailgate chrome hanging from his horn."

Warren rubbed his mouth like it was dry.

"In the end, the state trooper charged me with causing the accident by letting my bull run loose," the cowboy said, pulling a ticket from his front pocket and pushing it over in front of Warren. "I tried my best to tell him that I didn't LET the bull do anything. He just took it upon himself to get out of the trailer. The trooper wasn't impressed and just asked me for my insurance. I gave him the card and he studied it for a few seconds before he told me my insurance was expired by two months."

"Whoa," Warren said with concern.

"Five cars tore up in that little deal," the cowboy said. "Tore up real good."

The cowboy stopped talking and Warren figured it was the end of his story—or he hoped it was the end. He didn't think the man could take much more trouble.

"But who were the two cowboys?" Warren furrowed his brow.

"Didn't ask their names."

"I don't understand," Warren said.

"I don't know who they were; I didn't ask their names," the disgruntled dentist told Warren. "I called the Y O Ranch and told them to send two cowboys out here to the hotel and to meet me in the restaurant. I told them I wanted some guys who were good with ropes and who rode good stout horses. I also told them to bring a trailer. Those two guys showed up, and I gave them a bill of sale for the bull. I told them I couldn't afford to be a cowboy. It'll cost me everything I got to pay for the five cars that wrecked, to repair my truck, my neighbor's trailer, buy a new saddle and rope, pay all the tickets that the trooper piled on me, and to pay for the hospital bills."

"What hospital bills?" Warren looked like he had been pushed back into his chair.

"Oh, I guess I left that part out," the cowboy said. "When I was under the truck and that bull was stalking me, the sheriff showed up. When he stepped out of the car that bull turned on him, chased him back to his car, and before he could jump in the bull hooked him right up on top of the light bar. I think he'd have shot that bull but he lost his pistol. That may explain why the state trooper was so mad, that and the fact the sheriff was his brother-in-law. But the up side is we found the sheriff's pistol in the ditch. I wiped it off the best I could and gave it to the trooper. The sheriff left here cussing and with one of his deputies driving him to the hospital. I think he had a broken rib—I hope that's all that's wrong with him. It was, without a doubt, one ugly day."

Warren jumped to his feet and ran for the door. "Please excuse me," he shouted over his shoulder. "I'll be right back."

"What's with him?" the cowboy questioned Rose.

Puzzled, Rose shrugged. She watched as Warren disappeared out the door.

"Your guess is as good as mine," she said.

Rose and the cowboy watched the door, nothing. Just as Rose was about to go looking for her husband he came back through the door with a big smile painted across his face. He walked over to their table and extended his hand to his wife.

"Are you ready, Hon?" he asked.

Rose took his hand and stood up, and he pulled her close and kissed her. She laughed and hit him playfully with her fist.

"What was all that about?" she asked.

"I had some important business with those cowboys," Warren said with a smile. "I wanted to catch them before they got away."

"What kind of business?" she questioned.

"Cattle business."

"You didn't buy that bull?" she asked, stepping back and putting her hand over her mouth. "You're thinking about breeding that bull to your cows."

"No ma'am. I never thought of anything close to that," he laughed. "I was selling, not buying."

She said nothing, just looked at him with a million questions in her eyes.

"I just sold them my herd," he laughed. "If those cows are going to be bred to that bull, those boys can do it. Those boys bought my whole herd, all three of them."

"What?" Rose said, raising her eyebrows.

"They bought them all," he said. "I showed them the picture of the cattle and told them where they could pick them up. Range delivery. Well, hotel delivery. I took every dime those boys had."

"What?" Rose was shocked.

"Well, if you got a dime, you did better than I did," the cowboy said. "I was just glad to be rid of that bull. They got him for nothing."

"It cost them boys to get my cattle. I told them I'd sell my herd for all the money they had in their pockets," Warren said. "They took the deal."

"How much did they have?" the cowboy dentist asked.

"Well they tried to tell me all they had was eleven bucks," Warren laughed. "I was born at night but it wasn't last night. I made them boys check all the hidden compartments of their wallets. They had another thirty-five bucks squirreled away in there."

"You sold three registered Brangus cows for forty-six dollars?" Rose said with wide eyes.

"Well, they had some change, too," he said, holding out his hand to show her the change. "I got forty-six dollars and eighty-two cents. I cleaned them boys out."

"You spent a small fortune on those cattle and you sold them for forty-six dollars and eighty-two cents?" Rose fell back into her chair. "Babe, I thought you always wanted to be a cowboy?"

"Honey, do you know anyone who's lost that much money, that quick, in the cattle business?" Warren asked.

She had her hand up to her mouth and her eyes were filled with water. Warren couldn't tell if she was about to laugh or cry. To his question she only shook her head no.

"I'd say that more than qualifies me to be called a cowboy," Warren said, bowing at the waist as he removed his hat. "That might even qualify me to be a cattle baron."

"You're nuts." Rose wiped her tears and smiled up at him, "but I love you."

"Let's go to the movies," Warren said. "I got a pocket full of money, I just sold my herd, and now I want to go out with a beautiful woman."

"I'd go anywhere with you," Rose said, throwing herself into his arms, "cowboy."

Earl the Barefoot Bronc Rider

"Wasn't that sweet," Lee said.

"I liked the story," Pete said.

"You just woke up," Lee said. "You were snoring so loud I could hardly hear the sappy part."

"You're just antisocial," Malcolm said to Lee.

"Anti Social?" Lee laughed. "It was you that give old Suds Slaughter the devil every time you'd get a chance. I'd say if anyone was antisocial you would be getting the award for that."

"I've never done a thing to Suds Slaughter," Malcolm said in his own defense. "Well, nothing he didn't ask for."

A small smile crept from under Lee's mustache. He then started telling his story and Malcolm rolled his eyes.

Suds was a drunk. Earl was a monkey.

A man who is intoxicated every night without exception like Suds can safely be called a drunk without fear of numerous questions. Suds was not a mean drunk, but a drunk just the same.

Earl was a monkey. A real monkey. A spider monkey.

Suds was born Ronald Pete Slaughter and had hauled the nickname of "RJ" until he was mowed down in his prime by what some could only describe as a fatal case of mid-life crisis. Rhonda, his wife of thirteen years, maintained it was on the day of his forty-second birthday that he totally lost his mind. It was nearly a year to the day from his forty-second birthday that Randy Muvihill first called him "Suds" at a roping. RJ had fallen off his horse while holding on to a longneck bottle, and Randy had made the remark that he was full of suds. The name "Suds" just stuck.

Looking back, Rhonda could not remember one single day since his forty-second birthday that he was not drunk. Every picture she had of him since that day he was holding a beer or drinking from a longneck bottle. It was a very rare occasion that you could catch him without a beer in his hand, and if you did, the chances were he would be asleep.

Suds had grown wilder than ragweed, and Rhonda had developed allergies. It was three days after Suds' forty-fourth birthday that she waved good-bye as she drove Suds' new Dodge dully toward her newfound life with a computer salesman from Tulsa, a man who didn't know the first thing about horses, cattle, or cowboys—a very attractive thing in a man at this point in Rhonda's rocky life. Suds didn't take her leaving too awfully hard. In fact, he dug around in the glove box until he found a pen that worked, signed the title to his new truck over to Rhonda, and even handed her the pen.

As Rhonda had her foot buried in the carburetor and was laying down a perfect donut in the front yard of what was once their happy home, Suds held up a beer and yelled, "Adios, Baby." As the bed of the truck made the arch, throwing a rooster-tail of sod onto the porch, Suds stood up straight, snapped off a crisp salute, then threw his empty beer bottle into the back of the truck as a little reminder of his undying love. He fell backward into the door and stumbled back into the house to grab a fresh bottle of beer before she was out the front gate.

Earl could have had something to do with the breakup. In all honesty, Earl only had the misfortune of showing up on the scene, as Rhonda put it, "when RJ lost his mind."

It was on his forty-second birthday that Suds first met Earl. Suds woke up on his birthday and without a word of warning, jumped into his pickup and drove to Dallas. He wheeled in and took up two parking places in the long-term parking lot at the airport. Kicking the door shut with his boot, he walked straight to the airport bar like a man on a mission. For the better part of three hours, he hosted his own birthday party with the guest list consisting of anyone who wandered through the doors of the bar. RJ not only paid for but assisted in the drinking of three hundred and seventy-two dollars, not including tip, worth of longneck Lone Stars in celebration of his arrival to this world. After putting the bar tab on his gold card, Suds stumbled over and bought a ticket to Las Vegas. He had trouble convincing the girl behind the counter that he was not drunk but on tranquilizers—one of his better performances. Without so much as a thought of placing a phone call to Rhonda, he found himself behind a crap table on the strip and down five hundred bucks in less than four hours.

It was crowding 11:00 P.M. when the birthday boy, with a belly full of sloshing beer, found himself up seven hundred dollars in a private poker game with two Montana ranchers, a Korean businessman, and a circus act with banana colored yellow hair and faded tattoos that peeked out from under his dirty T-shirt. It was the circus act that owed Suds the bulk of the money. It wasn't until Suds attempted to cash out of the game that he learned that the skinny tattooed bag of gas had more tattoos than he had cash.

"I know what you're thinking, Circus Boy; if I drop your skinny tattooed butt on the asphalt, I won't get my money." Suds laughed as if he was demented while hanging the man off the rail of the twelfth floor. "I can live with it."

"Wait, please," the tattooed man whimpered, wetting himself.

"It's my birthday, Tattoo Boy," Suds laughed. "I don't have to wait."

"Please!" the man cried. "I can pay you. I will pay you. Just don't drop me."

Suds hauled the man back up over the rail and shoved his face up against the wall, bending his nose.

"Give me one good reason why I shouldn't drop you like prices at Wal-Mart?" Suds grunted foul beer breath on the guy's neck.

"I'm a married man."

"I said a good reason," Suds said, pushing the man toward the rail.

"I can pay you."

"The reasons are getting better."

It was at this point the tattooed man, being faced with the threat of a swan dive over the rail, came up with a structured payment plan involving a monkey. When the plan was first presented, Suds was still leaning toward giving Banana Hair the ride to the pavement until the man mentioned that the monkey could ride a horse.

"You mean a stick horse?" Suds grunted, pushing the man toward the rail.

"No, no," the man cried, clawing at the drapes. "The monkey can ride a real horse. He rides one every night in the circus. He likes horses," the man added, praying he would be allowed to take the stairs to the street, thus avoiding his before and after picture in the morning paper.

At 3:00 A.M., Suds laid his head back in the back seat of a taxi speeding toward the airport with his new friend Earl. Suds had named his monkey Earl because he felt it wasn't right to just keep calling his new friend "Monkey." When you are more than sixty miles from home, in the middle of the night, on your birthday, drunk, and looking into the deep brown eyes of a primate, Earl is the funniest name you have ever heard.

The cab driver didn't want to take the monkey with a stinky drunk anywhere. Suds was already in the cab when the driver started yelling, "Get out! Get the animal out."

Suds pulled the driver backward over the seat by his hair, and the monkey jumped onto the guy's throat and bit him. At this point, the cabby, fearing death, was more than glad to give the two a ride to the airport. In fact, if they had asked for the keys to the cab, the driver would have been on foot and running down the street without a word of protest. The cab bounced off the curb in front of the airport, and Suds threw a fifty over the seat, took Earl by the paw, and hit the revolving doors.

Although working in a town like Las Vegas and dealing with a drunk trying to board a plane with a monkey is somewhat out of the norm, it is nothing for a cop to get worked up about. The officer merely explained to Suds his three options. One, he could take his dirty monkey out of the airport, disappearing into the night. Two, the option the officer normally chose in any situation that would even come close to this one, Suds could go to jail. Since the officer was on his way to breakfast, he strongly discouraged option number two, as it would cost him several hours of paperwork. Or three, and the option the officer explained as the most reasonable, was to put the monkey in a cage and get on the plane and back to wherever he came from. Suds was drunk, but not that drunk, and he wisely chose option number three. Earl had no voice in the matter and went into the cage fighting, hissing, and showing his teeth. Earl in his cage was then checked as nothing more than a noisy piece of luggage.

Suds passed out and slept through the flight home. The flight attendant nudged him awake to notice he was the only one on the plane. He found his way to his truck and had his key in the door before he remembered he was now the proud owner of a spider monkey. Suds stumbled back to the baggage claim area and handed the wide-eyed attendant the claim ticket to recover his friend. The attendant never moved and only pointed to the cage where Earl was rocking back and forth, hissing in a feral attempt to escape. When Suds bent over to open the cage the attendant jumped up onto the counter, ran its length, jumped off, and with one movement was in the inter-office locking the door. Suds took Earl by the hand and walked out of the airport like any other mother and child.

To say that Rhonda was surprised when she first met Earl would be a gross understatement of fact. She rolled over in her bed, and one eye opened to greet the stream of sunshine drilling into her sleep. She was eye to eye with a beast that she knew fully well was about to end her life. Screaming to alert anyone within miles of a murder in progress, she jumped straight up onto her feet in the bed and fell against the wall, knocking a picture of her wedding day off the wall onto Suds' head. Wide eyed and with nostrils flared, Earl screamed, did a back flip off the bed, and ran into the closet. Suds never woke up and just laid there bleeding.

"What in the . . . ," Rhonda yelled, kicking Suds.

Suds moaned and rolled over, letting the blood from his open wound from the attack of the wedding picture drip onto the pillow.

"Wake up RJ," Rhonda yelled. "There's a gorilla in the closet."

Suds never moved.

She reached for a glass of water she kept by the bed and threw it into Suds' face. He rolled over, trying to get away. She kicked him hard with her bare foot, the blow landing on his shoulder. She kicked again, this time catching the side of his head. Suds opened his eyes, seeing the world through an alcohol-induced fog.

"Uhhhhh?" he moaned.

"There is a gorilla in the closet!" she screeched again. "He was trying to kill me."

Suds sat up, still wearing the clothes he had on when he fell into bed. Earl peeked around the door and looked to Suds for help from the crazed woman.

"That's Earl," Suds said, falling back onto the bed with no other explanation.

The morning Rhonda awoke eye to eye with Earl was as close as she would ever get to him. Even though Suds and Earl were inseparable, Rhonda kept her distance.

After Rhonda spun her donut on her way out of their life, Suds became really weird. Not that he wasn't weird before he saw her taillights, but now that she was gone, he must have felt it was his duty to pull out all stops. Suds did things like buying Earl his own horse. Tattoo Boy was right when he told Suds that the monkey liked horses. It was true. Earl had no fear of the larger animals. In fact, the monkey would jump up on any horse he came near, sometimes making for quite the show. If you were a horse and had never seen a monkey, chances are it would be somewhat of a shock to have the little furry creature jump onto your back. Earl would get a handful of hair, twisting the mane between his fingers, and grab the horse's loose skin and hair with his feet. The harder the horse bucked the better the monkey liked it. The monkey was a natural. He seemed to smile when a horse was bucking its hardest.

As Suds sped headlong down the "road of weird," he bought Earl a nice little mare at the sale. The mare had a good handle on her, but Earl was so small Suds had to work with both of them until Earl could rein his new horse. Suds even put Earl in the pickup and drove to Alpine, Texas, to have Gary Dunshee at Big Bend Saddlery make Earl a custom saddle.

Gary wasn't real happy with having the "nasty monkey" in his shop climbing all over the saddles, so he threw Suds and Earl out. Suds drove back home, and after three dozen or so calls to the saddle shop, Gary said he would make the saddle if Suds would rip his phone number out of his Rolodex. Suds promised that if Gary would make the saddle, he would never even drive through the county. Gary made the saddle.

If having a monkey with his own mount wasn't weird enough, when Suds worked on a neighbor's ranch he always loaded Earl's horse and took Earl with him. Earl would sit in the passenger side of the truck on a box so he could look out as they traveled. Earl had even been seen with his little arm resting on the window of the truck like the other cowboys would do as Suds drove down the road. Some said they saw Suds talking to Earl as they drove. Earl wasn't much of a hand and just rode along with the rest of the cowboys, but watching a monkey ride a horse was some good entertainment. Earl would be loping out across the sage, and if his horse didn't respond to the rein, the monkey would shoot out of the saddle and down the horse's neck, slapping his mount upside the head. Then like it was an act of normal horsemanship, Earl would crawl back up in the saddle and never miss a beat. This would usually put the cowboys on the ground with laughter.

At one spring roundup, Suds and Earl showed up and Earl had on a small pair of Wrangler jeans and a custom shirt Garth Brooks would have been proud to hit the stage wearing. Suds had Darryl Sullivan at the Thievin' Vaqueros Factory Outlet Store in Las Cruces make Earl a little hat with a stampede string. The one thing Earl was missing to top off his outfit was a pair of boots.

"I had him a good pair made, but they just hampered his riding," Suds said. "Earl likes to get a handful and a foot full of the horse when the pony gets rank."

After a while Earl even developed a bronc rider's swagger.

The first time Earl jumped up on a horse, grabbed a handful of hair, and rode the wild beast to a standstill it was great fun for all who watched. Now Suds was turning the bronc riding monkey into great sport. Every rancher, cowboy, and stock contractor was stepping up with what they felt was a horse that could buck the monkey to the ground. For years there were side bets on whether or not Earl could ride this or that horse. It seemed there was not a bronc out there that Earl could not top. He would just jump up and grab a handful of mane and foot full of hair, and it didn't matter how hard the horse bucked. The monkey was there to stay.

Suds starting taking all bets. It didn't matter whose horse it was. Earl could ride it. A bronc contractor came through once and bet Suds three hundred dollars that he had a horse Earl couldn't ride. The horse was unridden during National Finals in Las Vegas the year before.

"If the best cowboys in the world couldn't ride the horse, I'm sure your monkey won't make the whistle," the contractor boasted.

"Well, then let's make it five hundred," Suds shot back.

"We can make it a grand if you want," the contractor told Suds.

"A grand it is," Suds said, pulling a wad of money from his pocket. "You got the money?"

The horse was led to the chute, and Earl jumped on like he was sitting on a bar stool, something else he had considerable experience in doing. The chute was thrown open, and Earl looked like a tick on the horse's back. The dun horse fired twice in front of the chute, reared up, and spun around the other way. The contractor had never seen his horse buck harder, but the monkey seemed to be smiling. The monkey never moved. He just rode the horse jump for jump. The horse bucked for about a minute and a half before stopping in front of the chutes with his head down, played out. The stock contractor was slack jawed.

"I never seen anything like that in my life," the contractor said, filling Suds' extended hand with a thousand dollars in hundred dollar bills. "I want to buy the monkey."

"He's not for sale."

"I'll give you five thousand."

"He's not for sale!"

"OK, OK," the stock contractor said. "I'll go ten."

"What you'll do is go get your butt in your truck before I kick it," Suds snapped. "You can't sell a friend."

"He's a monkey," the contractor said just before Suds knocked him off the fence with a sweeping backhand that could have just as easily been a ham swung from a crane.

Suds made money nearly everywhere he went with Earl. There was always someone who thought they had a rank horse that could buck the bronc busting monkey off. Earl rode them all with little trouble. He rode wild horses fresh off the Nevada range, a mad turkey in a farmer's barn lot, the PRCA bucking horse of the year, and even a dog that ran in circles trying to bite the monkey. Earl would get his hands and feet full of hair, feathers, or whatever it happened to be, and there was no shaking him. He would ride them like he was glued to the animal.

Suds' boast of Earl's riding ability grew in proportion to the size of the bets. One day the bet was that Earl could not ride a bull. The result was the same. The monkey rode the animal easier than he rode a horse. It didn't seem to matter to Earl. He would just get a good hold and ride the animal to a standstill.

Malcolm and I were at the cafe when Suds and Earl busted through the door like the circus act they had become. Suds took a seat next to Malcolm. Earl jumped up on the jukebox and started gnawing at a grape our waitress had given him as he came through the door. Seeing a monkey dressed like Roy Rogers had lost its novelty, and Earl had become just one of the boys.

"I'm thinking of moving off," Suds started. We knew the conversation would end with the "greatest bronc rider to ever live," who just happened to be sitting on the jukebox behind us eating a grape.

Nobody bit, hoping Suds would take the hint and just order his breakfast. Our luck was not holding.

"I really think I'll move off," Suds started again.

Malcolm just nodded his head without looking up from his coffee.

"It's just no fun around here," Suds went on without encouragement. "Earl has rode every horse in the country. There is just no challenge anymore."

"You're right, Suds," Malcolm said. "If you need some help packing, just yell. We'll sure give you a hand."

"I just don't know where I'd go," Suds said.

"I'd make it at least 500 miles away so you wouldn't be tempted to make a day trip back," Malcolm said.

"I'm saying I'd need to move somewhere that Earl and I can find some horses that would challenge his great riding ability."

"That would be at least 500 miles away. I'm sure of it," Malcolm said.

"Earl needs the challenge."

"Earl doesn't seem to be too worked up about it," Malcolm said. "Fact is, he looks real content sitting up there on the jukebox fighting his grape."

"He told me the other night that he wished he had some real horses to ride." Suds shook his head, "It worries me."

"You worry me," Malcolm said, looking at Suds with a raised eyebrow. "Earl told you that, did he? You need to listen to what you're telling us—that a bronc riding monkey is talking to you?"

"Not in as many words."

"What were his words, Suds?"

"Well, he is just thinking there isn't a horse in this country that could throw him."

"He's just not trying on the right horses," Malcolm told Suds. "He has just been riding those bucking horses. Anyway, don't you think it's time you retire Earl from the hardships of bronc riding?"

"What are you talking about?" Suds questioned.

"I'm just saying Earl should retire at the top of his game," Malcolm said.

Suds pulled a can of beer out of his coat pocket, popped the top, and pulled a long drink. Malcolm shook his head at the thought of a beer this early.

"Earl is the greatest bronc rider this country has ever seen," Suds boasted.

"Suds, Earl is a monkey," Malcolm said. "A monkey. Granted he can hang onto a horse, but he is still a monkey and not Casey Tibbs. He's a monkey. A nice monkey, but a monkey just the same. Grab the reins, Suds, you're out of control."

"Earl may be a monkey, but there ain't a horse he can't ride," Suds shot back.

"He's a monkey," Malcolm laughed into his coffee. "He's a circus act. That's it Suds. Get a life. There ain't a horse that can't be rode, and there ain't a monkey that can't be throwed."

Suds was red as a beet and looked like he was about to pop a blood vessel in his forehead.

"This monkey can't be throwed!" Suds shouted, pointing at Earl.

"Settle down, Suds," Malcolm laughed.

"Admit it," Suds shouted even louder than before. "Admit it! Earl can't be throwed."

"I got a horse he can't ride," Malcolm said.

Suds beat his fist on the table and the coffee in his cup jumped.

"You talking about that young yellow horse of yours?"

"Any of them," Malcolm said softly. "Just pick one."

"Any of them?" Suds laughed out loud. "That old App horse you feed is so old he might be dead before we get Earl out to your place."

"You talking about Pecos?" Malcolm smiled. "Old Pecos is only about thirty years old. He has lots of good years ahead of him."

"I thought I drank too much," Suds said, still mad.

"If I was to put ol' Pecos in training, Earl wouldn't stand a chance of riding that fiery beast."

"In training," Suds scoffed. "That horse is about three hundred pounds overweight now."

"He's been retired for a few years," Malcolm said in his horse's defense.

"By the time you get him in shape, we'll all be retired."

"I'd need about two months to get him into razor shape," Malcolm said over the top of his coffee. "I'd want him in top form for that big event."

Everyone around the table was snickering, and that didn't do much for Suds' temperament. "I'm ready to put my money where my mouth is," Suds said, pulling a wad of money from his pocket, another irksome habit he had developed over the years. He always wanted to have the money to cover any fool's bet who thought he had a horse that could buck off Earl.

Malcolm looked up from under his hat as Suds counted out two thousand dollars into a pile on the table.

"If I'm going to take the time to pull ol' Pecos out of retirement and put him into training, it will cost more than you have in your pocket my friend."

Suds continued to count out money until he reached eight thousand dollars. "More than that?"

Malcolm never looked up. "More."

Suds laughed. "Right."

Malcolm tilted his head, looking at Suds.

"OK, big man," Suds said, raking the pile of money back into his pocket. "I'll cover anything you got. What's it going to be?"

"You put up Earl," Malcolm said.

"What are you talking about?" Suds asked.

"Put up Earl," Malcolm said.

"You ain't getting Earl," Suds said with anger in his voice. "Earl is my friend."

"I don't want Earl," Malcolm said. "You keep Earl. You retire him if he can't ride Pecos."

"What?"

"I'll uproot ol' Pecos from his well-earned retirement and put him into a rigorous training program for two months, and if Earl can't ride him, you retire the monkey. No more bronc rides. No more bragging about your monkey. No more bets. Nothing. Earl goes into retirement as the greatest bronc rider this country has seen—but you stop talking about it. We're sick of it, Suds."

"What do I get if Earl rides your old wore-out horse?"

"I'll put up two thousand bucks."

"Deal," Suds shouted, sticking out his hand to seal the deal.

Malcolm pumped Suds' hand. Suds had a smile that looked painted across his face.

"Two months," Suds threw his head back and laughed. "It'll take you more than two months to get enough weight off that horse just to get him in the chute."

"I wasn't planning on putting ol' Pecos in a chute," Malcolm said. "I was just going to lead him around in a light lope."

This caused Suds to howl. "This will be good. Two months."

As the days rolled by, Suds found himself swinging by Malcolm's place to see the horse in training, but he never caught Pecos working, training, or even out in the pasture. Suds asked around, and he couldn't find anyone who had even seen Pecos.

About a month after the bet was made Suds ran into Malcolm at the feed store.

"I haven't seen ol' Pecos training," Suds laughed.

"I been keeping him in the barn," Malcolm said. "It's been hot and I didn't want him to get overheated."

Suds rolled his eyes. "I guess you want more time?"

"No," Malcolm said. "As a matter of fact, I think ol' Pecos will be ready by Saturday. He is in peak form."

"Saturday?" Suds said. "Are you nuts?"

"Maybe," Malcolm said. "You're not backing out are you?"

"What time?"

"Let's make it early," Malcolm said, rubbing his chin. "Say eight."

At seven thirty Suds was in Malcolm's driveway, sitting on the tailgate of his truck, spinning a rope. Earl was chewing on the other end of the rope and hissing at Malcolm's dog, Mac, as he walked by on his way to the barn. A crowd was starting to gather to see the contest. Malcolm strolled to the back of Suds' truck, nursing a cup of coffee.

"Where's the old horse?" Suds said.

"Eating his breakfast in the barn."

"You wanting to call this off?"

"No," Malcolm said, sipping his coffee. "I just want to make sure that you keep your word if Earl can't ride ol' Pecos."

"Won't happen."

"If it does, you are going to retire Earl?" Malcolm asked. "We don't have to listen to any more of this nonsense about this great monkey bronc rider?"

"Won't happen."

"Do we have a deal?' Malcolm asked.

"Sure, we got a deal," Suds said. "If Earl can't ride your old horse, he retires. Are you wanting him to ride with a blindfold? With one hand? Should we get him drunk first?"

"He can ride any way he wants."

"You got the two thousand bucks on you?" Suds laughed.

Malcolm pulled a wad of money from his front pocket. "The boys took up a collection."

"I don't care where it came from, I just know where it's going," Suds said. "I just can't believe that there are others as nuts as you are to make this bet."

"They just wanted to see Earl retired," Malcolm said. "Enough is enough."

"Let's get on with this," Suds said. "I have to go shopping with your money today. Earl's ready."

Malcolm set his cup down and walked slowly to the barn. The door swung closed behind him and in about the time it took to halter a horse, he came out leading Pecos.

Suds' mouth fell open. The crowd that had gathered broke into laughter.

"What is going on?" Suds said, jumping to his feet.

"Is Earl going to ride or not?" Malcolm asked.

Suds tried to protest, but there was nothing he could think of he could say. Pecos stood ready to ride, and Malcolm held the lead rope. Suds gave Earl a hand up, and Malcolm started forward with Pecos and then broke into a trot. Earl rode the old horse five steps and then went to the ground. The crowd cheered, throwing their hats in the air. Earl was now going to be retired.

Malcolm went straight to the barn with Pecos and put him up. When he came out of the barn, Suds was gone. That was Earl's last ride. Not another bet was wagered on his riding ability. It was never spoken of again. Suds was never heard bragging about Earl, the bronc busting monkey. It was over. Earl would still ride with Suds but without his cowboy outfit. Earl was naked like God had intended a monkey to be.

Pete leaned forward, poking the fire and said, "So ol' Pecos bucked off the greatest bronc riding monkey of all time?"

"In less than five steps," I said. "He didn't even buck. Pecos just started into a short lope, and Earl rolled off into the dust."

"I don't get it," Ken said. "Why was Pecos able to buck him off?"

"I told you he didn't buck," I said.

"Why did the monkey hit the ground?" Pete asked.

"When Malcolm trotted ol' Pecos out, that horse was as round as an apple. Pecos had put on even more weight. His skin was as tight as a Navajo drum."

"What's that got to do with why the monkey couldn't ride him?" Dale asked.

"Malcolm had shaved Pecos slick-bald," I laughed. "Malcolm and some of the boys had lathered and taken a razor to the old fat horse. Every hair and even his mane was gone. They had even taped his ears back. There was nothing for Earl to hang onto. Pecos looked like a thousand-pound Chihuahua standing there smiling. It was the funniest thing I had ever seen. When Malcolm started to lope Pecos, Earl acted like he had been pitched up on a hot griddle. He was hopping from foot to foot trying to get some kind of a hold on the horse. That monkey bounced around like a rubber ball, fighting for something to hang onto. With no hair and skin so tight he couldn't get a grip, he hit the ground. The monkey never slowed and ran to Suds' pickup. He jumped in the open window, ready to go home."

"With the two thousand dollars the boys collected for the bet, Malcolm threw Earl a retirement party. Malcolm made a trophy for Earl," I chuckled. "Malcolm took a rubber monkey and glued it to a plastic bucking horse. But when we called Suds to tell him about the party, he hung up on us. So we just had a party without Suds or the monkey. We all toasted Earl, the famous bronc busting monkey."

"Antisocial behavior if I have ever heard of it," Lee said.

The Horse Race

"I was sick of that drunk and his furry bronc riding pal,"
Malcolm said. "Everyone was sick of him; the priest at my church
was sick of him. And he can tolerate anybody. Earl's alright, it's
just Suds that's a pain."

"But your behavior toward poor Suds would fall into the
antisocial category," Lee said.

"I get tired of hearing Suds' gas about his bronc busting crit-
ter and now I'm antisocial?" Malcolm said. "One time I bust
Suds, and you give me trouble."

"One time?" Dale laughed. "You bust his chops every time
you get within a hundred yards of him. Poor Suds has had a
tough life; you should give him a break."

"Right," Malcolm said. "I'm not that tough on him."

Dale started the next story, and Malcolm rolled his eyes.

It was in the sixth grade that Ronald Slaughter, or Suds as
he became known by later in life, was branded a bantam
brained braggart. A title that would haunt him to the end of his
stay on this earth.

Ronald, in a misguided attempt to impress a beautiful,
young, long-legged substitute teacher that he had determined
he was unquestionably and deeply in love with, boldly stood up
in the middle of second period math, with what appeared to be

a total lack of rhyme or reason, and cleared his throat to declare he could "whip anyone in the room."

The olive-skinned, dark brunette teacher ran her fingers through her hair, smiled sweetly, and asked him softly to stay after class.

It worked, he thought as he sat back down. *She loves me!*

After class the teacher gracefully glided across the room and over to Ronald's desk where he sat with an I'm-too-cool-for-school smile, proud of himself. She sat down on the corner of the desk, crossed her long shapely legs, and leaned forward. Her perfume lightly danced in the air between them as she leaned toward him. With her long fingers she brushed the hair out of his eyes as she licked her lips, preparing to speak.

So this is what love feels like, he thought.

As she leaned forward he thought about kissing her. She wanted him to kiss her. He knew it, young men know these things.

"Ronald, you're a troubled child. If you ever do that again," she said ever so softly, "you will not have to worry about anyone in the class beating you—I'll do it myself. Do you understand me?"

Crushed, he could only nod.

Looking back, it could be argued that this one incident changed his life. He was not able to admit to his friends that he had been belittled by his teacher for being stupid. Thus, he placed himself on the path of being a lifelong member in good standing of the Liars Club.

When asked what the teacher wanted, he told his classmates that she had said she loved him for his bravery. However, the distance between them in age was too great. He would explain, in a manner only a sixth grader with a long history of lying could, that although painful to both of them, there was nothing they could do about their age difference and it was best they forget about their love.

The real pain came in the next four consecutive afternoons. Each night after school, to assure him that he could not "whip anyone in the class," he was beaten to the ground for his bold talk. One of his assailants, the one who showed no mercy, was a girl. To make matters worse she was a fifth grade girl, and not a real big fifth grade girl at that. Ronald never lived down the tag of being a braggart.

From that misguided attempt to declare his love for an older woman, Suds began his journey down a reckless and boastful path he would travel the rest of his life. Even at that tender age he had become not just a braggart but an obnoxious braggart. The rest of his life he would brag that he had the best ranch, the best truck, best cattle, the best looking wife, and the fastest horses in the country. Not only would he brag about it, but he wanted to bet that it was true. He would bet anyone, anything, at any time. He had been known to bet a hundred dollars on which cockroach would reach the wall first.

Suds bragged about how good-looking his wife was right up until the day she spun the donut in the front yard on her way out of his life. After that day he never spoke of her again; it was as if the woman had never been born on this rock. He also stopped bragging about his truck since that was the mode of transportation his wife took as she exited his life. But he continued to brag about his horses. He always had the best roping horse, best cutting horse, and the fastest horse in the country—according to his drunken talk.

Suds' life had taken may strange and unexplainable turns as he approached a serious mid-life crisis, wide open and in full after-burn. When Suds was forty-five he discovered what he had sought his entire life, the thing that would make his fortune—armadillos.

It was a moonlit night as he literally stumbled onto his fortune. As he made his way to his truck, after last call, he tripped over an armadillo that had been rooting up some unknown plant by his front wheel. Suds fell and cracked his head on the bumper as the little Texas speed bump ran off into the night. As Suds laid on the ground cussing, in a drunken and blurry haze, the idea hit him—restaurants serving "armadillo on the half shell." He laughed out loud just thinking about a deep-fried creation served on the upside down shell of the West Texas mammal. The next day, without looking back, Suds threw himself into the armadillo business.

Suds did it big, as he did everything. He borrowed money from a banker, who mistakenly thought he was going into the cattle business. Suds bought fencing and placed an ad in the local "Dandy Dime" that read: *Armadillos - bought, sold, and traded. Top dollar for armadillos any sex, any age, any size.*

Not knowing what top dollar was, as there was no trade in the armadillo market up until Suds ran his ad, most people just took his first offer, not believing that anyone would actually buy the pesky varmints. It wasn't long before Suds had filled the pen he called the "armory" that he had built out behind his barn.

Your eye could not rest in the large pen without being on an armadillo's back. It was a sight. After word of the large herd of armadillos hit the community, people came from miles around to see it. Most of the reactions after seeing the herd were laughter, a shake of the head, and then they would just walk away, laughing again.

A problem soon developed that Suds had not expected. He discovered armadillos liked to dig, and every morning he was forced to round up the little land rats that had made good their escape from under the fence the night before. The problem got so bad he had to hire some boys to help hunt the creatures up and put them back, then mend the fence.

Suds was quickly becoming the Armadillo King, and he liked it. He had a custom belt buckle made with an armadillo head looking back at you. The mouth was open and looked like it was hissing at you. Suds had a local artist paint an armadillo on the door of his pickup truck and the words *West Texas Cuisine—The Other Red Meat* under the picture of the armadillo.

Needless to say, in spite of his hard work and planning the armadillo restaurant business did not rocket him to riches as Suds had hoped. It seemed he was the only one in the world who thought someone would order armadillo on the half-shell from a menu.

Suds had worked himself into a bad situation. Money was tight. He had put everything he had and everything he could borrow into the armadillo venture. He tried to sell the animals, but the bottom fell out of the market since he was the only known person in Texas to have paid money for an armadillo. He was forced into the unthinkable position of getting a job. Since Suds always thought manual labor was the president of Mexico, looking for gainful employment was somewhat alien to his thought process. He had never had a job. Well, unless you count the three hours spent at the brick factory. He had never received a paycheck, so he had trouble looking at that as employment.

He took the job the summer right out of high school. It was hot and dirty work, and he moved in slow motion. The second hour on the job the factory foreman jumped him about his slow movement and seemingly bad attitude toward his job. Suds acted upon the first thought that crossed his mind. He threw the brick he was holding. The foreman ducked, the brick exploded through the plate glass window of the front office, finding a home on the desk of the company's owner. The brick knocked the telephone that he was talking to his wife on into his lap. The red-faced factory foreman stood and, with a shaking finger, pointed toward the door, which Suds hit with no questions.

Since his miserable endeavor to become part of America's workforce, he had felt driven to search for some other method of bankrolling his stay on this earth other than working for someone else. Suds looked for angles, scams, and schemes to make a buck. He joined and quit every pyramid scheme known to modern man. He was the first to jump into any multi-level marketing plan to come down the pike.

After trying Amway, three different long-distance phone companies, a vitamin supplement program, and two term life insurance companies, he became the executive vice president of a company named "Pear Up." Pear Up was a company based in West Texas that sold a prickly pear aphrodisiac. Suds moved up the corporation ladder by selling a large number of sponsorships to Pear Up. These sponsorships allowed the buyer to sell the product and recruit others to do the same.

James Walker Gee, the president and founder of Pear Up, and the target of the Federal Grand Jury investigation out of Del Rio, Texas, reluctantly admitted there were no studies, doctor's reports, or scientific evidence that Pear Up would in fact improve the customer's sex life. He did, however, inject that based strictly on the volume of sales of the product "something must be working." The jury wasn't buying.

It was also learned through court testimony that James Gee was hiring illegal aliens, a crime low on the criminal food chain, to harvest, dry, slice, and package the prickly pear. James' problem developed when he touted the product as an aphrodisiac. Every time he sold a sponsorship over the phone, he was charged in Federal Court with one count of fraud by wire. For every time he mailed paperwork proclaiming the false claims, he was charged with a count of mail fraud. To Suds' dismay, every time James Walker Gee talked to him and they made plans to sell sponsorships, the thing that made Suds all the money and the title of executive vice president, it was a federal charge of conspiracy to commit fraud.

Ten minutes after the two men in suits, sunglasses, and a no-nonsense demeanor produced gold badges and said, "Mr. Slaughter, FBI, we need to talk," Suds turned states' evidence like some kind of low-level mob rat. The end result was James Walker Gee had his mail forwarded to the La Tuna Federal Penitentiary for the next few years.

To Suds' request of being placed in the Federal Witness Protection Program the FBI replied, "We're talking a prickly pear case here, pal. You didn't roll on the Teflon Don. Go home and milk your goats."

Despondent over his past experience as a common laborer but worried because his armadillo venture had gone bust, Suds was thinking of applying for a job. It was while he was at his lowest that he happened onto his real fortune. It was by accident, as was everything good in his life, that he came across what would make him a very wealthy man. He discovered hat grease.

It seemed that every major hat company, since they stopped using mercury in their hats, was having the same problem. The term mad hatter came from the use of mercury that found its way into the hatter's system, making him crazier than a peach orchard boar. Hat companies and hat makers stopped using the element in their process, and from that day on they were in search of something to replace mercury.

After a hat is felted, the body is stiffened using a liquid that is forced into the hat; this allows the hat to keep its shape after it's creased. The hat is then sent to the finishing shop where it is sanded to get a smooth finish. It's during the sanding process that more often than not the stiffening "pops," or comes to the surface, leaving blotches on the surface of the hat. When this happens the hat is ruined and becomes a loss for the hat company's bottom line.

Suds would tell everyone it was through years of research that he solved the hat finishing problem, when in fact he fell into the solution. He was fighting with a stubborn armadillo, with thoughts of shooting the beast. The animal was attempting to dig under the fence, in broad daylight, right in front of him. Suds had a death grip on the armadillo's hind legs and was pulling the little tank back into the pen; the animal was fighting and still attempting to escape. Suds lost his grip and fell backwards into a group of curious armadillos that had gathered to watch the struggle. Suds' hat was pushed down around his ears, and the armadillo made tracks for the barn. Suds let the creature go.

Later that night Suds noticed that where the armadillo rubbed up against his hat the hat took on a shiney and smooth look. There was a slight oil film on the hat, and it smelled sweet. The next day as Suds was patching the fence from last night's big exodus of shelled land rovers he bent to pick up a baby armadillo. The baby hissed from under its armor, and Suds shook him. Suds rubbed the small animal over the top of his old hat, and the hat took on a new appearance. Suds called a local hat maker and took him some armadillo oil, instructing him to rub it on some hats and see what he thought. It wasn't long until every hat manufacturer in the country was calling Suds and ordering the oil. Suds named his newfound bonanza "Hat Armor."

Business was booming and he was selling armadillo oil, or Hat Armor, by the barrel. This meant he needed more armadillos. Suds then entered into an aggressive breeding program. After years of studying the little ground diggers, Suds learned that when the armadillo was mad it secreted a clear, sweet-smelling oil. It was this oil that when applied to the hats gave them a shine unattainable since the use of mercury.

Suds built a building and set up a bottling operation to bottle the armadillo oil. He learned that armadillos hated loud heavy-metal music, and if he played it around them, they would start to secrete the needed oil. Suds build an "agitating room." He would herd the little animals into the agitating room and play loud rock music, working the armadillos into a biting frenzy. He discovered the animals would mill around like they were looking for the door, then they would start ramming their noses into one another and start to bite each other. At this point they were ready for "harvest."

His enterprise was not without problems. He thought since the media had picked up on his venture with the armadillos he would start to charge for tours of his plant. Since it was the only plant like it in the world it should have been a sound idea. Things went smooth for the first day of tours, and it looked like it would work into a moneymaker. However, on the last tour of the second day someone locked Suds into the agitating room. Suds was going to just run through the door and turn off the lights when someone caught him inside and locked the door on him. He pounded on the door but could raise no one; all his help had gone home. It wasn't until the next day that his shop foreman let him out. As a result of spending the night with the heavy-metal music pummeling his senses over and over, he lost twenty percent hearing in his left hear. He stopped the tours and put a panic bar on the door.

Soon, hearing loss and all, Suds was a wealthy man. Since Suds had money he was even more useless than he had been before, something Rhonda thought impossible. He fell into a nice lifestyle, always having money. He was a man of leisure, hiring hands to do all the work that was not automated.

A year after Rhonda gained her freedom, Suds began to look for something to fill his life so he joined the sheriff's posse. The sheriff's posse was a loose-knit group of guys who would meet and complain about local politics and high taxes, then they would drink. Sometimes they would have a morning ride serving breakfast, and in the afternoon they would drink. The posse was charged with carrying the posse and American flags into the arena during the local rodeo and then they would drink. They offered a combination of the three things Suds found most desirable in a club: drinking, lying, and horses. A deadly combination.

The second day of a two-day trail ride, hosted by the sheriff's posse, Suds wandered out of his tent, gathered his saddle and bridle, and hunted his horse for the morning ride. Suds, still in a drunken haze from the session the night before, found Cotton standing next to the hitching rail. Cotton, his big white horse, just stood, allowing Suds to walk up on him.

"You're a good hoss," Suds whispered, thankful that he didn't have to chase his mount like most of the other posse members. "You're a great hoss."

Suds threw the saddle over the horse's back, and Cotton didn't move. Suds leaned over to grab the cinch and, being lightheaded and still half drunk, nearly did a header, falling into Cotton's side. Cotton stood like a statue in the park. Suds pulled the cinch up tight. He put the bridle on, not noticing he had one of the horse's ears folded under it. Suds threw the reins up over Cotton's neck. The horse never offered to move. To keep from weaving, Suds leaned against Cotton as his head spun. Suds desperately groped, in the gray fog of his brain, for a reason, any reason, to get out of the ride. His head was swimming in what felt like a thick soup. Unable to think of a reason to back out of this ride, he stepped into the stirrup and swung his leg over the horse. Cotton didn't even take a step forward.

"You're a good hoss," Suds muttered in his low whiskey voice as he patted the horse's neck.

Suds leaned on the saddle horn, trying to get his balance as the rest of the posse gathered their horses. Suds sat his horse, dozing off. The next thing he knew he was awakened as the leader, a nondrinker and someone Suds felt could not be trusted, yelled, "Let's do it, boys."

The group started off. Suds spurred Cotton and, in anticipation of the horse's forward movement, leaned forward in the saddle and tumbled off, landing on his back at Cotton's feet. The horse never moved. A loud roar of laughter came from the other posse members.

Mike Lambert rode up beside Suds and said, "You have to leave the hitching rail here, we don't own it."

Suds had thrown his saddle over Cotton's back, and the cinch had gone over the hitching rail. Suds had saddled his horse to the rail.

Any one of the other members of the posse would have had a good laugh on themselves, but not Suds. He was still stinging from the incident that had happened the night before. Suds in his normal mode was bragging. He was bragging on what a "good hoss" Cotton was. Suds had bragged all day, and everyone was sick of it. When Suds stopped to unsaddle after their ride, he tied Cotton off to the mirror of his new pickup truck—the one he had to buy after Rhonda, his wife, left with his other one. Mike Lambert was the one who told him it was a bad idea to tie the horse like that, but in true Suds fashion he informed Mike and everyone near enough to hear his boast that Cotton was a "good hoss." Suds had no sooner gotten the words out of his mouth than the horse reared up and pulled the mirror off the door of the truck along with a healthy portion of painted sheet metal. The dangling mirror from the reins spooked the horse even more, causing a stampede. The mirror hammered the side of Suds' new truck as Cotton rounded the back. Suds had loosened the saddle just enough that it rolled up under the horse. Cotton knowing, without a doubt, that the "colt killer" was after him, kicked at the saddle and hung his right hind hoof in the rig. The horse went down, performing what others for years would describe as a perfect cartwheel.

The tree of Suds' new saddle, which he had owned for less than thirty days, broke at the cantle. The horse's hoof came loose during the cartwheel, and he came to his feet the next time they hit the ground. Cotton hit a wild-eyed run toward the creek with Suds' prize saddle swinging beneath the animal. The cantle could have been on a hinge the way it was flapping.

Three hours later Suds, sore footed because he had turned down all offers of help, came back into camp leading Cotton, without the saddle. When he had finely captured the horse,

Suds pulled his Barlow and cut his prize saddle off the trembling animal and threw it into the deepest part of the creek. The saddle floated lazily up under a log where it lodged and where it remained. To Suds' embarrassment, every straggler coming into camp late mentioned seeing a "brand new saddle floating in the creek."

As Suds laid on his back, with his head feeling the size of a number three washtub, he looked up under Cotton to see that the horse was saddled to the hitching rail. Even with all the laughter, the horse never attempted to move. It was then, in the dirt, that Suds decided the members of the posse were not his kind of people. His decision was clear—he needed to resign.

Without a word, out of character for Suds, he pulled himself up off the ground and unsaddled his horse from the rail. He led the horse to his trailer, dragging the backup saddle in the dirt, loaded the animal, and threw his saddle into the back of the truck. As he was reaching for the door handle, he glanced at the large hole in the driver's side of his pickup where the mirror had resided the night before. The anger pushed blood into his ears as he stepped into the truck and slammed the door behind him.

He started his truck, pulled it into gear, and put his foot into it, expecting to throw gravel as he left. The truck never moved; it only put out a loud whine as the motor raced. The transmission was shot. A new truck and the transmission was gone. Red-faced, Suds slid out from behind the wheel. Everyone watched and tried not to laugh, but it was too funny. The snickers came to a halt when they noticed that in Suds' right hand was a .45 single action Colt. With a blank stare on his dirty face, Suds cocked the pistol, raised it shoulder level, and put a round through the front fender and into the engine block of his new truck. The motor shuddered in an oil-spewing death rattle and gave up the ghost. Suds let the pistol slide through his fingers and drop into the dirt. Like a man on a mission, he took long strides toward the road, leaving his mortally wounded pickup, trailer, and bewildered horse behind.

The second he was out of sight, Mike Lambert looked at the rest of the posse with a grimace on his face. He stared up the road to make sure Suds had not decided to return, and when he was assured Suds was gone Mike raced over and pulled the jack out from under the back wheels. "Boys, maybe this wasn't a good idea."

The posse thought it best to adjourn the meeting and get out of there while the getting was good. Suds showed up in town in about a week with another new truck. He acted like the incident never happened. No one ever told him that his transmission was fine and that the truck would not move because they had jacked up the back tires until they were about an inch off the ground. Some things are better just left to die a natural death. However, the sheriff's posse fiasco did nothing to hamper Suds' incessant bragging. In fact, he could have been elected president of the Windjammer Club, unopposed.

It was during one of Suds' daily marathon cafe brags, this one about how fast his white horse, Cotton, was that Malcolm took all he could take.

"I've never seen this big white horse of yours, Suds," Malcolm said, leaning over the table. "I've never seen him run, I've never seen him walk for that matter, but I'm sure sick of hearing you race him across my eggs every morning."

"Are you sick enough to bet you don't have a horse that can beat him?" Suds said.

"I don't keep but one horse," Malcolm said. "Old Pecos has never been on a track, but I know he could beat anything you're riding."

That remark stopped all the banter at the table. Everyone knew Pecos, and no one could believe Malcolm would make a statement like that.

"You talking about that fat Appaloosa you ride?" Suds snorted, and threw his head back and held his ample belly as he laughed. "Cotton could outrun that old, U-necked plug of yours."

"It's not the horses, it's the rider that makes the difference," Malcolm said. "It doesn't matter if you're on a triple crown winner, you couldn't win, you old blowhard. You'd have to get off and brag to someone about how good a time you're making. You don't ride smart."

"I could be in a coma and beat that old wore-out horse of yours," Suds snorted.

Malcolm could feel his blood running hot. He wanted to reach out and grab Suds by the neck and pitch him out of the place. A feeling not uncommon to many who knew Suds.

"You're telling me that your horse Pecos could beat Cotton in a race," Suds laughed.

"That's just what I'm telling you," Malcolm shot back, knowing he was on real thin ice. "If it was the right kind of race, he could beat your horse."

"The right kind of race." Suds wiped the tears out of his eyes. "Please, Malcolm, you're killing me. This is too good. I've seen you on that horse plenty of times but have yet to see you break him into so much as a long lope."

"I'm sick of hearing you brag about everything from how fast your horse is to the amount of catfish in that muddy pond of yours." Malcolm wiped his mouth with his napkin and tossed it into his plate. "Can't you give it a rest just for one day? We'll call it a holiday, or maybe we could have just one place in the county where it would be against the law to brag. You know, a Blow-Free Zone. I'd buy the place and move in just to get away from your gas!"

"I can't give it a rest when you come on talking big like that," Suds snorted. "If you're so tired of hearing it, all you have to do is put your money where your mouth is."

"Would that shut you up about this horse?"

"I don't think that will be a problem," Suds laughed. "What's the right kind of race for your old horse? One to the grave? Do you want to race to the glue factory?"

It was all Malcolm could do to keep from reaching out and pinching the fat braggart's head off. "Pecos likes a long race."

"A long race?"

"A long race."

"How long of a race?" Suds asked.

"Thirty miles or so," Malcolm said, pulling on his hat. "Takes him that long to work the kinks out."

"Thirty miles?" Suds mouth fell open. "Are you nuts?"

"If it's too far for your horse, I understand," Malcolm said, fishing in his pocket for a tip.

"It's not too far for me if you can make it," Suds said. "I only see two problems."

"They are?"

"How much do you want to bet on this little horse race?" Suds asked.

"You make it light on yourself."

"How about a hundred bucks?" Suds said.

"No problem with me," Malcolm said. "What's the second problem?"

"I need some time to put Cotton in shape," Suds said. "I'm sure you need some time to see if Pecos can even make it that far."

"Whenever you're ready," Malcolm said.

"We need to get the rules lined out," Suds said.

"Rules?" Malcolm laughed. "What rules? It's a horse race. The one that gets there first is the winner. Is the concept beyond you, Suds?"

"Rules like what kind of saddle can we ride?"

"I'm riding bareback," Malcolm laughed. "A saddle just gets in the way of Pecos' fluid and never ending movement on those long hauls. I don't care what kind of saddle you ride. Put a lawn chair on his back if you want, I could care less."

"Alright, where are we going to race to?" Suds said.

"We'll start at my place and ride," Malcolm rubbed his chin, "to the sale barn. That's about fourteen or fifteen miles. Then we will ride back. We can have someone put two beer cans on a post there and we have to ride out pick them up and come back. Sound like something that will work?"

"It works for me," Suds laughed. "Bareback, is that what you're telling me?"

"Bareback," Malcolm said. "Just let me know when your old horse is ready."

"You're betting me that you can sit Pecos, that apple-round, fat horse for thirty miles," Suds laughed. "And bareback no less?"

"That's what I'm saying," Malcolm said. "If you're nervous just let me know, we can call it off. I wouldn't want to embarrass you, but I think that may be hard to do."

"And you're willing to bet one hundred American dollars on it?"

"American, Mexican, Confederate, I don't care, Suds," Malcolm said. "I'm just tired of hearing you go on."

"Malcolm, let me buy breakfast," Suds said in a loud voice. "You'll need your money to pay off that stupid bet."

"Thanks, Suds," Malcolm said, rolling his eyes.

Malcolm and Pete walked out of the cafe and jumped into Pete's truck. Pete's head fell to the steering wheel. "You've lost it," he said.

"I know," Malcolm said. "I know."

"Now what are you going to do?" Pete asked. "Pecos has never traveled thirty miles. And bareback? Where did that come from?"

"It sounded good at the time," Malcolm said, grinning. "I just got tired of hearing his gas."

"Everybody in this county is tired of hearing his gas. For that matter half the people in the state are sick of his gas. I know people out of this state who are sick of his gas, but none of them have made a bet like that. I'd just pay him if I were you," Pete laughed and started his truck.

"It's not over yet," Malcolm said. "Until the fat horse runs."

"I'd say it was over," Pete said. "Your fat horse don't run, or I have never seen it. There's no way you can put Pecos in shape to beat that young horse of Suds'. I've seen the horse and he is all that Suds says. Suds' horse will walk away with it. Trust me on this."

"Suds is a fat bag of wind," Malcolm said. "That horse can't carry him thirty miles."

"You're in shape and Pecos couldn't carry you to the end of the road on a run."

"Pete, I just couldn't stand to listen to any more of his bragging," Malcolm said.

"I have to agree with that, but I sure wouldn't have bet him a hundred dollars on winning some thirty-mile race, bareback, and on a fat old horse." Pete shook his head. "Yes my friend, I think it's over."

The next day Suds threw himself into training. He started working Cotton every day. Without fail Suds would ride Cotton, day in and day out. The weather didn't matter. Rain or shine Suds was in the saddle. It seemed that he forgot everything else. Nothing mattered other than putting Cotton in shape. For months Suds worked Cotton. Cotton was looking good, with not an once of fat on him. Suds even put himself on a diet. He bought a Jane Fonda workout tape and worked out at night in his dark living room in front of the TV. Suds watched what he ate. He still drank beer like he owned stock in the company, but he cut back on the fried foods and pizza.

Suds noticed that Malcolm was not working Pecos out. Anytime Suds drove by Malcolm's place Pecos was in the pasture with his head down in the grass. His belly seemed to get bigger with each day. Suds knew he had this bet won.

One afternoon Pete pulled into Malcolm's drive and in his rearview mirror saw Suds pass on his daily ground-eating lope to the sale barn. Shaking his head, Pete knocked and went into the house.

"I just passed Suds working Cotton out," Pete said to Malcolm. "He is serious about this. What are you planning?"

"Taking a nap."

"I mean about the race with Suds," Pete said.

"I was hoping that broken gas valve would forget about this nonsense," Malcolm said.

"I don't think he is going to forget anything," Pete said. "He just rode by. I've seen him every day riding like he and the white horse was headed for the Olympics."

"I've noticed that," Malcolm laughed. "Suds has even lost some weight."

"You think Pecos has a chance of winning?"

"Did you look over to see him as you came in the house?" Malcolm said, pouring Pete some coffee.

"Stupid question," Pete said, pulling the cup in front of him. "So what are you going to do?"

"Take a nap as soon as you drink your coffee," Malcolm said. "I'm tired."

"This is ugly," Pete said, blowing on the hot coffee. "Old Suds will never let you live this down. You'll have to move. What am I saying? I'll have to move, I'm your friend."

"There is a chance," Malcolm laughed. "As much as he drinks he could fall off Cotton, land on his head, and forget about the whole thing."

"Fall on his head," Pete said. "We're talking about Suds here. If he fell on his head, all it would do is recrease his hat."

"Another good point," Malcolm said. "We could be in trouble."

"We?"

"Remember, you're my friend," Malcolm laughed.

It was only a week and a half later that Malcolm got the dreaded news. He and Pete ran into Suds at the cafe again. Malcolm and Pete both thought it was safe to eat there because Suds had stopped coming in; after all he was putting he and Cotton both in shape and didn't have time to kill in the cafe. Malcolm looked up to see Suds standing in front of him with both hands on his hips and his hat pushed back on his head.

"Saturday morning," Suds said.

"What are you talking about?" Malcolm questioned.

"Saturday morning," Suds said. "The big race. Are you backing out? Don't have the money? What's the problem here big man?"

"There's no problem, Suds," Malcolm said in a calm voice. "You want some breakfast?"

"No I don't want any breakfast," Suds snapped. "I want to see your money. I want Dub over there to hold the money in case you don't show up."

"Don't show up? I thought we were going to race from my place. You think I wouldn't show up at my own place?" Malcolm laughed so hard tears came to his eyes. "Do you think I'd move to beat you out of a hundred bucks? Come on Suds, even you are smarter than that—well, maybe not."

Malcolm pulled out a hundred-dollar bill and slid it down to Dub. "You can rest easy now, Suds."

"Tomorrow, eight o'clock, let's do it!" Suds said and turned on his heels and threw open the door, letting it slam shut behind him.

"Do you think if I shot him a jury in this county would convict me?" Malcolm asked Pete.

"In this county," Pete said. "Not a chance."

Malcolm went back to his eggs.

The next morning Suds along with everyone who had ever ventured into the cafe and heard about the race was at Malcolm's place. Malcolm greeted Suds with a cup of coffee.

"I don't want any coffee," Suds snapped. "I want to get this race started."

"Well, let's get it started," Malcolm said as he took a sip of his coffee.

"You might want to get your old fat horse," Suds said.

"He's eating his breakfast," Malcolm said. "He doesn't like to be interrupted when he is having his breakfast."

Suds was instantly red-faced. "Why didn't you feed him sooner?"

"I don't like to wake him," Malcolm said. "He needs his sleep."

"I'm going to start without you if you don't get a move on," Suds yelled.

"I'd do that, Suds." Malcolm smiled. "We'll catch up."

"It's eight fifteen," Suds said from the saddle. "I'm not waiting. I'm going to start this race."

"Good idea," Malcolm smiled. "And Suds, that armadillo sweat looks good on that hat you're wearing."

"Who's going to start the race?" Suds asked.

"I'll do it," Malcolm said. "Go."

Suds huffed, put Cotton into a spin, lined him out toward the sale barn, and hung the spurs to the horse. Malcolm raised his cup in a salute to the rider, and everyone laughed.

"You'll never catch up, big man," Suds yelled over his shoulder as he spurred up the road, making a good show of it. Everyone knew he couldn't push the horse that hard the entire way or it would kill the mount.

Leaning over Cotton's neck, Suds followed the road up across the orchard. Suds looked back over his shoulder one last time and could not see Malcolm in sight. Suds knew that if he took the route he had planned there was no way Malcolm could win the race. Suds had planned his route for weeks, through the orchards, down by the river, up across the mesa, down a short stretch of highway to the feed store, then back the same way. It was a rough route, not like the highway, but it was about five miles shorter, and Suds had ridden it many times.

When Suds reached the feed store he found two squares of paper tacked on the fence with Dub's signature boldly across the front of each just as they had later decided. Suds thought it would be too easy to cheat just picking up a beer can sitting on a fence. The idea was that the rider would bring back to the finish line the paper with the signature on it to prove that he had been to the feed store and back.

Suds was sure Malcolm had not been there but he also felt that Malcolm must have something up his sleeve. Suds was winning the race.

Suds slid Cotton off the mesa and down to the river. The horse was in the best shape of his life. He loped along, eating up the ground with ease. Back up through the orchard and Malcolm was nowhere to be seen. The only tracks were his, meaning that Malcolm had taken the highway and had no chance at all of winning the race.

I got you now, Suds thought. *You'll never hear the end of this.*

Suds could see Malcolm's place at the end of the road and everyone came to their feet when someone yelled, "Here they come!"

Suds, being the showman he was, pushed Cotton into a dead run. He leaned over the horse's neck, letting the horse run at his full speed. It was beautiful.

The crowd started to cheer and throw their hats into the air. Over the cheering Suds heard someone yell, "It's going to be close!"

Close, Suds thought. *They must be nuts.*

Looking over his shoulder, he could see Pete's pickup bearing down on him. The motor roared and a cloud of dust from the dirt road licked at the back wheels. Behind Pete's truck was his old open top stock trailer. Pete pulled up beside Suds and the running horse and honked. Suds spurred Cotton harder and pushed the reins. He chanced one more look over his shoulder and he could see it.

In the back of the stock trailer stood Pecos with his head down. The horse was asleep. Malcolm was on his back, bareback. Malcolm's hat was pushed down hard on his head, and the front of the brim was folded up, pushed by the wind. Malcolm had a cigar in his mouth with sparks flying, giving him the look of a steam-fed locomotive. As Pete gave the old truck the gas and passed Suds on the right, Malcolm, sitting on the back of the sleeping Pecos, held up a brandy snifter in a salute, peeled off his hat, and threw it into the air as he gave off a hardy "hi ho Silver."

Suds put Cotton in a hock-sliding stop as Malcolm was waking Pecos up and unloading him out of the trailer.

"That was not a horse race," Sud screamed. "You cheated!"

"You laid down the rules," Malcolm said. "To the feed store and back. Here is Dub's signature." Malcolm pulled the square of paper from his shirt pocket and handed it to Suds. "You said I had to sit Pecos the whole trip. I did that and on top of it all I did it bareback. I don't see your problem, Suds."

"My problem is you cheated," Suds yelled, red-faced.

"I told you that you were not a smart rider," Malcolm said in a voice just over a whisper, making Suds all the more excited. "I rode smart."

Suds continued to complain and cry, but it was decided by an ad hoc committee of those within earshot that Malcolm had won the race. Nothing in the rules that Suds had laid down prohibited Malcolm from trailering Pecos if he rode him the entire way. There were witnesses who said in fact Malcolm sat Pecos the entire trip and seemed to enjoy the ride.

"Suds is nuts and you have to agree," Malcolm said. "All I did was shut him up for a while."

Big-Time Horse Traders

"I have to go with Malcolm," Ken said. "Suds is nuts!"

"Now, someone that is making sense," Malcolm nodded at Ken. "I hate to agree with the cantankerous old cook, but Ken is right. Suds is nuts."

"I'll tell you how nuts he is," Ken said.

If you were to subscribe to Suds' somewhat jaded assessment concerning the equine business, you'd be quickly convinced that the good horse trader was an artist. Not an artist in the sense one would think of a painter or sculptor, but an artist just the same. The horse trader, according to Suds' loud and vocal opinion, could be more closely compared to the artistry of a used-car salesman. The good horse trader, like the used-car dealer, had to buy right and make sure he sold to someone who didn't do the same. To be a good used-car dealer, or a good horse trader, you had to develop the ability to conceal any and all flaws and highlight the good. Since duplicity was one of Suds' strongest points, the ability of concealing flaws on a horse came natural and was something in which he took great pride.

Suds was not a professional horse trader, by any means, and would have gone broke had he attempted to turn his hobby into a profession. He bought and sold horses only as a side business, and still with that limited exposure he nearly went broke. Even though horse trading was not his full-time calling, when the urge came upon him to make a buck on a horse, Suds worked at it like it was a calling from God.

It was 2:00 A.M. and he had been sitting the bleachers of the sale barn, off and on, since 9:00 A.M. the day before. Buying horses at the sale barn at 2:00 A.M. was Suds' rule number three in a long laundry list of rules he possessed for buying and selling horses. He always liked to buy in the early morning hours when the rest of the "buzzard-wing-hat-wearing-dude-want-to-be-buyers" were already home in bed. At two o'clock in the morning there was nothing at the sale barn but killer buyers and serious horsemen. The latter was the category in which Suds placed himself. Some of the best buys Suds ever made at the sale barn came after 2:00 A.M.

This day, he had been through the pens just short of a dozen times and had chosen a handful of horses that he felt he could turn for a healthy profit. He had bid on these horses throughout the day with no success in buying any of them. Every horse he had picked out and bid on sold too high in his estimation.

In Suds' list of rules for buying horses, rule number one was to put a price on the horse you wanted to buy and never go over that price. Rule "1a" was never pay the seller's asking price. Rule number two was to never fall in love with the horse you are buying. If you violated rule number two, you would in turn be forced to abandon rule number one. The logic was that when you fell in love with a horse, it was like falling in love with a woman—your judgement went out the window. Love, no matter if it was in the case of a woman or a horse, blinded you to all flaws that were very apparent to others. Suds knew it didn't matter if you were talking about a woman or a horse, when you threw love into the equation you always paid a higher price than either was worth. Suds bought horses for one reason and one reason only—to sell and make a buck. Suds had a number of other rules, some of which he paid a great deal of attention to and others he would rewrite or completely disregard at will, depending on how it suited him at the time.

He had just raised his hand, making the last bid on a nice three-year-old buckskin mare. Admittedly, the little mare could have wore a few more pounds, she needed a good worming, her hoofs were in desperate need of trimming, she was cow-hocked, sported saddle marks from an ill fitting rig, her mane and tail needed pulling, and a good pair of clippers wouldn't have hurt her a bit. It didn't matter. If Suds bought her right he could fix it all, except she'd always be cow-hocked.

Before he called it a night Suds bought two other horses, outbidding the killers. At 4:00 A.M. he loaded his trailer and slammed the door on the buckskin mare. He fished his keys from his jeans, fired up his truck, and headed home, pleased with his purchases.

The sun was just peeking over the barn when he kicked the horses out in the lot behind the house. Suds was accustomed to rushing home like a vampire before the sun came up. This morning was no different. It was also no different in the fact he had hit the beer cooler he carried in the bed of his truck hard, and he was drunk.

He made it to the house, like he had many times in the past when he was drunk, threw his hat at the hall hat rack, missed, then stumbled to the shower. He stepped out of the shower and kicked the pile of dirty clothes he had dropped in front of the shower door across the floor and into the corner. After pulling on his white boxers and a T-shirt, he sat at the table eating his breakfast—a bowl of Sugar Pops. He had milk, but it had gone bad three weeks before so he pulled a college trick and poured a 12-ounce Bud over the contents of the bowl—not a new taste for Suds.

After his breakfast of champions Suds wandered to his dark bedroom and threw himself onto his unmade bed. He had only been in bed for about three hours when a pounding at the front door woke him from his light coma. He staggered to the door, pulled his hat from the floor, and shoved it on his head. He had tried to lay in bed and ignore the knocking, but whoever it was would not go away. Wearing his dirty hat, white boxers, and a gray T-shirt, he ripped the door open to be knocked backward by the flood of sunlight washing over him and racing straight into his eyes to burn holes in his retinas.

"Suds, you look like hell."

"That's the look I was going for," Suds snorted. "I feel like hell!"

Suds squinted, and by the outline of the person blocking the morning sun he could see the voice belonged to Norman.

"What do you want, Norman?" Suds grunted, pulling his hat off and putting it between his face and the sun, which he was sure was burning brighter than any time in the history of the world.

Someone was pounding, unmercifully, on an anvil in his head, and the background music for his day seemed to be an unrecognizable, nerve-racking, dull roar. Suds had always said he felt sorry for people who didn't drink. They knew when they got out of bed that was the best they would feel all day. A drunk's day almost always begins in a gray fog, leaving an abundance of room for improvement as he sobers up and the day progresses.

"Where did you get the horses?" Norman asked in a sing-song voice that Suds was sure was illegal in at least three states.

"What?"

"Where did you get the horses in the barn lot?" Norman sung again.

"Oh," Suds said, rubbing his eyes. "Sale, last night."

"Can I look at the buckskin?"

"I don't care what you do!" Suds slammed the door in Norman's face.

Suds leaned on the door to keep from falling on his face. When his head stopped spinning he pushed himself upright and dropped his hat back to the floor. Afraid to open his eyes again, he followed the wall down the hallway to his dark bedroom where he could hear his king-size bed calling his name. He flopped on his back, jarring his alcohol soaked brain and causing a low groan to find its way from his cotton dry lips. He was hanging, suspended and unconscious, between a major league hangover and a trip to the dark world of sleep, when he was yanked upright in bed by someone trying to knock the front door off its hinges.

"Go away!" he yelled. Mistake—yelling hurt his head, bad. Yelling could kill a man in his condition.

The knocking continued—the knocking hurt bad, also. The thought of firing a round down the hall toward the front door passed through Suds' throbbing head. The only thing that squelched the idea was knowing that if yelling caused his brain to bleed like it did, firing a pistol in his bedroom would kill him for sure. He pulled himself upright and staggered toward the door again, picked up his hat, held it up to block the sun, and wrenched the door open.

"What is it?" he whimpered pathetically.

"How much do you want for the buckskin?" Norman asked, again in that annoying I-don't-drink singsong voice he had working this morning.

"Go away."

"I want to buy the buckskin horse."

"Go away," Suds slurred, drooling on himself. "You don't have money and I don't have time."

"I'll give you four hundred and fifty dollars," Norman said, thinking he was making a joke.

"Sold," Suds said. "Now go away. I'm sick."

Norman's mouth hung open. "Really?"

"I'm really sick."

"No, really will you sell me the horse?"

"Yeah, now get out of here before I get my pistol."

Suds would have said anything to get rid of Norman and get back to the sanctuary of his bed.

"Let me get my checkbook," Norman said, jumping off the porch and running toward his truck.

Suds pushed the door closed with his bare foot. He knew Norman was nuts. Norman had always been nuts. Suds also knew that Norman didn't have any money. Suds rubbed his eyes. He was in no mood to be standing in the doorway in his underwear, with a headache, listening to some nutcase with an annoying singsong voice blab.

Again he followed the wall to his dark room, and with closed eyes he found his bed by feel and dropped into it, but easy this time so he would not slosh his brain. He opened his eyes and looked toward the ceiling. He made the decision that if Norman knocked on the door one more time, he'd pull a pillow over his head against the noise and risk a shot down the hall. Sleep washed over him like a muddy river, washing away the torment in his head, and to his relief the door remained quiet.

At seven that night hunger pains gnawing at his stomach woke Suds up. He tugged on a clean pair of jeans, a starched white long sleeve shirt, fresh from the cleaners, and a pair of worn boots. On his way out the door he stopped for his hat, still on the floor. When he bent to pick it up he nearly did a header into the wall. He was still dizzy. Suds steadied himself with both hands on the wall, letting his head drop between his arms holding him upright. He blinked several times to put the world back into focus and noticed something on the floor at his feet. When the blood slowly came back to his head and he pulled himself together he picked up the paper. It turned out to be a check written to him from Norman, in the amount of four hundred and fifty dollars.

The buckskin, he thought, *Norman wanted to buy the buckskin.*

Suds pushed himself upright and slowly made his way to the kitchen window to look toward the back lot. Only two horses stood in the lot waiting to be fed—the buckskin was gone. He'd have to deal with this after he ate. Right now his stomach thought his throat had been cut—he was starved.

The two horses in the lot threw their heads up and ran toward the fence as Suds approached. He disappeared into the barn, and when he returned he threw a few flakes of hay into the rack and walked to his pickup.

Suds drove to the cafe, but they were closed.

Must be a holiday or something, he thought.

As a second choice, he pulled his truck into the drive-through of the new fast food joint just off the interstate. The place was ten years old, but everyone still called it "new" because it was the last thing built in the town.

Suds pulled up alongside the smiling plastic clown, located at the back of the building. The clown didn't seem to care that his right arm had been knocked off by a truckload of kids who had cut the corner too short and clipped him with their mirror two years before. Suds shouted his order into the clown's plastic, painted, smiling face and in return received what sounded like static from a ham radio blaring back at him loud enough to set him back in his seat. He had no idea what the person said, so he just grunted and pulled forward as the static blared again from the clown. In less then a minute a pimpled-faced kid, with braces that must have set his parents back a year's wages, opened the window and told Suds he owed five eighty. Suds handed the kid six bucks. The kid stuck the money in the cash register, then passed Suds the heart-attack-in-a-sack and a large drink. Suds drove off before the kid could hand him the twenty cents change.

Suds turned up the radio and unwrapped the burger. He drove with one hand and stuffed the greasy cheeseburger into his mouth with the other. He had two bites down when he noticed the mustard just below the third button of his fresh shirt.

"Ughhh," he grunted. He tried to wipe the mustard off with the paper napkin that was already soaked with grease from the burger. He only succeeded in smearing the yellow stain across his starched white shirt, making more of a mess. Mad, he shoved the burger back into the sack and threw the whole thing out the window, to be followed by his drink.

Suds was still mad by the time he reached Norman's apartment, and to add to the mad he already had working Norman was nowhere to be seen. There was only one other place Norman would be. Norman's entire world consisted of only three places. He was home, at work at the ranch, or he was eating at the cafe—nowhere else. Since the cafe was closed and he was not at the apartment, he had to be at the ranch. Suds drove out to the catch pen on the ranch and found Norman brushing the buckskin. Suds stepped out of the truck and walked to the fence.

"Hey, Suds," Norman said, waving cheerfully.

Suds only nodded. As he walked toward Norman, Suds pulled a pack of cigarettes from his shirt pocket and flipped a filtered tip from the box, making a show of putting it between his lips. From his jeans he pulled an old Zippo that was his dad's, and was about to light up.

"I saw on NBC news last night," Norman said, as he got a faraway look on his face like he forgot what he was talking about. "I like NBC news. They have a pretty girl on that channel that does the news. She has dark hair and brown eyes. I like her brown eyes. I've got color TV and her eyes are real brown. That channel comes in a lot clearer. I have been watching . . . . "

"Is this going somewhere or is it intended to just bore me to tears?" Suds said.

"Oh!" Norman said, pulling himself back to the original thought that Suds was certain he'd care nothing about. "They said secondhand smoke was even worse for you than first hand."

"I guess I made the right decision, then," Suds said as he lit his cigarette and drew deep.

Suds blew smoke in Norman's face as he fished Norman's check from his jeans pocket and held it up. Norman's entire focus was on the smeared yellow stain across the front of Suds' white shirt.

"What's that?" Norman questioned.

"Your check."

"No, that," Norman said, pointing at the stain on Suds' gut.

"Supper," Suds said, waving the check in front of Norman's nose. Norman then focused his attention on the check.

"I think we have made a mistake," Suds said. He would have come on stronger and ordered Norman to take the horse back to his place, but there was a group of cowboys sitting on the fence talking. Suds thought the wisest tactic was to play it easy.

Norman said nothing, looking cross-eyed at the check, just inches under his nose.

"I didn't think you were really going to buy the mare," Suds said. "I thought you were just joking. You know what kind of funny guy you are."

"I like the mare," Norman said, lifting his gaze and painting a big smile across his face.

This guy is dumber than I gave him credit for, Suds thought.

"I already have her sold." Suds shifted to plan "b"—the lie. To be fair, it wasn't a total lie, the kind Suds normally told. He had, in fact, thought about cleaning the buckskin up and running her by Mike Morgan, a rancher who he knew was looking for a young roping horse.

"I think she would be a good heading horse," Norman said.

Suds threw a glance over at the cowboys on the fence, who had quit talking and were now listening to the horse deal taking place in the catch pen. Suds put his arm around Norman's neck and guided him to the other side of the pen.

"Look," Suds said just above a whisper. "This morning when you came by I had just got in and was asleep. You woke me up, and I was sick. I didn't know what you were even talking about. I have that mare sold. So here is your check and you can just put the mare back in the pen behind my house."

"Suds, I really like this mare," Norman said. "I want to keep her."

"Are you listening to me?" Suds snapped, checking his anger. "I have her sold. I'd let you have her if I hadn't already sold her."

Norman was dejected, and before he could come back with a convincing argument to keep his mare, Suds cut him off.

"I'll give you $500 for the mare," Suds said. "You just made fifty bucks on a horse that you haven't owned twelve hours."

"I don't know," Norman said. "I really like the mare."

Suds shoved Norman's check into his shirt pocket and peeled off a fifty-dollar bill, waved it in front of Norman's face, then put it in his front pocket.

"You're a pal," Suds said as he walked away. "You can just kick that mare out into the lot where you got her whenever you get a chance. There's no hurry."

As usual, Norman did as Suds had told him and took the mare back to Suds' ranch that night.

The next day, at the crack of noon, Suds drug his saddle out into the pen and threw it up onto the buckskin. The mare never offered to make a move. Suds cinched the saddle up tight and dropped the stirrup, a little harder than he intended, down on the mare's side. She stood, with her head down, like she was asleep. Suds smiled. She was sweet. He pulled the bridle off the horn of the saddle, and the mare took a noncommital look back. She released her lower jaw and took the bit like a pro. Suds was feeling very good about his newly acquired mount. She would make him some money.

Just as he was about to mount, Norman pulled up, coming to stop in a dust cloud that had chased him up the ranch road. Norman walked over to the fence, climbing to the top for a better view.

"Howdy, Norman," Suds said busting with pride. "You got here just in time to see her maiden voyage. She could care less. Someone has put some saddle time on this mare."

Norman secretly wished he hadn't let Suds bully him into selling the mare back to him.

Suds put his left foot into the stirrup, stepped up, and found his seat. The mare stood rock solid. Suds smiled wide and threw his chest out with pride. He eased some slack into the reins, giving the mare her head, and nudged her forward with a light touch of his spurs. The mare took a step forward, threw her head down between her hoofs, and bucked straight into the air like she had been kicked out of a chute at the tenth round of the National Finals. Her front feet hit the ground with a teeth-loosening jar, throwing Suds over the dashboard. He landed on his hat and was knocked colder than a banker's heart. He only spent a few seconds in the darkness of unconsciousness, and as he broke its surface his first blurred sight was of Norman hovering over him, fanning him with his hat.

"Get away from me, you bag of nuts," Suds hissed, sitting up and then falling back to the ground with a thud that removed the little breath he had left in his lungs.

Suds' eyes widened and then crossed. He wheezed as his nostrils clawed desperately to drag air into his lungs. Norman still hung over him, fanning him with a hat, an action that helped Suds not one bit.

"Get my pistol. I'm going to kill that horse." Suds' eyes then rolled back into his head and he passed back out, falling backwards into the dirt.

"Man, that horse can buck," Norman said. Suds heard nothing.

When Suds woke up and his head cleared enough that he was able to understand English again, Norman wasted no time attempting to buy back the mare.

"I'll pay you $550 for the horse," Norman said. "You can make fifty bucks on her."

Suds didn't care about the fifty bucks, but he'd be more than happy to be rid of that man-eating, killer horse. Suds could only nod his agreement and Norman took Suds' limp hand and shook it. The deal was struck and Norman loaded his new mare in his trailer.

That was the last time Suds saw the mare until summer had passed, and with the turning of the leaves along the river, Suds found himself driving out to the ranch where Norman worked. Suds had bought a load of calves from the ranch and was on his way to pick them up. As Suds drove along the ranch road he noticed Norman, off on the mesa, with the buckskin in a long ground-eating lope toward the ranch headquarters. Suds couldn't take his eyes off the buckskin as she ran. She moved as smooth as ten-year-old bourbon, and bourbon was something with which Suds had undisputed, extended experience.

By the time Suds had loaded the calves, Norman came loping into the ranch headquarters, and Suds went over to meet him.

"That mare sure looks good, Norman," Suds said.

"I've kept her saddle blankets wet all summer," Norman said. "I've rode her every day, and she is working out good. She just needed someone to ride her every day."

Suds walked around the animal, running his hand over her rock hard muscles. He ran his hand down her right hind leg and lifted her hoof, she never moved. He ran his hand up over her rump, stopped at the saddle, then went to the front of the horse. He rubbed her neck and grabbed her ear; she never moved.

"Mind if I take her a turn?" Suds asked.

"Be my guest." Norman stepped off and handed Suds the reins.

Suds pulled himself up into the saddle and got himself set. He nudged the horse forward. Suds was fully expecting her to blow up and buck with him. He'd be ready this time. She wouldn't put him on the ground this time. She stepped out with no problem, without a thought of pitching. Suds kicked her out along the fence. He took her down the fence line about a hundred yards and then turned her back into the fence. She set back on her hocks and spun around, handling it like a pro. She was responding to his leg cues and reined like a dream. It was evident that Norman had put a lot of hours into this horse.

"I want to buy her," Suds announced as he stepped off her back.

"I couldn't sell her," Norman protested. "I really do like her."

"Yeah, yeah, yeah, whatever. I'll give you six hundred bucks," Suds said, peeling off several one-hundred dollar bills from a wad he produced from his front pocket. "I'll pay you cash, right now, right here for her."

"I really like her, Suds," Norman said.

"I really like her too," Suds said. "Boy, you just made fifty bucks on her. You are quite the horse trader."

"I don't know." Norman pulled off his hat and rubbed his head, then pulled it back on. "I really like her, a lot."

"Fifty bucks," Suds said. "I know you're broke and you won't get paid for another two weeks. Better take the money. Six hundred bucks would make your truck payment, give you some lunch money, and you might have money for a date."

Norman was still shaking his head no.

"I guess money for a date doesn't mean anything to you," Suds laughed. "You'd have to find some woman to go out with you."

"I had a date last...."

"Not since the Kennedy administration," Suds laughed again.

"I went out with Norma Watkins," Norman shot back, embarrassed. "We had a good time, too."

"Her car was broke down and you picked her up walking to town."

"We had lunch," Norman said. "I bought her lunch."

"OK, OK," Suds said, cutting him off. "If you want to call that a date it's fine with me. You better take the money. Who knows, Norma may break down again, and there you'd be broke and unable to take her to lunch. It might be another ten or twelve years before you have another date."

Norman looked to see if the boys on the fence had heard Suds' loud talk. They had not, but Norman lowered his head in embarrassment.

Suds counted out the money and pushed it in Norman's pocket. "Take the money, boy. You never know when a date might come your way."

"I guess," Norman said with hesitation.

Suds pushed the calves to the front of the trailer and closed the division gate. He then loaded his new mare behind the calves and pulled away a happy man.

The day of the spring branding, a day that Suds had been looking forward to for months, he proudly unloaded the buckskin mare. She looked good. He couldn't wait to show her off and had her groomed and clipped to where she looked like a show horse. She was shod and had the manners of Ann Landers at her mother's house.

As Suds and Norman rode out toward the breaks along the river, Suds caught the sight of a wild steer busting through the brush in an attempt to escape. Suds, seeing a chance to show off, shook out a loop and put the spurs to the buckskin. The little horse stretched out into a run, and she hit the brush with her head down, splitting the thicket like a diver entering the water off the high board, never slowing down. The steer ran through the mesquite and then jumped into a clearing. The little buckskin was right on the wild beast. Suds was rolling a rope, ready to make the catch. He took two spins on his rope and cast his line at the steer. The loop settled on the steer's head, one of Suds' luckier catches, and Suds reined the buckskin up.

The horse sat down on her hocks and slid to a stop. The line went tight, the steer flipped over backward, and the buckskin blew up. Her eyes widened, her nostrils flared, and she humped in the middle, ready to buck. Suds spurred her forward and she jumped. The steer came to his feet as the mare was running forward, and she attempted to jump over the steer. She didn't clear the steer and came down on his back. This scared the steer even more, and he jumped to the right, throwing the buckskin to the ground. Suds came out of the saddle, and the mare jumped to her feet. Suds had his left foot stuck in the stirrup. The mare broke into a run. Suds was flipped over on his stomach as he was drug through a patch of cactus. He was slammed against the base of a mesquite, and the force threw him back into the back hoofs of the mare as she ran in fear.

When the mare had traveled just a few feet she came to the end of the rope that was still attached to the steer. The rope had become wrapped around her hindquarters and it flipped her to the ground again. She hit the ground and bounced, coming to her feet. Suds' boot came off, releasing him from the jaws of death. The mare again took off in a run, with his boot still in the stirrup. When she came to the end of the rope this time it broke about three inches behind the saddle horn. She ran in one direction and the steer, pulling the broken rope raveled on one end, ran back toward the river.

Suds' eyes opened to see the blue sky. He was alive. He knew he was alive because he felt like he was going to die. He pushed himself up onto his elbows then fell back to the ground in pain. He had begun to hate the mare yet again.

Norman spurred up next to the running mare, leaned over, and took the reins off the horse's neck. He dallied the reins around his saddle horn and made a circle, loping back to where Suds lay in the dirt. As Norman rode up Suds was sitting up, staring straight ahead; his eyes had that "no one's home" look about them.

"You OK?" Norman said, leaning over the saddle horn and looking down at Suds on the ground.

Suds didn't move. Norman stepped off and walked over to Suds.

"You OK?" Norman asked again, leaning over to look Suds in the eye.

"I should have killed that horse the first time she drove me in the ground," Suds squeaked. He blinked to focus, pushed his hat back on his head, and attempted to catch his breath.

"She's never had anyone throw a rope off of her," Norman said. "I would have told you but I didn't think there was a chance you'd catch anything in this brush."

Norman held the buckskin's reins out to Suds as he struggled to his feet.

"I'll just walk back," Suds said, bending over and leaning on his knees. "Can't take anymore today. Take her back and I'll be along shortly."

Suds came limping back to the truck and found that Norman had loaded the buckskin into the trailer. Norman was sitting on the tailgate eating an apple.

"Let me take the buckskin and teach her what a rope is all about," Norman said. "I think she would make a good roping horse."

"I think she would make good glue, she almost killed me today," Suds said. "I'll just sell you that horse."

"How much?"

"Seven hundred bucks."

"I'll give you six fifty," Norman said, knowing Suds was wanting to unload the mare. "That will give you a fifty-dollar profit, our standard deal."

"Just get that horse out of my trailer and it's a deal," Suds said, rubbing a purple knot that was growing on his forehead. Both his eyes were turning black and a trail of dried blood came from his nose.

Norman put the mare into a pen and did nothing with her for three days. When he started working with her on the fourth day she was fine. On the second day of working with her he was throwing a rope off her. On the third day he was catching calves off her. After a little work the mare seemed to really take to roping. She seemed to like it, busting out of the box and overtaking the calf like she had done it for years. That spring and summer Norman made a few local rodeos and more often than not took first place in calf roping, giving him some pocket money.

Suds started watching the mare with interest again. She was nice, and all she had needed was some work. Norman had the mare looking like she had been raised in the roping box.

It was just a week after the Fourth of July rodeo, where Norman had won every roping he entered on the buckskin mare, that Suds laid awake thinking about the mare. Norman had her working behind the rope, and the mare never looked better. The next day Suds dressed and hunted Norman. He found Norman at the cafe. Suds marched in with a mission—he wanted the buckskin mare back.

Suds pulled out a chair beside Norman. "What's up, Norman."

"Getting ready to go to work," Norman said. "We have some heifers that need to be moved off that pasture by the river."

"Norman, I was wanting to talk to you about the buckskin," Suds said. "I want to buy her back. I'll give you seven hundred dollars for her. You can make fifty bucks on her, our standard deal."

Suds pulled a wad of hundreds from his jeans pocket and started counting them off.

"Can't do it."

"Alright," Suds said, going back to his counting. "I'll give you seven fifty."

"Still can't do it."

"Alright, alright," Suds said. "One thousand bucks, but don't try to rob me on this deal."

Suds was in love with the buckskin mare, a clear violation of his own rule number two—never fall in love with a horse, it will cost you too much.

"I'll give you ten fifty," Suds said. "But not a penny more. I mean it." He was willing to pay more but was playing his best bluff, hoping Norman would sell.

"I can't do it," Norman said.

"Alright, eleven hundred," Suds said.

Norman shook his head.

"Eleven fifty."

Norman shook his head again.

"Norman, give me a break here. Twelve hundred," Suds said. "I want that horse."

"I can't . . . ," Norman said, trying to explain. Suds wouldn't let him.

"What do you want?" Suds said with a touch of panic in his voice. "I'll throw in that big dun horse I ride. I want that buckskin horse!"

"I can't sell you the mare," Norman said, holding up his hand to stop Suds' next offer. "I sold the buckskin to Malcolm; he wanted a good roping horse."

"Malcolm? Are you nuts?" Suds yelled as the veins in his neck stood at attention and he came close to having a stroke. "You couldn't have sold our horse to Malcolm. Have you lost your mind, you little moronic goof. Why did you sell our mare to Malcolm?"

"He wanted a good roping horse."

"She's a nice horse." Suds looked up to see Malcolm sitting two tables over with Pete; they were both laughing.

Suds' face turned red, and he grabbed Norman by the ear and pulled him out of the chair.

"We need to talk," Suds said as he drug Norman to the door.

"When you're done with your meeting come on back and I'll buy you breakfast, Suds," Malcolm yelled to Suds just as he reached the door. "I want to hear about her bucking you to the ground."

Suds pushed Norman out the door and over to his pickup truck.

"He wanted a roping horse, he wanted a roping horse," Suds shouted, pushing his blood pressure into the danger zone.

"He paid me nine hundred dollars for her," Norman said. "Why are you so mad? You sold her to me a bunch of times."

"You're even dumber than you look," Suds said, sitting on the bumper of his truck. "How could you sell our horse? You just ruined the best deal we have had going in a long time. We were both making a good living on that horse!"

Wild Cow Milking

"Suds is nuts," Pete said. "I don't think you'll find anyone around this fire who will argue with that."

Malcolm stretched and yawned like he was about ready to go to bed.

"He's nuts alright," I said, "but Malcolm still goes out of his way to bust his chops."

"So I beat him at the horse race," Malcolm said. "He needed it bad."

"That's true," I told him. "But you still bust him every chance you get."

"Win one horse race," Malcolm laughed. "Beat him at a bet that his monkey couldn't ride Pecos, and you guys think I do it all the time to poor old Suds."

"You do it all the time to him," I said.

"That's not true."

"I guess you forgot about the rodeo," I said.

Malcolm rolled his eyes again. "I'm starting to feel like Suds. You guys should leave me alone."

"You are like Suds," Pete said. "You're too easy a target."

"As I remember, Pete," Dale said, "you are just as bad. Let's hear about the rodeo, Steve."

Stanley Slaughter, or Slick, as everyone knew him from his horse trading days, was a smoker and died early in life. However, smoking had nothing to do with his untimely departure from the bonds of this world. He was three months and six days past his forty-sixth birthday when the death angel brushed past the entire earth's population to secure Slick's legacy of being the first human being in documented history to be killed by a meteor.

To be factual, once a meteor enters the Earth's atmosphere it becomes a meteorite, and most meteorites burn up in just a few seconds, never reaching the Earth's surface. Another undeniable fact is that it doesn't matter how old you are or what name you choose to tack on the projectile, when you get beaned by a fastball the size of a Volkswagen, moving at speeds over 128,000 miles per hour, regardless what inning you're in—you're out of the game.

On that fateful day, if Slick had caught a red light, he would have caught a break that would have spared his life. Anything at all that would have delayed his trip would have made the difference in how his day ended. If he'd made the block on his way out of town, adding just one minute to his driving time, the meteorite would have missed him completely. Which is precisely how you want a meteorite to miss you—completely. Something the size of an automobile, burning hotter than a Pittsburgh steel furnace and moving faster than the speed of sound tends to fall in the category of horseshoes and hand grenades—meaning, a near miss still counts. As it was, Slick Slaughter was the unlucky soul to have been at the right place at the right time to receive a direct hit by an object originating in the darkest corners of the cosmos and light years away, driving him into the earth and into history.

In essence, an argument could be made that cigarettes did contribute to his death. Without knowing it, when Slick stopped for the cigarettes he placed himself in the path of the death rock from outer space. It could be argued, admittedly with immense difficulty, that cigarettes had killed Slick Slaughter at the age of forty-six. An argument with which, Suds soon discovered, no attorney was willing to tackle the tobacco industry.

Slick was on his way to meet his twenty-three-year-old son, Suds, at the pasture where they were attempting to pen a small herd of wild cattle. Slick had bought the cattle "range delivery," meaning they had to pen the wild beasts before he could haul them off. Since they were wild cattle and had been missed during the last two spring gathers, Slick bought them right, having faith in the ability of he and his son to be cowboy enough to catch them.

Suds had arrived first, unloaded his horse, saddled him, and not wanting to wait for his dad, rode off toward the big pasture. He had loped up to the wire gap used as a gate, some two hundred odd yards from the road, and looked back over his shoulder as his dad drove up. Slick's truck came to a stop, and he took what would become his last long drag off his cigarette. The last vision Suds had of his father was of him turning to his left and glancing out the driver's side window as he exhaled a blue puff of smoke from deep within his lungs.

Slick could have just as easily been beamed aboard the starship *Enterprise* by Scottie and not disappeared any quicker. Not only was he gone but so was nearly every trace of his new three-quarter-ton red truck. Nothing was left on the dirt road but a cloud of dust, the horse trailer, and the back bumper of the truck with the license plate still attached.

The paint was burned off the front half of the matching red horse trailer, and the paint on the back half of the trailer was bubbled and brown from the extreme heat of the passing meteorite. The trailer was facing the opposite direction it had been

just a split second before. Slick's truck had been peeled from the road, stripped from the trailer, and the trailer had been spun around, much like a kid's play top. The smoldering trailer came to rest sitting upright, two feet left of center and engulfed in a cloud of dust from the dirt road.

Slick's big, gray, green-broke colt was standing with his legs wide apart, resembling a newborn—his eyes were even wider. The colt violently trembled with the fear of knowing, in his walnut-sized horse brain, that the "colt killer" had come for him and was lurking just outside the trailer door. The extreme heat of the passing meteorite had singed the hair off the colt's face, head, ears, neck, and shoulders. A faint blue smoke rose from the smoldering horse in the fashion of a strange dance, and the smell of singed hair hung heavy in the air of the enclosed trailer.

The gray, even though burned and terrified, had survived in the scorched trailer. However, it could be said that the meteorite did in the end claim the colt also, as he was never the same and had to be put down just a few weeks following the impact of the asteroid.

Suds was never the same and quite possibly should have been put down along with the horse but was not. It was the consensus of most that after witnessing such a freak and historic accident, Suds lived with the ever gnawing fear of being ripped from this earth at any given second. It was also common belief that it was this fear that caused Suds not only to work at cheating death but cheating everyone with whom he came in contact.

Suds had been a different breed of cat since grade school, and with every passing year he seemed to wander farther and farther off the graph of normal. He was also somewhat of a eccentric magnet, drawing to him other like souls who resided on the other side of the equator of the norm. To put it in the very nicest of terms, every one of his friends possessed a unique quality of being different from the rest of the world's inhabitants. Without exception, they were all nuts.

It was one of Suds' abnormal friends, Norman Chastaine, who brought it to Malcolm's attention that Suds was cheating and had been for years. Since Malcolm had no doubt that Suds' sole purpose for existing on this earth was to cause him irritation and bother, Malcolm could not let information of Suds' cheating pass without some type of response. Malcolm felt, no, knew, it was his duty to follow up and find out how Suds was cheating. Suds was not only an obnoxious braggart and a compulsive liar, but Malcolm now knew him to also be a cheat.

Norman Chastaine was going nowhere in life, but he was making extremely good time in his travel. By no stretch of the imagination could he be labeled one of the community's more intelligent citizens. This point could be easily proven by citing the fact that he went from the sixth grade into the army. It was in boot camp where he and Suds met for the first time. On day one of service to their country, both Suds and Norman appeared wearing cowboy hats. This gave the drill instructor fodder for a barrage of insults and nicknames for both men that followed them through their entire military careers.

The army was not the worst thing Suds had ever endured in his life. The fact is Suds didn't mind being in the army at all and managed to save quite a bit of money while serving. Norman was instrumental in playing a major role in helping Suds' savings program. Most of the money Suds saved belonged to Norman in the first place. Every payday Suds would lure Norman into a poker game or some other ploy or scheme to separate him from most of his earnings. This would only bolster the belief, in Norman's dim mind, that Suds Slaughter was the smartest man on the planet.

Since Norman was under the mistaken belief that Suds was the most brilliant man in the world, it was only natural for Norman to follow Suds through the army and then back home after they were discharged. Norman took an apartment in town—an apartment for which he paid approximately twice what it was worth; an apartment that Suds had inherited from his late father just after Slick's ride into immortality on the back of the meteorite. Norman, not being an interior decorator or having even met one, furnished his apartment with a lime-green lawn chair; a black & white TV perched on two cinder blocks; a saddle, bridle, and two well-worn ropes; two pair of boots, one for work and one for good (only Norman could see the difference between the two pair); two pair of jeans, both with holes; and three shirts, two with holes and one without, all three to five years out of fashion.

Although Norman was not the sharpest knife in the drawer, he had one thing going for him, he was a "hand," or in other words a good cowboy. Norman's greatest aptitude lay in his unequaled proficiency with a rope. Since he was such a hand with a rope he had little trouble landing work on a nearby ranch. He was one of the best ropers to have stepped off the bus in years—another reason Suds liked having him around. Always with an eye open for a quick buck, Suds made something of a career betting on Norman's roping ability. Norman never saw any of the winnings, but this one-sided arrangement never seemed to bother him.

Every Fourth of July, Suds would enter Norman in every roping contest the local rodeo offered. Norman usually won every event where he roped alone, but in the events where Suds' talent was required they never fared so well. In the team roping event Norman always caught the head and cocked the steer for Suds, but Suds was not always so successful at heeling. However, for the past six years, without exception, Suds and Norman had won the wild cow milking contest.

It was in the event of wild cow milking that Malcolm learned Suds was cheating. Malcolm was enlightened at breakfast one morning late in November when Norman was talking too much. Since Norman was not running with the pack when it came to his intellectual shrewdness, he had no clue he had let Suds' guarded secret slip.

Suds was on his way out the door when Malcolm bumped into him.

"You're late," Suds said. "Sleepin' in?"

"You leaving?" Malcolm asked.

"Yeah," Suds laughed. "Already had my breakfast. I don't sleep all day."

"If you're leaving, then I'm right on time," Malcolm shot back.

"Let's meet like this every morning," Suds said. "I'm beginning to like it this way."

"Suds, I think we may have something in common after all," Malcolm said, tipping his hat. "We just don't like each other."

Malcolm pulled out the chair across from Pete, sat down, and dropped his hat to the floor beside him.

"What are you doing today?" Malcolm asked, directing his question toward Pete over the top of a menu.

"Jackie has me doing honey-do's today," Pete said. "Stuff I've put off for months. It caught up to me today. I must have been asleep when she brought it up; I couldn't think of any way to get out of it."

"Then why are you here eating breakfast?" Malcolm asked, studying the menu like it was the first time he had ever seen it.

"I'm running with the story that I needed some bolts to hang the front gate," Pete smiled.

"Good story."

"The one I'm sticking with," Pete laughed. "I really did need some bolts, but I wanted to see if anything was going on."

"You were hoping someone had some greater need for your services," Malcolm said. "Something that would save you from a day of work around the house?"

"Maybe," Pete answered, "but Jackie sees right through my ploys."

"And she lets you come to town anyway?"

"She's a wonderful woman," Pete said. "She knows how to keep me in line. She knows I'll loaf around here for about an hour then I'll wander home to do my chores."

Sara May came over and slid a cup of coffee in front of Malcolm—he always drank coffee—then she took his order for a breakfast burrito. Sara May had just disappeared behind the counter when his radar picked up Norman, two tables over, bragging about Suds' superior brain power. No one ever paid much attention to Norman, just as they never paid much attention to Suds, but Malcolm picked up something that raised his interest. Norman said, and only in passing, that Suds had a foolproof plan to always win the wild cow milking contest. No one around Norman questioned him or even grunted for fear he would keep talking about a subject they had no interest in—Suds Slaughter. Not getting anyone to bite on that subject,

Norman passed onto his next topic. He started to explain, to no one in particular as no one was really listing, how Suds' armadillo ranch would have worked had anyone else had any vision. According to Norman, Suds was way ahead of his time—words that everyone knew came straight from the lips of Suds Slaughter at one time or another.

When Norman paid his bill and headed out the door to go to work, Malcolm decided he would chase him and question him further about his remarks about Suds' "foolproof plan" to win the wild cow milking contest.

"Be right back, Pete." Malcolm stood up, taking one last sip from his coffee. "I need to grab something from the truck."

Malcolm caught Norman just as he was about to start his dent riddled and rust ridden pickup truck.

"Norman, where you headed to?" Malcolm shouted after him.

"Malcolm," Norman said, flashing a big toothy grin. "Gotta go to work."

Malcolm leaned into Norman's truck. "I heard you say something about Suds' armadillo ranch. I think you're right, that Suds had a good plan on that armadillo ranch."

"He should have made a train load of money on that deal," Norman said.

Malcolm knew where that came from. He'd heard Suds brag that he was going to make a "train load" of money on that venture.

"Suds is one smart cowboy," Malcolm said.

"You can say that again."

"Suds is one smart cowboy," Malcolm said again.

"Yeah." Norman missed the lame humor.

"That plan he came up with to win the wild cow milking was a great one," Malcolm said. "Only Suds could think up something like that one."

Norman just nodded his agreement.

"Well, I need to get to work," Norman said. "We're branding today. I like branding. I get to do a lot of ropin'. I like to rope."

"I know you do, Norman, but before you go tell me again how it worked," Malcolm said, putting his hand on Norman's arm to stop him. "His plan to win the wild cow milking, I mean. I don't think I remember it all. I'm not near as smart as ol' Suds."

"I don't think anybody's as smart as Suds," Norman said.

Then without hesitation, Norman, speaking in a quick and choppy rhythm, laid out Suds' trick to win the wild cow milking. A trick, according to Norman, Suds had employed for the past six years. Malcolm could only shake his head; the ploy was pure Suds.

"Good to talk to you, Norman." Malcolm waved as he went back into the cafe. "Adios."

Malcolm sat back down to finish his breakfast just as Pete pushed his plate away.

"I was going to wait on you but decided I better get back to the ranch," Pete said. "Jackie is not above coming to look for me."

"She doesn't trust you?" Malcolm laughed.

"Not since the time I told her I'd be back in an hour and ended up calling her from Nevada," Pete laughed.

"You should have known better than that," Malcolm said.

"As I remember it, you and Dale were the ones who picked me up in town saying there was a big horse sale in Nevada and they had a paint horse I needed to buy," Pete said. "It was you two fools that I trusted to be doing the right thing. Poor judgement on my part, I know."

"You should have known better than that," Malcolm said again.

Pete fished a buck from his front shirt pocket and pitched the dollar on the table for a tip.

"Sit down," Malcolm said. "I got something to tell you."

"I'm not going to Nevada today."

"You're not going anywhere," Malcolm said. "But you are going to want to hear this one."

"It better be good and it better be quick," Pete said, flopping back down in his chair. "If Jackie catches me in town loafing with you, she'll skin us both. You know that she wouldn't hesitate skinning you, ever since we pulled that Nevada trip."

"You mean ever since you dropped a dime on me with Jackie and painted me with all the blame in your lame attempt to escape the wrath of your bride," Malcolm said as he took his first bite of his burrito, which was by now cold.

"That too," Pete laughed.

"You know why you can't beat Suds at the wild cow milking?"

"Yeah, Norman ropes like he is possessed by some sort of supernatural power," Pete said.

"Norman can spin the hemp, I can't take that away from him," Malcolm said, sipping his coffee, which was also cold.

"But Suds couldn't milk a plastic jug in the dairy department of Kroger. Suds for the past six years has been cheating."

"What?"

"Suds has been cheating at the wild cow milking," Malcolm said as he waved for Sara May.

She looked up and raised her eyebrows.

"Could I get some more coffee?" Malcolm shouted.

Sara pursed her lips like she was throwing him a kiss, picked up the coffeepot, and walked toward the table. She poured Malcolm's coffee from his cold cup into Pete's empty cup and refilled Malcolm's cup. "Honey, if you'd stay put and drink this it wouldn't get cold," she said. Malcolm never looked at her and only waved to her over his shoulder.

"What are you talking about?" Pete asked, as Sara walked away.

"Suds has been cheating," Malcolm said. "That's how the fat slug has been winning the wild cow milking."

"How?"

"Suds fills his mouth with milk, and when Norman drops a loop on the cow Fat Boy runs up and gets under the cow and spits the milk into the bottle," Malcolm said. "He then turns and runs back to the line, and the judge pours the milk out on the ground while everyone else is trying to milk their cows."

In the wild cow milking event one man of a two-man team ropes the wild cow. Once the cow is roped, the second man, who is on foot, runs up to the downed cow to milk her. The milker has to run the bottle containing the milk back to the judge who stands under the announcer's stand. The milker hands the bottle to the judge and the judge turns the bottle upside down, and a visible amount of milk must pour to the ground. The first team to perform this task wins the event. Suds and Norman had won the event for the past six years without fail.

"Suds has stooped to an all-time new low here," Pete said. "That's low, even for Suds. How do you know all of this?"

"Norman just got through telling me," Malcolm said. "That's what I was doing outside. I wanted to talk to him. I heard him blowing about some foolproof plan Suds had came up with to win the wild cow milking. So I chased him down, and he was very happy to tell me about it."

"Are you going to tell the rodeo committee?"

"Got a better idea," Malcolm said with a grin, tapping his temple as though he had just hatched a plan of his own. "Let's beat Fat Boy at his own game."

"Norman ropes like superman," Pete said. "If Suds isn't milking the cow, how are we going to beat him? Even if we do the same trick with the milk, even if we put the milk in our mouth to spit into the bottle, Norman will still beat us with his rope. I don't think we can pull it off; Norman's just too quick."

"I'll come up with something," Malcolm said. "The one thing Suds likes is being a big man. If we expose him somehow or if we can beat him even if he's cheating, he'll hate that."

"Look, if you have some deviate and sneaky plan rolling around in your head, well, all I can say is count me in," Pete said. "A deviate plan in the making. Whatever you come up with, if it's underhanded and beats Suds at his game, just count me in. I haven't been in trouble in over a week."

"Works for me," Malcolm said.

"I need to get out of here," Pete said, standing up and pushing his chair under the table. "I have to run before Jackie comes through the door and catches me dodging her work and then my streak of not being in trouble will come to a screeching halt."

"I'll have the plan worked out quick, and when I do I'll let you know," Malcolm said. "It needs to be a good one, so I need to think about it for a while. I'll run it by Peggy, she loves this sort of thing."

"Poor Suds," Pete laughed. "He just can't help himself. He would lie when the truth sounded better. He would cheat when he could win without it."

"But the point is he can't win without cheating," Malcolm said, "and we are going to prove it to the world."

Malcolm, true to his word, came up with a plan that he put into motion during the week of the Fourth of July, when the town was in full celebration. Norman, not surprising anyone, had won the calf roping and steer roping. He and Suds lost the team roping when Suds missed one hock, something else that surprised no one. When it came time for the wild cow milking, Suds had already built up a good brag and was boasting to everyone who made the mistake of slowing down long enough to listen. With not a hint of humility, he told the rest of the contestants that they could just sit the fence so they wouldn't get in his way.

"With Norman's quick rope and my unhuman milking speed, you farmers don't stand a chance," Suds said to Malcolm, poking him in the chest with a fat index finger.

Malcolm's face reddened and he was having trouble suppressing the urge to reach up with a firm c-clamp and choke the fat braggart.

"I notice you have made the grave mistake of entering the wild cow milking," Suds said, pushing his luck to the very brink of disaster. "Malcolm, what in the world were you thinking? Where was your mind?"

"I thought you were having it too easy against these amateurs," Malcolm said. "I thought I'd take the buckle home with me this year."

"You think Pete can outrope Norman?" Suds howled.

"Pete may not be as fast as Norman, but I'll make up the time with my nimble milking fingers," Malcolm said through clinched teeth.

"Pete better come a ropin' if you think you have a chance to come in a close second on this deal," Suds giggled.

"We've been practicing," Malcolm said, again suppressing the bile that was building in the back of his throat. A bile caused by a mounting need to grab the fat boy by the neck and choke him into the blackness of unconsciousness. "We're ready."

Suds just roared with laughter in Malcolm's face, pelting little drops of spittle into Malcolm's red face.

He must have had onions with his high-fat lunch, Malcolm thought. *He really needs a good old-fashioned Navy style beating!*

Malcolm's hand, hanging limply at his side, opened slowly, and before he realized what was happening, his hand, acting solely on its own, moved upward toward Suds' throat. Pete grabbed Malcolm's collar and pulled him backwards before he could harm the fat man. Pete could see that Malcolm was about to detonate into a beat-Suds-into-the-ground meltdown.

"Let it ride," Pete whispered into Malcolm's ear. "I can't think of another soul who needs his attitude adjusted by a good beating more than Suds Slaughter, but today's the day he pays the fiddler. Let's do it right."

"Let's rope!" Malcolm spit the words at Suds and then spun on his heels and walked away.

"Let me beat the boy," Malcolm whispered to Pete as they walked away. "Just a little beating. Just let me beat him around the edges."

"Beat him," Pete said. "Beat him bad, but beat him in the arena like we talked about. If we pull this off he'll never forget it, and that will be the end of his cheating at the wild cow milking."

"I know, but just let me beat him a little before we beat him in the arena," Malcolm said. "It'll soften him up some. You know he needs it bad."

"No one I know needs it more than Suds," Pete chuckled. "But I didn't bring bond money to bail you out of jail, and I'd be forced to find another partner. Then you'd get all worked up and be mad at me because you missed your chance to go down in local rodeo history."

"Sounds good," Malcolm said, looking over his shoulder at Suds, "but I still think he needs a little beating before we stomp him in the arena. It's only right."

The cows were in the pen, and the mounted ropers were at the far end of the arena with their ropes tucked under their arms ready to rope. Beside them stood their milkers, with empty Coke bottles in their hands. When the judge raised a single-action Colt pistol containing blanks and fired off a round, the gates came open and the cows ran out; the wild cow milking was underway.

The ropers spurred their horses and charged the cows, sending cows spilling into every corner of the arena. Norman rode up behind the nearest cow and with one spin dropped his hemp around the horns. Like it was just another day at the office, Norman spurred up beside the cow, flipped his rope up over the cow's back, and galloped on by the beast. When Norman hit the end of his slack, the rope pulled the cow's head around toward his rump and down she went. Suds was on top of the downed cow before any of the rest of the teams had even roped their cows. Suds went down under the cow, out of sight of everyone, and spit a mouthful of milk into the Coke bottle.

He came up with milk in his bottle and looked toward the announcer's stand where the judge stood. He started to run toward the judge, and the crowd came to their feet in a cheer. It was then Suds noticed Malcolm was racing toward the judge also, and Malcolm might have a step or two on him.

How could he have roped the cow and milked her that quick? Suds' mind raced as fast as his feet.

Suds ran for all he was worth and dove into the circle that the judge was standing in; he had beaten Malcolm by just one step. Suds came to his feet, spit dirt from his mouth, and handed the judge the bottle containing the milk. With great ceremony the judge tipped the Coke bottle upside down, and milk ran out onto the ground. The crowd cheered louder. It had been a close race, but Suds had won again. For the seventh year in a row he had won.

"You'll have to give it a better effort than that to beat a real pro," Suds shouted over the roar of the crowd and pointed at Malcolm. "Admit it, you were beat by the best."

Malcolm only grinned as Suds made a show of pulling off his hat, waving it to the crowd like some movie star. He then took a long and theatrical bow. First, he bowed to those who sat on the right side of the arena, then to the stands on the left side. Suds was working the crowd and soaking in applause like a washed-up vaudeville actor with one last taste of the footlights.

"Ladies and gentlemen." The announcer's voice boomed and echoed through the arena. "You have just witnessed history in the making."

The crowd cheered even louder. Suds took another bow and blew them all a kiss.

It was a good run, he thought. *I must have broken the arena record. Cool!*

"Today, you have witnessed a feat that no other human being has ever achieved," the announcer articulated the words slow and in a tone reserved for professional announcers. "No one else has done what you have just witnessed. Suds Slaughter is the first cowboy in recorded history to have successfully milked a STEER!"

The crowd broke into a roar of united laughter. Suds' mouth fell open, and he shot a glare to the announcer and then to Malcolm, who was bent over with tears in his eyes from laughter.

"If you'll look closely at the cattle in the arena," the announcer proclaimed, "you will notice that they are all steers. Suds Slaughter is quite a cowboy to have just milked a steer. Ladies and gentlemen, give ol' Suds a rousing rodeo hand."

Suds' head whipped toward the center of the arena and saw that all the animals that had gathered and were milling in the center of the arena were males.

IT'S TRUE, his panicked thoughts screamed. *THEY ARE ALL STEERS!*

The crowd was laughing so hard no one heard his cussing as he spun on his heels and stomped out of the arena.

Pete rode up and slapped Norman on the back, "Good job of roping, Norman."

Norman was grinning wide as he stood up in his stirrups and waved his hat at the crowd proudly.

Suicide, Murder, or Cowboy Entertainment?

"I'm sick of hearing about Suds," Malcolm said.

"I'm about sick of it all," Ken said, standing up. "I'm going to make some bread pudding. That is if any of you guys want some."

"We'll force ourselves," Dale said.

"Admit it. You don't like Suds Slaughter," Lee said, pointing his finger at Malcolm. "You can admit it, we're all friends here."

"Name someone that does like Suds Slaughter."

"Norman," Lee said.

"Someone sane," Malcolm shot back.

"We don't know anyone sane," Lee said.

"Let me tell you a funny story that Suds Slaughter had nothing to do with," Malcolm said.

"Make it good," Pete said. "The Sandman is beating me to death. I need some rest if I have to endure any more of this nonsense. You guys are wearing me out."

"I've heard some sure enough Puncher Pie tonight," Malcolm said. "This story is true, I assure you."

"Did you ever work for the government?" Dale asked. "If not, you missed your calling because I want to believe you. Knowing it's a lie you're about to tell, I still want to believe you."

Malcolm never broke stride.

Truth is a relative concept—ask any lawyer. It's all a matter of one's perception of the world that surrounds him. Thus explaining why two completely honest and sane individuals can sit next to one another and witness the same event, yet report it as two completely different occurrences. Because one story is different from the other doesn't mean that one individual lied. It only points out that their perceptions were different.

Years before Colombus sailed the deep blue sea and accidentally ran aground onto what we now call America, it was thought that the world was as flat as a table. At that period in time if someone were to pass that information on to you, they would not be telling a lie. They believed the information to be true, in fact were convinced of it, and were giving you an honest accounting of their perception of the shape of their world.

Webster's II dictionary defines a lie as "an untrue statement made *deliberately*." Making the point that if two honest men see the same thing and tell two different stories, believing their account to be true, neither is a lie, just a different perspective.

Such was the case of Ned Reed and the kid.

Ned was the foreman of the Rafter A Cattle Company—had been for years. Fact is, no one living could remember who was the foreman before Ned. When you thought of the Rafter A you thought of Ned Reed. He was in his seventies, but no one knew just how deep into his seventies Ned really was. However, he looked more like he was twenty when he rode. He sat a horse like he was born to it, mainly because he was born to it. Ned came from a ranching family, and before he could walk his daddy had him sitting a slick-fork saddle looking at the world through the ears of a cow horse.

Ned had more natural cow sense than most of the men working for him. He was one of the best hands in the country of any age, but Ned had his shortcomings as do all men. Ned couldn't balance a checkbook, but it didn't matter, he never had a checking account in his seventy odd years. He never had a credit card, he had no use for one. On those rare occasions that he felt the need to buy something he would merely save his money and put down cash. In his entire life he never owned a truck or a car—if he needed to go somewhere he rode his horse as he had all his life. He never watched television because he thought it was a sin to waste time. "Idle hands are the devil's workshop," he would say. He never listened to a radio, not even to hear the cattle prices. If he needed to know what cattle were selling for, he would ask someone. Everyone he ever talked to talked about cattle and horses, and the price would come up eventually in the conversation. However, he would read a newspaper if he found one in the bunkhouse, but that was seldom because none of the other punchers read anything.

Ned never married. He had never found the woman with whom he cared to be hooked tandem, well, excluding Clair Jane Gentry. It had crossed his mind to court her after he returned from the war. To be quite honest, it more than crossed his mind—he dwelled on it, constantly. It was all he thought about when he reached the front and the enemy's shells exploding overhead forced him to pray facedown in the mud of his foxhole. In the tough times, such as when he was pinned down for two cold days and nights, unable to so much as lift his head, it was the clear memory of her big brown eyes and beautiful face framed in dark hair that pulled him through. She would never know how many letters he wrote to her declaring his love but never posted, how many foxholes her memory warmed, or how many times her face stepped between him and some truly horrible sight.

Upon his return to Texas from the war, he found out she had already married Jappy Hardgrove. He discovered a rumor had circulated that he had been killed in France. The rumor was almost true, they *tried* to kill him. Clair Jane had been brokenhearted. She couldn't pry any word, one way or the other, from the War Department, and near the end of the war she married Jappy. When Ned returned, she had a family on the way. Ned never completely recovered. He hated it that he could survive a war but something as silly as a nasty rumor could ruin his life. From that day he was straightforward and would never listen to rumors or gossip. Clair Jane was the last woman Ned ever allowed into, or for that matter near, his heart.

When he learned that the love of his life had married another man, Ned began to drink. He pretty much stayed drunk for the better part of three months. It was Jason Mayberry, the owner of the Rafter A, who drug Ned back to reality. Jason found Ned passed out, facedown, in one of the local bars. Ned's father had worked for Jason, and Jason had thought highly of him, so he couldn't allow this to go on any longer. Jason paid

Ned's tab, drug him out of the bar, and threw him in the back of his truck. Ned woke up the next morning in the ranch yard with Jason kicking his feet. Jason sobered the boy up and worked him until his hands bled. Ned never looked back.

He moved out to the Rafter A Cattle Company because it was remote. The ranch was at the end of the road. He couldn't think of another place that would take him farther from the world that had scarred him so deeply. Ned never drank again, and his entire life revolved around cattle and horses—he was a cowboy. He moved up fast in the ranks of the cowboy for no other reason than he took pride in his work. Work was all he allowed in his life. He did nothing that didn't have to do with his work, never riding to town with the boys, and hardly ever leaving the ranch.

Ned didn't have time for the foolishness the kids indulged in these days. The kids who came to work for the outfit were not the kind of cowboys he was when he was that age. When they were not in the saddle, they wore basketball shoes that cost them better than a week's wages. They wore caps with stupid sayings printed on the front, or what he thought was the front; half the time they wore the hats with the bills toward the back—he couldn't tell if they were coming or going. They didn't have the knowledge of cattle like when he was a kid—they were always crowding the cattle, never handling them gentle, like he was taught. They were hard on the horses, always jerking on their mouths. Worst of all, they would shake out a rope at the drop of a hat. They liked to dab a rope on anything that moved. They'd rope cats at the barn, chickens that were not paying attention, and calves that didn't need roping. To Ned's way of thinking, the rope was the last tool you wanted to pull out of your bag of tricks, but it was clear he was the only one in the outfit who thought that way.

Mike Samson was one of the kids who worked for Ned. He had been working for Ned for less than a month, and Ned was sure the kid didn't have what it took to be a cowboy. The kid never listened. As Ned put it, "he was always running his yap hole." The kid was always talking when his ears should have been big. To make it worse, the kid wore one of those weird haircuts that the kids today wore, and wore a baseball cap all the time, and not the western hat that Ned grew up seeing on real cowboys.

In the city they would say it was the middle of the night. On the ranch, even though it was still dark, it was early morning. The darkness of the early morning found Ned kicking the kid's bunk, bringing the kid straight up in his bed.

"Didn't you hear the bell?" Ned asked in a gruff voice. "Boy, you're going to get bed sores. Get up. Didn't your daddy ever tell you if you eat breakfast after the sun is up it'll kill you?"

The kid's bloodshot eyes attempted to focus enough to see the big face of the noisy windup clock sitting on the floor beside his bed. It was 4:00 A.M.—4:00 A.M.!

"Ugh," the kid sighed as he fell back into the bed and pulled the pillow up over his head. "Unless the place is on fire, come back in about four hours. Never mind, just come back in four hours even if the place is on fire."

"Roll out, boy," Ned said, kicking the bunk again. "We have to ride out to the river today. It's seven miles out there. So get up, feed your horse, and get something to eat. We're pulling out in forty-five minutes."

Ned kicked the bunk again. "Start looking like a cowboy, son."

"Why don't we just trailer the horses out there," the kid said, his voiced muffled under the pillow. "It ain't like we don't have trucks and trailers. We ought to use them now and then. Why do we always have to wear out saddle leather for no good reason?"

"That's what's wrong with you snot nose kids these days," Ned grunted, kicking the bunk again. "Always the easy way. It'll do you good to ride out there, and it'll give your horse time to get loosened up some. Now get up before I beat you with that shovel against the wall. And since we're talking about shovels, what's that shovel doing in here, anyway? It ought to be in the toolshed. So be sure to put it back when you feed the horses. Next time I need a shovel I don't want to look all over the darn ranch for one."

Ned walked off as the kid's feet hit the cold floor and he expelled a long, deep groan. His pounding head fell into his hands, and he rested on the side of the bunk for just a second.

That old man was nuts, he was sure of it. The old man did everything like the calendar told him it was still the 1800s. The old man would never let them trailer the horses out to work as long as they were working on the ranch. If they were working far enough away that they couldn't ride back and forth, rather than trailer the horses, the old man would have them pull the wagon, and they would be sleeping in the teepees on the ground. It didn't make a nickel's worth of difference what the weather was like either. If it was too far to ride back, the old man would have them sleeping on the ground. The weather never was a concern. If it rained you wore a slicker, if it snowed you wore a coat. The old man never seemed to even notice the weather. Hot or cold, clear or rain, they worked. The old man never seemed to know what day it was. They worked every day, with the exception of Sunday. On Sunday they would not ride out but would only do the work they had to do, such as feeding the stock and maybe shoeing a horse for tomorrow's use. The kid wasn't religious, but he thanked God for Sundays.

The kid painfully crawled to his feet and yanked on his jeans, which felt like someone had just pulled them out of the freezer. The old man didn't like a fire at night; he said it would make you sick. The kid shivered, pulled on his shirt, and stumbled over to wash the sleep from his face—he hoped the bucket wasn't frozen. He dressed as quick as he could and stepped out into the dark to feed the horses. He fed them quick, and when they had their heads down he jogged back in to smell the bacon the cook was frying up. It had warmed up some in the bunkhouse from the cook's fire. The kid's stomach was churning, he was hungry. After he wolfed down a half a dozen eggs and a quarter pound of bacon, washed down by four cups of strong black coffee, the kid put his plate in the washtub and went out to saddle his horse.

He could hardly buckle the bridle because his fingers were numb. He thought if he could just stay alive until the sun came up he might make it. The sun would warm him up. It was the same thing every morning. Jump up early, do the chores, saddle up, and ride out to some mesa to wait for the sun. The old man was really nuts—he was sure of it.

After the kid saddled his horse in the dark, he walked him past the bunkhouse to meet the rest of the boys. As the kid passed the bunkhouse door he was stopped cold in his tracks by someone yelling at him.

"WHAT IN THE SAM-HILL ARE YOU DOING?"

The kid turned to see Ned standing in the doorway of the bunkhouse. When the old man used the word "Sam-Hill," he was cussing. The old man's fists were balled up in a tight clinch, and his arms were board stiff at his sides. The kid noticed the old man was shaking like he was cold. It *was* cold. The kid didn't know what was making the man shake, but he feared it didn't have anything to do with the temperature. The old man's face was lit by the bare lightbulbs hanging in the bunkhouse, and the kid could see his face was beet red. The veins on the sides of the old man's neck bulged to the point the kid thought he might have a stroke.

"I asked you what you thought you were doing?" Ned said with more control in his voice.

The kid frantically searched his memory but had no idea what the old man was talking about. He was stunned that Ned was so angry, and he had no clue as to why.

"I was about to meet up with the boys," the kid said. The kid found nothing in Ned's face to tell him why he was mad. "Ahhh, I was going to work."

"Not on my night horse you're not!" Ned yelled and pointed a bony, accusing finger at him. "Just what are you trying to pull, kid?"

The kid spun on his heels to face the horse he had in tow. His stomach fell and his knees went weak under him. It was Ned's night horse, his favorite horse. The dun gelding he had on the end of his reins looked like one called Slick, a horse the kid had in his string.

"Ned, Uhhhh. I'm sorry." The kid shuddered; he knew he had just committed the unforgivable sin from the cowboy's bible. That being, you never saddle another man's horse—NEVER.

"In the dark he looked like Slick," the kid said in a nervous tone. "I thought he was my horse, Slick."

"Boy, that ain't Slick," Ned snorted. "Are you blind along with being stupid?"

"No sir," the kid said, ducking his head. "I just...."

"You just what?" Ned yelled, taking a step down off the steps. "You just didn't think? You just didn't pay attention? You just felt like saddling my horse? You just what, kid? You just what?"

"I didn't mean...."

"I guess you'd like me to believe that your saddle came to life and just jumped up on MY horse when you weren't looking?"

"Uhhh, no sir...."

"I should have whipped you with that shovel this morning," Ned yelled. "Is that what this is all about? Are you mad because I woke you up this morning?"

"Ned, I didn't know I had your horse," the kid said. "Honest, I would never have...."

"I'd advise you to get my horse back to the corral," Ned said. "Unless you want me to take this shovel to you, like I should have this morning."

The kid turned and walked toward the corral with Ned yelling behind him, "You better not have ruined him."

"I didn't hurt your horse," the kid said over his shoulder, getting a little braver. "All I did was saddle him."

"Don't back sass me, son," Ned shouted at the kid. "You're in the wrong here, and you good and well know it. You need to start thinking about what you're doing. Grow up, boy."

"Yes, sir."

That day was one the kid prayed he would never have to live again. He should have known it was going bad by the way Ned yelled at him about the horse mix-up. The rest of the day, Ned was ruthless the way he rode the kid. The entire trip to the river that morning, Ned was on the kid's back about one thing or another. The old man yelled at the kid for jerking on the horse's mouth, for cutting another cowboy off on the trail, for having a bad attitude. At one point Ned yelled at the kid to "wipe that stupid grin" off his face—it was still too dark for Ned to see if the kid was grinning, which he was not, but Ned yelled at him anyway, just in case. It didn't matter what the kid did that day, Ned was down his throat with both feet about it.

That morning the wagon rolled out with them and lunch was cooked over a fire by the cook. The kid was the last one in because Ned had him on drag to eat the dust—Ned felt it might help his bad attitude. When the kid came riding up to the wagon, Ned stepped out from the other side and with his hat, swatted the kid square in the face, nearly knocking the surprised boy out of the saddle.

"You know better than to ride into camp like that," Ned said with anger in his voice. "You're lucky Cookie doesn't take a chunk of wood and wear your hide out with it; you're getting dirt in his stew. What's wrong with you, kid? That horse has got more brains than you do."

"Sorry, sir," the kid said, reining his horse around and spurring off.

With a red face the kid rode off to tie his horse to the tree where the rest of the cowboys had tied their mounts. The kid sheepishly walked over to the wagon, giving Ned a wide berth, and took a plate from Cookie, who winked at him. Without a word and embarrassed by his transgression of cowboy etiquette, the kid walked over to a stump and plopped down on the ground by himself. He never looked up. Keeping his head down, he ate in silence the double portion of stew Cookie had spooned on his plate. Some of the boys tried to get him to talk but he just nodded, said nothing, and continued to eat his dinner as quietly as he could.

However, he was not quiet the entire time. The noon hour talk was interrupted when the kid let out a blood curdling scream. He jumped to his feet and threw his plate into the air. The kid began to dance and whimper like a beat pup. The whimper started off as a low groan, then grew in intensity until it was laced with loud screams of pain. The kid ripped off his hat and started swatting and beating it against his leg as he continued to scream.

"What in the Sam-Hill," Ned yelled as he came to his feet unnerved by the kid's sudden disturbing outburst.

The kid yanked down his pants and fell back as one of the pant legs caught on his spurs. He jumped back up and jerked off his boots, throwing them to the ground. He tugged off his pants and then pulled his shirt over his head. In short order the kid was jumping around naked. He did what some of the older guys there described as a dance akin to a fast Chubby Checkers twist as he made two turns around the stump and then cut a line for the river at full tilt. The kid never broke stride and sprinted off the bank into the muddy waters of the river. He broke the surface screaming and disappeared under the water once again. When he surfaced the second time he stood up in water just waist deep, rubbing his arms violently.

Wes, the wagon boss, hustled, as fast as one could hustle in cowboy boots with a two-inch riding heel, over to the riverbank and yelled to the kid, "What in the devil's got into you?"

The kid never answered, he just kept yelling and rubbing his body like a madman.

Ned, shoveling the last few bites of his stew into his mouth, ambled up beside Wes. The wagon boss, with a slack jaw and questions in his eyes, turned to Ned.

"Fire ants," Ned said around his last mouthful of stew. Wes nodded and turned back to watch the show that was going into its second act in the river.

Ned stepped down the bank until he reached the edge of the water where he bent to wash his plate off.

"Kid, did your mama have any other kids that lived?" he said as he straightened back up and flipped the water from the clean plate. "You don't pay attention. You don't listen. You don't do anything right. What am I going to do with you?"

Ned then turned around and walked over to the wagon and put his plate on the tailgate, where Cookie reached over, dried it on his apron, and then put it away. Without another word Ned walked over to his horse and with a quick move tightened the cinch, stepped up, and slowly rode off, heading back toward the cattle.

Ned didn't allow it to show, but inside he was fuming. The kid was driving him nuts. Ned's anger steady grew along with the shadows of the dying day. Ned yelled at the kid every time he came within shouting distance. Before long it was obvious to everyone, with the exception of Ned, that the kid was beat and broken by his abuse. The kid never uttered another word the rest of the day, to anyone. He didn't do his normal joking with the boys as they rode back to the bunkhouse. He just rode with his head down and a strained look painted across his face.

When the cowboys reached the ranch the kid hurried to unsaddle his mount. He curried and fed his horse while the rest of the boys were still talking and currying their horses. The kid took his saddle to the saddle shed where he hung it up and then he quietly slipped off unnoticed to the bunkhouse.

The kid didn't make his escape unnoticed; Wes had been watching him all day and saw that he had slipped away from the group. Wes could see the boy had been hurt by Ned's continuous abuse, loud rebukes, and daylong reprimands. Wes knew he had to step in and do something so he walked up to Ned and put his hand on the older man's shoulder.

"Pard, you've been awful hard on that kid today," Wes said. "What's up? It's not like you to be yelling at the boys. Even if they do pull some stupid stunts."

"Have I been hard on him?"

"You know good and well you have."

Ned dropped his head and sighed, "You're right."

Ned pulled off his hat and rubbed his head. "I just don't understand these kids nowadays," Ned said.

"They surely are a different breed," Wes said. "So what's up, my friend?"

"You're right. I've been steamed all day," Ned said. "It all started with the kid saddling my night horse this morning. He would have rode off on him if I hadn't seen him."

"Well, that's a cowboy sin for sure," Wes said. "But I don't think you're riding roughshod on that kid like that over your darn night horse. I saw Jappy Hardgrove's truck here last night. He didn't stay long. What's going on, Ned?"

Ned cleared his throat and paused a beat before speaking.

"He came out to tell me that Clair Jane passed away last week," Ned said as he turned his head so Wes wouldn't see the water forming in his eyes. "He said he knew I loved her. He also thanked me for never coming between them. He felt that gave me the right to know."

"I'm sorry, Ned," Wes said, clamping his friend's neck with his gloved hand. "I'm truly sorry. I know it's got to be rough."

"He told me she spoke of me often." Ned said, wiping his face with his open hand. "Jappy's a good man, I have to give him that. I'm just glad she married a good man. I never had a quarrel with him."

"You're right," Wes said, "Jappy's a good man."

"He didn't have to drive all the way out here to tell me, Wes," Ned said. "I'm just sorry I didn't go see her before she died, but Jappy said she just took sick and was gone before he knew it."

"I'm sorry," Wes said. "I'm really sorry."

"Thanks, Wes," Ned said, pulling himself together. "I guess I was too hard on that kid. He didn't deserve what I dished up to him today."

"You did ride him hard," Wes said. "Maybe you shouldn't have threatened him like you did."

"Threatened him?" Ned said. "What are you talking about?"

"I heard you threaten to beat him with a shovel this morning," Wes said.

"I guess I did," Ned said, shaking his head.

"When he started to rope that calf by the river do you think you should have told him that you were going to shake out your rope and hang him if he pulled one more boneheaded deal?" Wes chuckled. "I think he believed you."

"Then he's not as stupid as he looks, because he should've believed me," Ned laughed. "I was thinking serious about hanging him."

"I'm just saying you were a little hard on the boy," Wes stated. "He doesn't know that you are just an old windbag, and he had no idea about your loss. He didn't know anything was wrong, none of us did. You've got to admit you do lean to the tight-lipped side."

"What would you have me do," Ned said, puffing up. "Ride around all day crying like some baby?"

"It might not hurt if you did cry for a woman you loved," Wes said. "It don't make you less of a man."

"She was another man's wife."

"But you still loved her," Wes said, gripping his friend's neck. "It's alright to feel the pain when she's gone. Ned, you hard-headed old puncher, it's normal for a man to feel pain when someone he loves dies."

"I'll shake out a rope and hang you if you keep running your yap hole," Ned said, loosening his saddle. "Maybe you're right. The kid isn't that bad. After all he is just a kid, but I'll still never understand him."

"Why don't you go talk to him," Wes said.

"Yeah, I guess I should," Ned said, throwing his saddle on the fence. "As bad as it pains me I think you're right. I'll go talk to him."

"I'll keep the boys out here," Wes said. "We'll give you some time with him. Just remember he's a kid and you don't have to understand him, just don't lose your temper."

"I'm fine," Ned snapped.

"Sure you are."

Ned walked to the bunkhouse with his head down, pulling his thoughts together. It was the loss of Clair Jane that had made him act the way he was acting. He needed to admit it. Last night after Jappy left, Ned had gone though all the Christmas cards Clair Jane had sent him. He had kept them all. She had never missed one year since he returned from the war. One year she even sent him a picture of the entire family. He kept the picture on the dresser and looked at it every day of his life. He wondered if Jappy had noticed the picture when he came to see him last night. How could he have missed it—it was right there in plain sight.

Wes was right, he had rode the kid hard today. Maybe too hard. It wasn't the kid's fault he had been a failure with the woman he loved. Maybe he just needed to forget about how different these kids are. If they do the job, that's all he could ask of them. Even if they didn't do it like he would have done it. He knew he was getting too old; this was wearing him out. He just didn't understand the kids nowadays. He reached the bunkhouse door, stopped, and took a breath; he wanted to calm down before he approached the kid. He'd rode the kid too hard. Threatening to hang him was a little much, and maybe he shouldn't have threatened to beat him this morning.

As Ned stepped through the door he was shaken to his soul. In a panic, Ned's eyes went from the kid to the shovel that he had told the kid to put in the toolshed this morning. Ned grabbed the shovel, screamed, and ran toward the kid. With all his might he hit the kid, whose back was turned. The shovel hit the kid's shoulder with a powerful glancing blow and then hammered into the kid's skull. The kid went down like he had been shot. His head ricocheted off the wood stove and bounced before coming to rest in a pool of blood on the wooden floor. The kid's lifeless body lay facedown as his blood found its way across the floor before dripping down between its boards. He was unconscious with his arms folded up under him.

Hearing Ned's scream, the boys poured through the door and observed Ned standing, with a shovel in his hands, over the unconscious and bleeding kid. A blood splatter ran up the wall. The old man was red-faced and shaking.

Wes pushed his way through the boys, who had crowded at the doorway. When he saw the boy on the floor and Ned over him with the shovel Wes raced forward to take the shovel from the older man's hands. Wes pried the shovel from the old man's grip and threw it toward the wall. The shovel bounced off the wall with a loud clatter. Ned, wide-eyed and stunned, took two steps backwards and fell to his bunk. Beads of sweat ran from under his old faded hat. Ned had a look of disbelief on his face as he stared at the downed boy's bleeding body. The old man pulled off his hat and ran his fingers through his gray hair.

"Get the truck," Wes yelled to one of the boys. "Be quick about it."

The cowboy turned and ran out the door. Wes and the rest of the boys picked up the kid and carried him out to the waiting pickup. Before they could get the kid out the door, he came around and began to scream with fear and pain. Wes tried to calm the boy as they loaded him in the back of the truck on a mattress they had pulled off an empty bunk. The kid was bleeding profusely and screaming loudly. Wes yelled for the boys to get the kid to the hospital and that he would be along in a minute.

After the makeshift ambulance left with the screaming kid, Wes turned and walked in and sat down on the bunk beside Ned. Ned was laying on his back, wide-eyed, looking up at the ceiling.

"What happened?" Wes asked. "The kid was hurt bad."

"I don't understand kids nowadays," Ned said. "I just don't understand them."

"What happened, Ned?"

"I had to do it," Ned said, sitting up.

"Do what?"

"Is he alright?"

"He's on his way to the hospital, with a hole in his head," Wes said. "That's all I know."

"Then he's OK?" Ned said. "If he is going to the hospital he'll be OK. He's not dead."

"No, he's not dead," Wes said. "Now what happened, Ned?"

Ned was sweating and pulled his bandana from his back pocket and wiped his face. He was white. Ned shook his head, then lowered it into his hands.

"What happened, Ned?"

"I came in and he was trying to kill himself," Ned said.

"What?"

"The kid was trying to commit suicide," Ned said. "I couldn't believe it. It was all my fault. I rode him too hard. I should have cut him some slack. I pushed him too hard. It's my fault. Because I had a problem I pushed it off on the kid, and now this happens."

Wes leaned over and put his hand on Ned's knee.

"Settle down, Ned," Wes said, trying to comfort his friend. "Take your time and tell me about it."

"I came through the door," Ned said as he blew out a deep breath, "and I saw the kid over there." Ned pointed with a crooked finger to the wall. "The kid had some electric wires attached to his head. It was horrible. I have never seen anything like it in my life. He was screaming with his head thrown back, and the electricity had his arms drawn up over his head; he was convulsing and shaking all over. His scream was the most frightful thing I have ever heard."

Ned wiped the sweat from his head again. "Will he be alright?"

"I think so," Wes said.

"I knew if I grabbed him I would get electrocuted too," Ned said. "I saw the shovel leaning against the wall and I grabbed it and knocked him away from the wires. I hit him hard enough that the wires came off his head."

Ned pointed to the wires that were sticking out from under a bunk against the wall.

"I know I hit him hard," Ned said. "I saw no other way to save him. I just don't understand these kids anymore. What could he have been thinking? I know I rode him hard today, but was it that bad? Did I ride him too hard? It was my fault."

"Calm down," Wes said. "He'll be fine. The boys will have him to the hospital and we'll go in and check on him in just a bit. But you need to get it together."

Wes pulled a plug of tobacco from his shirt pocket, and with his knife he cut off a chew and handed the plug and knife to Ned. Ned cut off a good size chew and pushed it into the corner of his mouth.

"Thanks," Ned said as he handed the knife and tobacco back to his friend.

"What do you think was going on?" Wes said.

"I rode him too hard," Ned said. "I should have cut him some slack. I had Clair Jane on my mind and the kid just pushed me over the edge when he saddled my night horse. It was just an excuse to pile my trouble on the kid, and I just stayed on the boy's back. I don't know why he would try to kill himself. He should have just punched me in the nose if he was that mad. But why kill yourself? I just don't understand these kids. What have I done, Wes?"

Wes walked over to the bunk where the wires the kid had attached to his head lay. He bent and picked them up and walked back to Ned and sat down.

"Ned, you're just under a lot of stress. With the death of Clair Jane and all. Besides, you and I are just two old cowboys," Wes said. "I know you and I will never understand these kids. Their life is different. You never watch TV with them; they go to town to the movies and you stay here and work on your saddle or mend harness. They listen to that new music and it drives you nuts so you leave the bunkhouse. You and I, my friend, are a dying breed. We're dinosaurs on horseback. All we know is cows and horses. These kids wear high-dollar running shoes when they don't ride; they even use words we have no clue what they mean."

"What are you getting at, Wes," Ned said, looking up puzzled.

"You have never seen a Walkman?" Wes said, holding a small tape player in his hand. "The kid was listening to his music. The screaming you heard was him singing. He was listening to music and singing."

"What?" Ned said. "I never heard any music."

"That is because he was wearing earphones," Wes said. "Only he could hear it. The kid was not trying to kill himself, he was singing and dancing when you saw him. He was not trying to kill himself. When we loaded him in the truck he was screaming that you tried to kill him. He thinks you're nuts. He was crying that he didn't know what he had done this time to make you use a shovel on him. Then he screamed that you must have wacked him with the shovel he forgot to put in the toolshed like you told him to."

"He was singing?" Ned said. "He was listing to music when I hit him?"

Wes held the earphones out to Ned, turned on the music, and turned it up loud so Ned could hear it.

"What in the world is that?" Ned shouted and jumped back.

"ZZ Top," Wes said. "The kid was singing and dancing while he listened to rock and roll."

Ned stood up and spit a line of brown tobacco juice that hit the wooden floor between his boots. "Well, I guess this'll take me off the kid's Christmas list."

"That's it," I said, jumping to my feet. "Stick a fork in me, I'm done. If God loved a liar, he'd hug you to death."

I hauled my saddle over to the pickup and shoved it up under the bed in case it rained during the night, as the rest of the boys got up and started to stretch.

"Let's ride the Dark Canyon tomorrow," Pete said. "I'll show you some nice old ruins."

"Works for me," Lee said. "Ken, where's that pudding you were blowing about?"

"Right here," Ken snorted. "But I'm not sure I've got enough for you."

"Cranky old man, ain't he?" Lee said.

Everyone was gathered around Ken's cook table where he had spooned out the hot bread pudding. I took a bowl and poured milk on it. Ken did know how to cook—we knew how to eat. A marriage made in heaven.

"Tomorrow night, remind me to tell you boys about the other bet that Malcolm and Suds made a few years ago," Pete said.

"What bet?" Malcolm stopped with a spoonful of bread pudding a half inch from his mouth and looked at Pete like he was some kind of demented escapee from a sanitarium.

"One day Suds was bragging that everyone in the country knew him—that he was famous," Pete said. "Like normal, Malcolm got tired of listening to his gas and told him he was more famous. Malcolm said they couldn't go anywhere that people didn't know who he was. That everyone in the world knew him. Well, Suds couldn't resist and bet Malcolm a thousand dollars he could find someone within a week who didn't know him. Malcolm took the bet, because he had already planned a vacation to Rome the next week and knew he wouldn't be around for the test. For the next two days, Suds followed Malcolm around, and sure enough everyone they ran into knew who Malcolm was. In fact, they called ol' Malcolm by name."

Not knowing where this was going, Malcolm continued to look at Pete like he had lost what little sanity he had left.

"On the second day of the week bet, Malcolm and Peggy drove to Dallas to catch their plane and Suds followed them, looking for someone who didn't know Malcolm. While Suds followed Malcolm around Dallas he found that everyone in the city knew Malcolm. People would honk and wave, they shouted from their cars at Malcolm and stopped on the street to talk to him." Pete paused to take a few bites of his pudding. *"Everyone knew Malcolm. Well, the next day Peggy and Malcolm were leaving for vacation. They flew to Rome."*

"You'll never guess who they ran into in Rome?" Pete said in a very serious tone.

"Suds," Ken said.

"How did you know?" Pete laughed.

"I must have STP."

"You mean ESP," Dale said.

"Yeah, that too."

"Well, there Suds was and he followed Malcolm all over Rome," Pete said. *"Everyone Suds ran into knew Malcolm. People in Rome were stopping to talk to Malcolm; everyone waved and called his name."*

Malcolm was rolling his eyes again. Pete had lost it.

"All day Suds stopped people and asked if they knew Malcolm, and without exception they knew his name. As Suds followed Malcolm they ended up at the Vatican," Pete said, nodding to convince us it was all true. *"Suds couldn't believe what he was seeing. The Pope came out onto the balcony to bless the people, and who do you think was next to him wearing his cowboy hat, but Malcolm Burdett.*

"Well, old Suds nearly passed out. The Pope even knew Malcolm. Suds couldn't believe his eyes," Pete continued. *"As Suds was standing in the crowd, looking up at the Pope and Malcolm he heard this guy next to him say, 'Who in the world is that guy in the hat?' Suds jumped back, astonished. The guy was looking toward the Pope and Malcolm with a puzzled expression. 'You*

don't know that guy?' Suds asked. The guy squinted up at the balcony and said, 'never seen the man in my life.'"

Malcolm put his pudding bowl down on the table and watched Pete. Pete had stopped telling the story and was finishing his pudding.

"Well, let's hear it," Dale said.

"Yeah," Malcolm snapped. "Let's hear it."

Pete put his bowl down and finished.

"Good pudding, Ken," Pete said.

"I'll be pudding something up side your head if you don't get on with the story," Lee said.

"Well, not believing he had finally beat Malcolm, Suds asked the guy again if he knew the man in the hat up on the balcony, and the guy again told Suds he had never seen him in his life and had no clue who he was. Suds had beat Malcolm. The thousand bucks was his. Here was someone who didn't know Malcolm

Burdett. Suds laughed out loud, and people in the crowd turned to tell him to be quiet.

"Suds whispered to the man, 'The guy with the hat is an American, his name is Burdett.' The guy turned and looked Suds square in the eye and said, 'I know who Malcolm Burdett is, but who's the guy in the big tall hat with Malcolm?'"

"That's it," I said, pitching my empty pudding bowl in the wash. "I'm full of Puncher Pie. See you boys in the morning."

Other books from

Mysteries and Ghost Stories

Best Tales of Texas Ghosts

Ghosts Along the Texas Coast

Phantoms of the Plains: Tales of West Texas Ghosts

Spirits of San Antonio and South Texas

Spirits of the Alamo

The Great Texas Airship Mystery

Unsolved Texas Mysteries

Unsolved Mysteries of the Old West

When Darkness Falls: Tales of San Antonio Ghosts and Hauntings

Humor and Trivia

A Treasury of Texas Trivia

At Least 1836 Things You Ought to Know About Texas But Probably Don't

Bubba Speak: Texas Folk Sayings

First in the Lone Star State: A Texas Brag Book

Fixin' to be Texan

From an Outhouse to the White House

The Funny Side of Texas

Good Times in Texas: A Pretty Complete Guide to Where the Fun Is

I Never Wanted to Set the World on Fire, But Now That I'm 50, Maybe It's a Good Idea

Just Passing Through

More Wild Camp Tales

Only: The Last Dinosaur

Pete the Python

Puncher Pie and Cowboy Lies

Rainy Days in Texas Funbook

Humor and Trivia (cont.)

Texas Wit and Wisdom

Texas Highway Humor

That Cat Won't Flush

This Dog'll Hunt

This Dog'll Really Hunt: An Entertaining and Informative Texas Dictionary

Wild Camp Tales

History

A Cowboy of the Pecos

Alamo Movies

Battlefields of Texas

Daughter of Fortune: The Bettie Brown Story

Death of a Legend: The Myth & Mystery Surrounding the Death of Davy Crockett

Etta Place: Her Life and Times with Butch Cassidy and the Sundance Kid

Exploring the Alamo Legends

Eyewitness to the Alamo

Lawmen of the Old West: The Good Guys

Letters Home: A Soldier's Legacy

Red River Women

Return of Assassin John Wilkes Booth

Return of the Outlaw Butch Cassidy

Spindletop Unwound

The Star Film Ranch: Texas' First Picture Show

Tales of the Guadalupe Mountains

Texas Tales Your Teacher Never Told You

Republic of Texas Press

History (cont.)

Texas Ranger Tales: Stories That Need Telling
Texas Ranger Tales II
The Alamo Story: From Early History to Current Conflicts
The King Ranch Story: Truth and Myth
The Last of the Old-Time Cowboys
The Return of the Outlaw Billy the Kid
The Last Great Days of Radio

Volunteers in the Texas Revolution: The New Orleans Greys

Cooking

Dirty Dining: A Cookbook, and More, for Lovers
Making it Easy: Cajun Cooking
The Ultimate Chili Cookbook
Top Texas Chefs Cook at Home: Favorite Recipes

Recreation/Field Guides

A Trail Rider's Guide To Texas
Critter Chronicles
The Texas Golf Guide

The Texas Golf Guide (2nd Ed.)
Horses and Horse Sense
They Don't Have to Die: Home and Classroom Care for Small Animals
Your Kitten's First Year
Your Puppy's First Year

Travel

Dallas Uncovered (2nd Ed.)

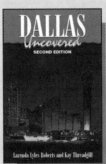

Exploring Branson: A Family Guide
Exploring Dallas with Children: A Guide for Family Activities
Exploring New Orleans: A Family Guide
Exploring San Antonio with Children: A Guide for Family Activities

Exploring Texas with Children
Los Angeles Uncovered
Seattle Uncovered
Salt Lake City Uncovered
San Francisco Uncovered
Tuscon Uncovered
Twin Cities Uncovered

Top sellers from Republic of Texas Press

1-55622-648-9 • $15.95

1-55622-537-7 • $16.95

1-55622-569-5 • $18.95

1-55622-613-6 • $16.95

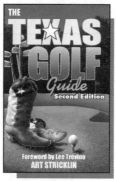

1-55622-575-X • $14.95

1-55622-624-1 • $18.95

1-55622-536-9 • $16.95

1-55622-377-3 • $16.95

1-55622-571-7 • $18.95